English Grammar and Composition

First Course

John E. Warriner

FRANKLIN EDITION

Harcourt Brace Jovanovich, Publishers

New York   Chicago   San Francisco   Atlanta   Dallas *and* London

THE SERIES:

English Grammar and Composition: First Course
English Grammar and Composition: Second Course
English Grammar and Composition: Third Course
English Grammar and Composition: Fourth Course
English Grammar and Composition: Fifth Course
English Grammar and Composition: Complete Course
Test booklet and teacher's manual for each above title.

CORRELATED SERIES:

English Workshop: First Course
English Workshop: Second Course
English Workshop: Third Course
English Workshop: Fourth Course
English Workshop: Fifth Course
English Workshop: Review Course

Composition: Models and Exercises, First Course
Composition: Models and Exercises, Second Course
Composition: Models and Exercises, Third Course
Composition: Models and Exercises, Fourth Course
Composition: Models and Exercises, Fifth Course
Advanced Composition: A Book of Models for Writing, Complete
   Course

Vocabulary Workshop: First Course
Vocabulary Workshop: Second Course
Vocabulary Workshop: Third Course
Vocabulary Workshop: Fourth Course
Vocabulary Workshop: Fifth Course
Vocabulary Workshop: Complete Course

John E. Warriner taught English for thirty-two years in junior and senior high schools and in college. He is chief author of the *English Grammar and Composition* series, coauthor of the *English Workshop* series, general editor of the *Composition: Models and Exercises* series, and editor of *Short Stories: Characters in Conflict*. His co-authors have all been active in English education.

ISBN 0-15-311880-6

To the Student

Have you ever thought about how important language is? Can you imagine what living would be like without it?

Of all creatures on earth, human beings alone have a fully developed language, which enables them to communicate their thoughts to others in words, and which they can record in writing for others to read. Other creatures, dogs, for example, have ways of communicating their feelings, but they are very simple ways and very simple feelings. Without words, they must resort to mere noises, like barking, and to physical actions, like tail wagging. The point is that one very important difference between human beings and other creatures is the way human beings can communicate with one another by means of this remarkable thing called language. When you stop to think about it, you realize that language is involved to some extent in almost everything you do.

Since you live in an English-speaking part of the world, the language you use is English. Unless your family and childhood friends spoke another language, you learned English even before you went to school. You learned to speak it and to understand it. In school your language ability grew rapidly as you learned to read and to write. Each year you study English in school so that your language ability will continue to grow, to keep up with the increasingly complicated ideas you need to express as you acquire more knowledge.

This textbook will be a valuable aid in your study of English. In it you will find an explanation of how the language works, which is something you need to understand if you are to learn to express yourself correctly and effectively. You will find exercises and writing assignments that you need for practice. The book will teach you the difference between an effective sentence and an ineffective one, between strong writing and weak writing. You will learn to express yourself in correct, clear, and interesting English. Nothing you learn in school is more important than this.

J.W.

Contents

3. The Parts of Speech 53

Verb, Adverb, Preposition, Conjunction, Interjection

4. The Prepositional Phrase 83

Adjective and Adverb Uses

PART TWO: Usage

PART FIVE: Composition

15. Manuscript Form 279
Standards for Written Work

16. Narration and Description 284

17. The Paragraph 303
Structure and Development

18. The Whole Composition 333

Planning and Organizing a
Longer Piece of Writing

19. Writing Explanations and 349
Reports

Steps in Organizing Information

PART SIX: Aids to Good English

PART SEVEN:
Speaking and Listening

Grammar

PART ONE

Chapter 1

The Sentence

Subject and Predicate;
Kinds of Sentences

All people need to express their thoughts and feelings to others. Expression may take many forms other than words. For example, a smile may show happiness. A shrug may express uncertainty. A siren indicates a fire or an accident. An arrow points out a one-way street.

Of course, the two most common forms of communication—speaking and writing—depend on words. When words are combined in a meaningful arrangement, or pattern, communication takes place. The patterns used in speaking and writing often differ. When we speak, we very often depend on gestures and facial expressions to help communicate thoughts and ideas. But when we write, we have only words and punctuation. To make ideas clear and easy to read, we must construct good sentences and punctuate them properly.

Look at the following groups of words spoken at one end of a telephone conversation:

Yes.
Sure.
This afternoon.
I'll bring my skates.
Don't be late.

Although you know each word in the first three lines, you do not know exactly what is meant because in each case the thought is incomplete. Some words — those of the other speaker — are missing. The first three lines do not express complete thoughts; therefore, they are not sentences. The last two groups of words do express complete thoughts; they are sentences.

1a. **A sentence is a group of words expressing a complete thought.**

Here are four sentences. Notice the capital letter at the beginning of each sentence and the mark of punctuation at the end.

> Harper Lee won a prize for her book.
> Please fasten your seat belt.
> Why did you stop running?
> Watch out for the car!

The following groups of words are not sentences because they do not express complete thoughts. Each one leaves out something you need to know in order to understand what the writer means to say.

> after they pitched the tent and built a campfire [Then what happened?]
> because Anna won the 100-meter race [What was the result?]
> sailing around the world [What about it?]
> on her hike through the Grand Canyon [What did she do on the hike?]

EXERCISE 1. The following groups of words have no capital letters at the beginning and no marks of punctuation at the end. Some groups are sentences; some are not. Write the numbers 1–20 on your paper.

Copy each sentence, adding a capital letter at the beginning and a mark of punctuation at the end. Write *NS* after the number of each group of words that is not a sentence. Do not write in the book.

EXAMPLES   1. a mountain stream full of trout and slippery rocks
    1. *NS*
    2. we caught three trout and cooked them for dinner
    2. *We caught three trout and cooked them for dinner.*

1. my sister spoke about saving the whales
2. on the other side of the basketball court
3. after collecting the papers, the teacher walked out of the room
4. the quick and clever magician
5. the whales in the Pacific Ocean
6. whales are the largest mammals
7. found by hikers walking on the beach
8. only a few people saw the whale
9. she climbed slowly up the side of the hill
10. they flew kites in the park
11. fought for the right of free speech
12. when she wrote the story
13. fishing with her aunt
14. although everyone could vote
15. because of the loud buzzing
16. after a short rest the beaver began building again
17. have you heard about the strange area called the Bermuda Triangle
18. apparently many ships disappear in this region
19. searching for a reason
20. and even blame UFO's

EXERCISE 2. Ten of the following twenty groups of words are sentences although the capital letters and marks of punctuation have been purposely omitted.

Write the numbers 1–20 on your paper. After each number, if the group of words is a sentence, copy it, adding a capital letter at the beginning and a mark of punctuation at the end. If the group of words is not a sentence, write *NS* after its number.

1. you can take an exciting boat trip on the Colorado River **2.** running the rapids **3.** as your boat drifts through the Grand Canyon **4.** when it drops suddenly **5.** the river becomes foaming rapids full of dangerous boulders **6.** which may break a boat **7.** your boat may be a wooden dory five meters long **8.** with one guide and four passengers **9.** large inflated boats with outboard motors can carry eighteen persons **10.** these boats move very fast **11.** and are less likely to be broken by boulders **12.** than the smaller boats **13.** some rapids contain dangerous holes **14.** a hole is a sink **15.** caused by water plunging over a hidden boulder and forming a great wave **16.** which can overturn a boat **17.** if a boat flips **18.** you are kept afloat by your life jacket **19.** you drift to the tipped boat **20.** you turn it over and climb back aboard

SUBJECT AND PREDICATE

Every sentence has two essential parts: a *subject* and a *predicate*.

1b. The *subject* of a sentence is the part about which something is being said.

In these sentences, the subjects are in heavy type.

> **Jane** painted.
> **The girls on the team** were all good students.
> **Margaret Bourke-White** was a famous photographer.

In any sentence, you can find the subject by asking yourself who or what is doing something or about whom or what something is being said.

EXERCISE 3. Write the numbers 1–10 on your paper. After each number, write the subject of the sentence.

EXAMPLE   1. Mountain climbing is an exciting sport.
              1. *Mountain climbing*

1. Mount Everest is the highest mountain in the world.
2. Many people enjoy mountain climbing.
3. Falling rocks present a danger to climbers.
4. Snow slides are also feared by climbers.
5. Expeditions often attempt to scale mountains in Alaska.
6. Some great mountain peaks contain volcanoes.
7. The lava from a volcano is very dangerous.
8. The seeming quietness of a volcano crater is misleading.
9. One volcano in Japan was silent for more than a thousand years.
10. A gigantic outburst occurred in 1888.

The subject does not always come at the beginning of a sentence—it may be in the middle or at the end. Notice the position of the subjects in the following sentences.

> Did **the pitcher** strike her out?
> After practicing for hours, **Timmy** bowled two strikes.
> For centuries **the earth** was thought to be the center of the universe.
> Hiding in the tall, dry grass was **a frightened rabbit.**
> Have **you** called Isabel yet?

EXERCISE 4. Write the numbers 1–10 on your paper. After each number, write the subject of the sentence.

1. Many stories have been written about Paul Bunyan.
2. In his North Woods one winter a blue snow fell.

3. The animals of the forest fled even farther north.
4. Because of the extreme cold, some bears became polar bears.
5. During the storm Paul discovered a blue calf.
6. The big logger nursed the calf back to health.
7. Soon the calf grew to be very large.
8. Its horns were forty-two ax handles and a plug of chewing tobacco apart.
9. Linked forever with Paul Bunyan was Babe, his Blue Ox.
10. With Babe's help Paul Bunyan became the greatest logger of all time.

EXERCISE 5. Write the numbers 1–10 on your paper. Make sentences out of the following groups of words by adding subjects where there are blanks. Subjects may be one word or more than one word. Begin each sentence with a capital and end it with a mark of punctuation. Do not write in the book.

EXAMPLE   1. —— is very heavy.
            1. *A bag of cement is very heavy.*

1. —— is a difficult game to play.
2. —— works in the post office.
3. Luckily for me —— was easy to read.
4. —— manufactures automobiles.
5. At the end of the parade came ——.
6. —— will make you sick.
7. After the game —— were talking with the coach.
8. —— was destroyed by fire.
9. —— are dangerous.
10. Did —— help you?

Complete Subject and Simple Subject

The part of the sentence that you have been writing is called the *complete subject*. Among the words of the complete subject, there is always a main word. This main word is called the *simple subject*.

1c. The *simple subject* is the main word in the complete subject.

EXAMPLE   The four new students arrived early.
  Complete subject   The four new students
   Simple subject   students

EXAMPLE   A round walnut table with five legs stood in the middle of the dining room.
  Complete subject   A round walnut table with five legs
   Simple subject   table

Note that the key, or main, word of the subject (*students, table*) cannot be omitted. Without this word the sentences do not make sense.

> The four new . . . arrived early.
>
> A round walnut . . . with five legs stood in the middle of the dining room.

EXERCISE 6.   Write the numbers 1–10 on your paper. Copy the complete subject of each sentence. Then underline the simple subject. Remember that the subject of a sentence may come at the beginning, in the middle, or at the end of the sentence.

1. A typical five-year-old child is sometimes outwitted by a chimpanzee.
2. The average chimp can easily be taught to eat with a fork.
3. The friendly chimp enjoys a meal at a table.
4. In the middle of the meal, the playful rascal may put its feet on the table.
5. No self-respecting chimp enjoys a cage.
6. Unexpected jailbreaks have been carried out by chimps.

7. One very clever chimp dug a tunnel under the walls of its cage.
8. This difficult act required many hours of patient work.
9. The job had to be done without attracting attention.
10. Hidden in the chimp's mind are many such tricks.

Sometimes when the subject is very short, the simple and the complete subject are the same.

EXAMPLES **Jets** break the sound barrier.

Aunt Carmen owns a grocery store.

Maud Martha is a novel by Gwendolyn Brooks. [*Maud Martha* is the title of a book; therefore, all the words make up the simple subject; they are also the complete subject.]

From now on in this book, the term *subject* will mean "simple subject," unless otherwise indicated.

EXERCISE 7. Write the numbers 1–10 on your paper. Copy the complete subject of each sentence. Then underline the simple subject.

1. H. G. Wells was a writer of history and fiction.
2. *The Time Machine* is one of his best books.
3. The main character in that book is called the Time Traveler.
4. He journeys into the future to the year 802,701.
5. In that distant year this imaginary traveler meets two kinds of creatures.
6. One kind dwells above ground.
7. These individuals live peaceful but unproductive lives.
8. The other creatures live below the earth's surface.
9. Because of their dark surroundings, this second group cannot bear any light to strike their eyes.

10. These apelike creatures work machinery under- ground to support the dwellers of the upper world.

EXERCISE 8. Write five sentences about school, your family, or your favorite hobby. Underline the simple subject of each sentence. Try to make some of your subjects come in the middle or at the end of your sentences.

The Predicate

Predicate comes from a Latin word meaning "to proclaim." Thus, a predicate proclaims, or says, some- thing about the subject.

1d. The *predicate* of a sentence is the part which says something about the subject.

In these sentences the predicates are in heavy type.

> Old Faithful **is a giant geyser in Yellowstone National Park.**
> Jade Snow Wong **wrote about growing up in San Francisco's Chinatown.**
> Sarah's sister **took us bowling yesterday.**
> The hot sun **blistered the berry pickers.**

The predicate in the first sentence, *is a giant geyser in Yellowstone National Park,* says something about the subject, *Old Faithful.* In the second sentence, *wrote about growing up in San Francisco's China- town* tells what the subject, *Jade Snow Wong,* did. You can see that the predicates in the other sentences also tell something about their subjects.

EXERCISE 9. Write the numbers 1–10 on your paper, and copy the predicates from the following sentences.

EXAMPLE   1. Daily life was different 100 years ago.
             1. *was different 100 years ago.*

1. Families had to make their own home entertainment in the 1880's.
2. Homes did not have radios, television sets, or record players.
3. No one could go to a movie.
4. A movie machine was not invented until 1894.
5. Electric appliances like refrigerators and washing machines had not been dreamed of.
6. Very few homes had a telephone.
7. The main source of horsepower was the horse.
8. A world without automobiles and airplanes is hard for us to imagine.
9. Doctors practiced medicine without X-ray machines or painkillers.
10. The zipper had not been invented.

Just as the subject does not always come at the beginning of the sentence, so the predicate does not always come at the end. When the subject comes in the middle of the sentence, a part of the predicate usually stands before it; when the subject comes at the end of the sentence, the whole predicate stands before it.

Notice the positions of the predicates in the sentences below.

> **Late in the night** we **heard a noise.**
> **Quickly** we **jumped to our feet.**
> **Outside the tent was** a baby bear.

EXERCISE 10. Write the numbers 1–10 on your paper and copy the predicates from the following sentences. Remember that a part or all of the predicate may come before the subject.

1. Roberto Clemente won four National League batting titles in his career.
2. He was his league's Most Valuable Player in 1966.

3. Clemente played right field for Pittsburgh.
4. He had a lifetime batting average of .317.
5. Clemente was chosen for twelve All-Star teams.
6. Twice Clemente helped lead the Pirates to World Series victories.
7. Clemente never went hitless in fourteen World Series games.
8. Roberto Clemente was elected to the National Baseball Hall of Fame.
9. Clemente died in a plane crash off the coast of his native Puerto Rico.
10. On the plane were people flying to Nicaragua to aid earthquake victims.

EXERCISE 11. To each of the following subjects, add a predicate to fill the blank or blanks marked. Write the complete sentence on your paper.

EXAMPLES   1. The tides of the oceans ——.
           1. *The tides of the oceans are influenced by the moon.*
           2. —— we ——.
           2. *One day we visited a planetarium.*

1. My favorite television show ——.
2. The path in the woods ——.
3. Finger painting ——.
4. A powerful locomotive ——.
5. The Buzzell twins ——.
6. —— our television set ——.
7. Five sailboats ——.
8. —— the little bay pony ——.
9. A four-leaf clover ——.
10. The skyline of Chicago ——.

The Simple Predicate

The predicates you have been studying are called *complete predicates.* Each complete predicate contains a *simple predicate,* which is the main word in the predicate. The simple predicate is the *verb* of the sentence.

1e. The *simple predicate,* or *verb,* is the main word or group of words in the complete predicate.

EXAMPLE   The pilot broke the sound barrier.
    Complete predicate   broke the sound barrier.
Simple predicate (verb)   broke

EXAMPLE   Arkansas has the only diamond field in the United States.
    Complete predicate   has the only diamond field in the United States.
Simple predicate (verb)   has

Look at the following sentences. The complete predicates are underlined, and the simple predicates (verbs) are in heavy type.

The dinosaur **is** a prehistoric animal.
The puppy **walked** across the sofa with muddy feet.
Laura **found** two birds' nests in the hedge.
The city of Washington **has** many monuments.

The simple predicate is always a verb. In this book, we will usually refer to the simple predicate as the *verb.*

EXERCISE 12.   Copy the complete predicate of each sentence. Then underline the verb.

EXAMPLE   1. Nobody knows the creator of our flag.
    1. *knows the creator of our flag.*

1. Historians are unsure about the history of the Stars and Stripes.
2. The Continental Congress approved a design for the flag in 1777.

3. The design included thirteen red stripes and thirteen white stripes.
4. The top inner quarter of the flag was a blue space with thirteen white stars.
5. The designer of the flag is unknown.
6. Congress said nothing about the placement of stars.
7. George Washington wanted flags for the army.
8. The flags arrived after the Revolutionary War.
9. According to a popular legend, Betsy Ross made the first flag.
10. Historians doubt the Betsy Ross story.

The Verb Phrase

Some verbs consist of more than one word. Even so, these verbs are still the simple predicate of a sentence. When a verb is made up of more than one word, it is called a *verb phrase*. Notice the verb phrases in these sentences.

Kathy **is riding** the Ferris wheel.
The carnival **has been** in town for two weeks.
Bernice **should be** here somewhere.

EXERCISE 13. Copy the verb or verb phrase from each of the following sentences.

1. Alaska became the forty-ninth state of the Union.
2. It was admitted to the Union in 1959.
3. Alaska is two and one-fifth times the size of Texas.
4. Statehood brought some new problems to the people of Alaska.
5. Tourists can drive to Alaska along the Alcan Highway.
6. Thousands of gold prospectors rushed to Alaska between 1897 and 1899.
7. Many of them died from exposure.

8. Others were forced into trading or farming.
9. The people of Alaska must endure extremely cold temperatures.
10. The weather during an Alaskan summer may be hot.

EXERCISE 14. Write ten original sentences using these verbs or verb phrases.

1. roars	6. poked
2. learned	7. demands
3. was dancing	8. have been warned
4. will need	9. shuddered
5. begs	10. has teased

Finding the Subject

You have probably found that in some sentences it is easy to identify the subject at once. By now you should have no difficulty in locating the subject in these sentences:

The **movers** arrived early Saturday morning.
The math **test** was easy.

In other sentences, however, you may have trouble in locating the subject. Sometimes it is a help to find the verb first and then to ask yourself, "Who ——?" or "What ——?" Study the following examples:

In high school we will have more homework than ever.

What is the verb? Clearly, it is *will have.* Ask yourself, "Who will have?" The answer is *we. We* is the subject of the sentence.

Can you untie this knot?

What words in this sentence express action? *Can untie,* of course; *can untie* is the verb. Ask, "Who can untie?" *You* is the answer, and *you* is the subject of the sentence.

> The peak of Mount Everest was first reached by a British group.

The verb in this sentence is not difficult to identify: *was reached.* "What was reached?" The answer is *the peak. Peak* is the subject of the sentence. If you thought that *Mount Everest* might be the subject, you will see the value of first finding the verb and then asking yourself, "What ——?" The answer to that question is always the subject. If you use this method, you will not be misled by other words in the sentence that look as if they might be the subject.

Diagraming Subjects and Predicates

One good way of showing that you know the parts of a sentence is to use a diagram. The diagram of a sentence is really a picture of its structure. It shows how the subject and verb fit together.

A sentence diagram begins with a straight horizontal line, divided by a short vertical line. The horizontal line is for the main parts of the sentence—the subject and verb. The vertical line separates the subject and the predicate. In making a diagram you keep the capital letters but omit the punctuation marks.

PATTERN

subject	predicate

EXAMPLES   Horses gallop.   People think.

Horses	gallop

People	think

Examples such as these are easy because the sentences each contain only a simple subject and a verb. Let us look at a longer sentence.

> Many countries cooperate in the scientific investigation of space.

To diagram the subject and predicate of this sentence, follow these three steps: (1) Separate the complete subject from the complete predicate. (2) Find the simple subject and the verb. (3) Draw the diagram.

	complete subject	*complete predicate*
Step 1	Many countries	cooperate in the scientific investigation of space.

	simple subject	*simple predicate*
Step 2	countries	cooperate

Step 3

countries	cooperate

Following the same steps, we can diagram the simple subjects and the verbs of the following sentences.

1. Roger Maris hit sixty-one home runs in one season.

Roger Maris	hit

2. Lena was named to the team.

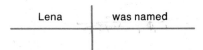

Think of the horizontal line as the base of the sentence, holding the main words — the simple subject and the verb. The vertical line divides the sentence into its two main parts — subject and predicate.

EXERCISE 15. Find the simple subject and the verb in each of the following sentences. Then make a sentence diagram of the simple subject and the verb. Use your ruler for the lines. Leave plenty of space between diagrams.

EXAMPLE   1. Hot **weather** **came** early this year.

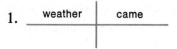

1. Some people have strange pets.
2. In city apartments, small pets are popular.
3. However, some large dogs live in cities.
4. They walk quietly along the crowded streets.
5. A Great Dane on the sidewalk may startle pedestrians.
6. Some children like hamsters as pets.
7. Wild creatures may be trained for domestic life.
8. Farm families often have a variety of animals about the place.
9. At some time during childhood, nearly every youngster wants a pony.
10. A quiet, untroublesome pet is the goldfish.

Questions may seem more difficult to diagram. However, if you look carefully for the subject and verb, you will have no trouble. Remember that in a question a part of the predicate comes before the subject. Notice this question, for example:

Are you going to the party?

Make the question into a statement.

You are going to the party.

You will recognize *are going* as the verb. To find the subject, ask "Who?" The answer is *you*.

In a diagram the subject always comes first on the horizontal line.

EXERCISE 16. Diagram the simple subject and verb in each of the following sentences. Use your ruler and allow plenty of space between diagrams.

1. Have you visited a wax museum?
2. The figures seem almost alive.
3. Can you imagine a house full of life-size wax "people"?
4. For many years England has specialized in wax museums.
5. Many rulers of the past have been re-created in wax.
6. Famous criminals have been shown at the scenes of their crimes.
7. Each wax figure has real hair.
8. Even the wrinkles on the face are in the right places.
9. How can a lifeless dummy look so realistic?
10. Museum visitors often ask that question.

COMPOUND SUBJECTS AND PREDICATES

Often we wish to show that two or more subjects are performing the same action or that the same subject is doing two or more things. To do this, we connect subjects or verbs with words like *and* or *or*. Subjects or verbs connected in this way are said to be *compound*.

Compound Subjects

1f. A *compound subject* consists of two or more connected subjects that have the same verb. The usual
connecting words are *and* and *or.*

EXAMPLES   **Paris** and **London** are favorite tourist attractions. [The two parts of the com-
pound subject have the same verb, *are.*]

Costumes, makeup, scenery, and
props are needed for the production of
a play. [The four parts of the compound
subject have the same verb phrase, *are
needed.*]

Marie Ellis or **John Schwartz** will go
on the field trip with us. [The two parts
of the compound subject have the same
verb phrase, *will go.*]

EXERCISE 17.   Copy the compound subjects from the
following sentences. Watch for subjects in the middle or at the end of sentences.

EXAMPLE   1. The pilot and the navigator are in the
cockpit.
1. *pilot, navigator*

1. The northwestern states and the southeastern
parts of the country receive heavy rainfall each
year.
2. The flowers and the trees in these areas depend on
this for their growth.
3. Golfers and vacationers are not pleased by all the
rain.
4. The people of India and those living in Southeast
Asia experience heavy rains for several months at
a time.
5. The warm air and the constant rain produce a
wind called a monsoon.

6. A good monsoon or a bad one can be measured by the amount of rain that falls.
7. The crops and the animals need the heavy rains in order to live.
8. The temperature of the land and the temperature of the surrounding water are quite different in May, the start of the monsoon season.
9. The air and its water vapor rise and condense into heavy rain.
10. An encyclopedia or an atlas will tell you more about monsoons.

EXERCISE 18. Make sentences by adding compound subjects to these predicates. Write the complete sentence on your paper. Use *and* or *or* to join the parts of your compound subjects.

1. —— are competing in the race.
2. —— amused the audience.
3. —— make good pets.
4. —— planned the hayride.
5. Yesterday —— sailed into the harbor.
6. —— are fun to collect.
7. Staring at us through the window were ——.
8. At the ocean —— found a starfish.
9. —— can water-ski on one ski.
10. In the attic —— were piled.

Compound Verbs

Just as a sentence may have a compound subject, so it may have a *compound verb*. When two or more verbs or verb phrases are joined by *and, or, nor,* or *but,* the combination is called a *compound verb.*

1g. A *compound verb* consists of two or more connected verbs that have the same subject.

EXAMPLES   That dog either **barked** or **whined** all night.
Ginny **pitched** well but **lost** the game.
The rain **has fallen** for days and **is flooding** the low areas.

A sentence may have both a *compound subject* and a *compound verb*.

EXAMPLES   A few **vegetables** and many **flowers sprouted** and **grew** in the rich soil.
Pam and **Sue bought** peanuts and **fed** the bears.

Note that in such sentences both subjects carry out the action of both verbs.

EXERCISE 19. Copy the verbs and verb phrases from the following sentences.

EXAMPLE   1. The largest crowd of the season attended the game and cheered for the teams.
1. *attended, cheered*

1. The team played well but lost the game.
2. John went out early in the morning but came home late in the evening.
3. At dawn heavy rains and strong winds struck the southern coast of the island.
4. Jenny is worrying about her grades and is studying very hard.
5. In the afternoons, most campers either swim or play softball.
6. Mrs. Ortiz listened to my story and offered me some good advice.
7. Some of the test questions were easy.
8. The passengers had fastened their seat belts and were waiting for takeoff.
9. Depending on the weather, Maria and Joan either walk to school or take the bus.

10. During our absence, someone had obviously entered the house but had taken nothing.

EXERCISE 20. Make sentences by adding compound verbs to these subjects. Try to use some compound verb phrases. Write the complete sentence.

1. The trained seal ——.
2. At the fair we ——.
3. The doctor ——.
4. Last week my next-door neighbor ——.
5. The birds ——.

EXERCISE 21. Make two columns on your paper, headed *Subject* and *Verb*. After the number of each sentence write its subject and verb in the proper columns. Some of the subjects and verbs are compound.

1. Settlers faced and overcame many dangers.
2. Mt. McKinley and Mt. Whitney are two very high mountains.
3. Sacajawea of the Shoshones helped open the West.
4. Many famous racehorses have been raised or trained in Kentucky.
5. Each year many people rush to New Orleans for Mardi Gras.
6. The bright lights and tall buildings of New York City thrill and delight tourists.
7. Boiling springs, mud volcanoes, and petrified forests can be found in Yellowstone National Park.
8. The Carlsbad Caverns are located in New Mexico and have the largest natural cave room in the world.
9. *Kansas* comes from a Sioux Indian word and means "south wind people."
10. An education in colonial history awaits the visitor to New England.

Diagraming Compound Subjects and Verbs

To diagram a compound subject, you place the subjects on parallel lines. Notice that the connecting word is put on a dotted line between the parallel subject lines.

EXAMPLE Sharks and eels are dangerous.

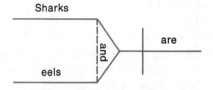

A compound predicate is diagramed in a similar way. The two verbs go on parallel lines with the connecting word on a broken line between them.

EXAMPLE The cowboy swung into the saddle and rode away.

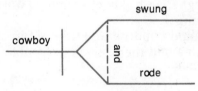

A sentence with both a compound subject and a compound verb combines the two patterns.

EXAMPLE Paul Revere and William Dawes saw the lantern in North Church and warned the Americans of the approach of the British troops.

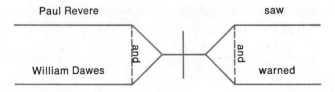

EXERCISE 22. Diagram the subjects and verbs in the following sentences. Many of them are compound. Use your ruler and leave plenty of space between diagrams.

1. Everyone knows and loves the bears at the zoo.
2. Cubs and adults entertain the onlookers.
3. They stand on their hind legs and beg appealingly for peanuts.
4. The koala is a native of Australia and looks like a teddy bear.
5. This little bear measures about two feet long and has large, hairy ears and gray fur.
6. Some bears are extremely large and can be vicious.
7. The polar bear may stand fourteen feet tall and can kill a human being with a slap of its great paw.
8. Visitors should not tease or mistreat the animals at the zoo.
9. Signs and guides plainly warn visitors of the danger.
10. Some children and adults forget the warning and later find themselves in trouble.

SIMPLE AND COMPOUND SENTENCES

1h. A *simple sentence* **is a sentence that has one subject and one verb.**

The sentences you have been studying so far are *simple sentences.* Each sentence has one subject and one verb. (A compound subject is considered one subject, even though it has two or more parts. Likewise, a compound verb or a verb phrase is considered one verb.) Here are some examples of simple sentences:

A good, soaking rain would help the farmers.

Sally and Diane are the best players on the junior varsity team.

Susan read *The Planet of Junior Brown* and reported on it last week.

1i. A *compound sentence* is a sentence that contains two or more simple sentences, usually joined by a connecting word.

When two or more simple sentences are joined into one sentence, they form a compound sentence. The words *and, but, or, nor, for,* and *yet* are used to combine simple sentences into a compound sentence. Here are some examples:

In the last fifty years scientists have conquered many diseases, **but** the common cold persists.

Citrus fruits and green vegetables should be a part of everyone's diet, **for** they supply needed vitamins.

He called the children to supper, **but** John refused to leave the ball game, **and** Jo didn't hear.

EXERCISE 23. Write the numbers 1–10 on your paper. Read the following sentences carefully. If a sentence is simple, write *simple* after its number. If it is compound, write *compound* after its number. Be prepared to explain your answers.

1. Ruth Benedict was a great anthropologist, and Margaret Mead was one of her pupils.
2. The pine tree is native to many parts of America.
3. Seals and porpoises are great performers.
4. The House of Representatives can impeach the President, but the Senate must carry out the trial.
5. In Europe students attend high schools voluntarily, and they usually pay admission fees.

6. *Circus* comes from a Greek word and originally meant "ring" or "circle."
7. Joan Sutherland, Leontyne Price, Martina Arroyo, and Beverly Sills have all sung before huge audiences.
8. To the east of the United States is Europe, and to the west is Asia.
9. George Washington did not sign the Declaration of Independence or participate in the Boston Tea Party.
10. Did you read *Hedda Gabler* or see the play?

Diagraming Compound Sentences

Learning to diagram a compound sentence may help you to see how its parts are related. The diagram of a compound sentence is like the diagrams of two simple sentences put together.

The first step is to find the subject and verb in each part of the compound sentence. Then make a diagram for the first part of the sentence. Write the subject and the verb on the horizontal line with a vertical line between them. Below that diagram, make a diagram for the second part of the compound sentence. Join the two diagrams by a broken line drawn from the verb in the first part to the verb in the second part. On the broken line, write the word that connects the two parts.

EXAMPLE   Crocodiles look slow, but they can move swiftly.

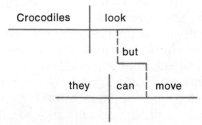

EXERCISE 24. Diagram the subjects and verbs in the following compound sentences. First diagram the two parts; then join the verbs with a broken line on which you write the connecting word.

1. Napoleon was a brilliant general, but he made several costly mistakes.
2. The President of the United States is elected for a four-year period, and he may serve only two terms.
3. The giraffe has a long neck and long legs, but it is a very graceful animal.
4. During the War Between the States many naval battles were fought, and the battle between the *Monitor* and the *Merrimac* was one of the most important.
5. Do you recall earlier battles between ironclad ships, or was this the first?
6. The sides of the *Merrimac* were twenty-eight inches thick, but only part of that was iron.
7. The *Monitor* had a turret in the middle of its low, flat deck, and many people called the ship a "cheesebox on a raft."
8. The smaller *Monitor* could turn easily, but the *Merrimac* was difficult to maneuver.
9. The two ships fought on March 9, 1861, and the battle lasted all day.
10. Did the *Monitor* sink the *Merrimac*, or was the outcome different?

CLASSIFYING SENTENCES BY PURPOSE

The following examples illustrate the main kinds of sentences: those that make statements, those that give orders or make requests, those that ask questions, and those that express strong feeling. Sentences may be classified according to these purposes.

A storm warning has been issued. [a statement]
Get into the storm cellar. [an order]

Are you afraid of the storm? [a question]
Here comes the tornado! [an expression of excitement]

1j. Sentences may be classified according to their purpose.

(1) A *declarative sentence* is a sentence that makes a statement.

EXAMPLES   Our library has several encyclopedias.
Willa Cather was born in Virginia.

The declarative sentence is used more frequently than all of the other kinds combined. It is always followed by a period.

(2) An *imperative sentence* is a sentence that gives a command or makes a request.

EXAMPLES   Be quiet during the play.
Please give me another piece of melon.
Don't miss the bus!

An imperative sentence may be followed by a period or an exclamation point. Ordinary requests take a period. Commands and strong requests take an exclamation point.

The subject of a sentence that is a command or a request is the word *you,* understood but not expressed. The first sentence means: *You* be quiet during the play. The second means: *You* please give me another piece of melon. The understood *you* may refer to one person or to a group of persons.

Sometimes an imperative sentence consists of only one word, as in the following:

Stop! [The subject *you* is understood.]
Hurry! [The subject *you* is understood.]

The word *you* is still the understood subject when the person spoken to is addressed by name, as in:

Mary, [you] please answer the door.

(3) An *interrogative sentence* is a sentence that asks a question.

EXAMPLES   When did Thurgood Marshall become a Supreme Court justice?
How much did the surfboard cost?

An interrogative sentence is always followed by a question mark. Notice that in an interrogative sentence a part of the verb always comes before the subject.

(4) An *exclamatory sentence* is a sentence that expresses strong feeling. It exclaims.

EXAMPLES   Imagine the look on her face when she won first prize!
How terrifying that movie was!

An exclamatory sentence is always followed by an exclamation point.

EXERCISE 25.   Decide whether the following quotations are declarative, imperative, interrogative, or exclamatory sentences. Write the numbers 1–10 on your paper. After each number write the kind of sentence it is. (Be careful of the spelling of declar*a*tive, imper*a*tive, interrog*a*tive, and exclam*a*tory: notice the *a* before the *t* in each word.) Then write the proper mark of punctuation to follow the sentence.

EXAMPLE   1. If Winter comes, can Spring be far behind — SHELLEY
1. *Interrogative ?*

1. I want to be alone — GARBO
2. Take time for all things — FRANKLIN
3. Where are the snows of yesteryear — VILLON
4. Art is too long and life is too short
— GRACE PALEY
5. What a piece of work is man — SHAKESPEARE
6. Pardon my dust — DOROTHY PARKER
7. Do you like me more than you don't like me or don't you like me more than you do
— SHELAGH DELANEY
8. Life was meant to be lived, and curiosity must be kept alive — ELEANOR ROOSEVELT
9. No path is wholly rough — ELLA WILCOX
10. Keep true to the dreams of thy youth — SCHILLER

REVIEW EXERCISE A. Some of the following groups of words are sentences; some are not. Copy the groups of words which are sentences, adding capital letters and punctuation marks. If a group of words is not a sentence, add whatever is needed (subject or verb or both) to make a sentence. Write the sentence.

EXAMPLES
1. the students read English ballads
1. *The students read English ballads.*
2. over the glowing coals
2. *We toasted marshmallows over the glowing coals.*

1. wrapped the presents and put them under the tree
2. the snow fell for two days
3. just after the War Between the States
4. the people jogging along the path
5. how happy the senator was to be re-elected
6. a detective story keeps you guessing until the end
7. do you know the distance from the earth to the sun
8. draw a picture of a castle
9. working every Saturday during the summer

10. about a half mile below Niagara Falls is a great whirlpool

REVIEW EXERCISE B. Copy the following sentences. Underline the complete subjects with one line and the complete predicates with two lines. Circle the simple subjects and verbs. If your teacher prefers, diagram the simple subjects and verbs.

1. Switzerland is the most mountainous country in Europe.
2. The Alps have about seventy peaks.
3. Can you name a famous Swiss lake?
4. The Rhine and Rhone flow from Switzerland.
5. The country produces much machinery and manufactures more than half of the world's watches.
6. Salt is the principal mineral.
7. Large amounts of chocolate and cheese are exported from Switzerland.
8. Switzerland is a republic and is governed by a Federal Council of seven members.
9. One member serves as president for a one-year term.
10. In Switzerland dialects of German are spoken by most of the people, but French and Italian are also spoken.

REVIEW EXERCISE C. Some of the following sentences are simple; others are compound. After each number on your paper, write *S* if the sentence is simple or *C* if it is compound. Then write the simple subjects and verbs.

EXAMPLE   1. Manufacturers are making smaller cars.
          1. *S Manufacturers are making*

1. After the storm, telephone repair crews worked all night.

2. The others fished from the dock, but Helen and I went in the boat.
3. You may go downtown with your father, or you may go to the park.
4. Susan won the race with a powerful sprint.
5. Traveling cross-country with the family was fun, and we learned a lot about the United States.
6. My sister plays the drums in our combo, and I play the clarinet.
7. In tennis, strength is necessary, but speed and skill are more important.
8. The Voyager 2 spacecraft sent back valuable pictures of the planet Jupiter.
9. On rainy days we may bake a cake, make a batch of candy, or play checkers.
10. The result of our efforts was a disaster.

REVIEW EXERCISE D. The following sentences are declarative, interrogative, imperative, or exclamatory. Copy each sentence, adding the appropriate mark of punctuation at the end. Then underline the simple subject once and underline the verb twice in each sentence. If the subject is *you* understood, add it in parentheses.

1. Flowers and insects depend on each other for life
2. Have you ever watched a bee in a garden
3. The bee flies from one blossom to another
4. Notice the pollen on the bee's wings and body
5. The bee is carrying pollen from one flower to another
6. What a remarkable process it is
7. Think of other carriers of pollen
8. Could the wind do it
9. Pollen of corn plants is carried by the wind
10. How many food products come from a tiny grain of pollen

Chapter 2

The Parts
of Speech

Noun, Pronoun, Adjective

Words, which are the building blocks of
language, are used in eight different ways. They have,
therefore, eight different names, called *parts of speech.*
These parts of speech are noun, pronoun, adjective,
verb, adverb, preposition, conjunction, and interjection. In this chapter and the next one you will discover two things about each part of speech: what it
is and how it is used.

THE NOUN

Look around your classroom and name the things
that you see. All the objects that you have named are
nouns. Many things which you associate with your
classroom but which you cannot see or touch are also
nouns: *interest, thought, education, instruction, coop-
eration.* A noun is the *name* of something, something
which it may or may not be possible for you to see
or touch.

2a. A noun is a word that names a person, place, thing, or idea.

Persons Mother, Dan, Maria, Mayor Dawson, teacher, brother, woman
Places Grand Canyon, city, Nevada, kitchen
Things train, lamp, canary, year, bread
Ideas grief, desire, democracy, speed, bravery

EXERCISE 1. There are twenty nouns in the following paragraph. Make a list of them on your paper. Before each noun, write the number of the sentence in which it appears.

1. The *Titanic* was supposed to be an unsinkable ship. **2.** The captain and the crew had great trust in its strength. **3.** The passengers, too, were convinced that the ship was indestructible. **4.** Then the liner struck an iceberg off the coast of Newfoundland. **5.** About fifteen hundred persons drowned because few lifeboats had been provided. **6.** Only the children, most women, and a small group of men were saved. **7.** The whole world was shocked by this senseless tragedy.

EXERCISE 2. There are twenty-five nouns in the following paragraph. Make a list of them on your paper. Before each noun, write the number of the sentence. Some of the nouns will be listed more than once.

1. Rebecca Motte was a great patriot. **2.** During the Revolutionary War, British soldiers seized her mansion in South Carolina and set up defenses. **3.** General Harry Lee told Motte that the Americans would have to burn her home to smoke out the enemy. **4.** Motte supported the plan and was glad to help her country. **5.** She even supplied fire arrows and a bow for the attack. **6.** The enemy raised the white flag, and the house was saved. **7.** That night, Motte invited both sides to dinner.

Proper Nouns and Common Nouns

You may have noticed that some of the nouns you have been identifying begin with a capital letter. These are called *proper nouns*. Nouns that do not begin with a capital are called *common nouns*. A proper noun names a particular person, place, or thing. Here are some examples of proper nouns:

Persons	Ms. Frankel, Neil Armstrong, Rita, Aunt Gladys
Places	Kansas City, Idaho, Egypt, Australia
Things	Eiffel Tower, Old Faithful, Jupiter

A common noun does *not* name a particular person, place, or thing. These are common nouns:

Persons	child, teacher, movie star, uncle
Places	town, meadow, street, valley, gym
Things	book, airplane, scissors, typewriter, shed
Ideas	friendship, consideration, justice, anger

Proper nouns are always capitalized. Study the following lists of common and proper nouns until you are sure you understand why each word is classed as it is.

COMMON NOUNS	PROPER NOUNS
document	Bill of Rights
mayor	Mayor Hudson
girl	Kay O'Neill
desert	Sahara
country	Canada
people	Finns

Nouns of more than one word, like *White House, living room,* or *Colorado River,* are considered one noun.

EXERCISE 3. List the twenty-five nouns in the following paragraph. Before each noun, write the number of the sentence in which it appears. After each noun, write *C* if it is common or *P* if it is proper.

1. Early one morning Charles A. Lindbergh left Roosevelt Field in New York in his plane, the *Spirit of St. Louis.* **2.** Lindbergh was attempting a nonstop flight to Paris. **3.** The pilot was in the air for about thirty-three hours. **4.** The plane flew through rain and fog. **5.** Lindbergh finally reached the designated landing field in Paris. **6.** The whole world celebrated his heroic achievement. **7.** On his return to the United States aboard a cruiser, the young hero was welcomed by President Calvin Coolidge.

EXERCISE 4. Rewrite the following sentences, substituting proper nouns for all common nouns. You may need to change some of the words which precede the noun.

EXAMPLE   1. An ambassador visited a local school and spoke about his country.

1. *Ambassador Rios visited Jackson High School and spoke about Brazil.*

1. Two friends water-skied on the lake.
2. The doctor turned right at the street beyond the department store.
3. The twins, who are from a large city, are vacationing near a lake.

4. A teacher asked a student to report on a country.
5. The architect says the building will be completed next month.
6. Our school newspaper comes out in three days.
7. The girl bought a book at the bookstore.
8. That state borders on the ocean.
9. The principal of our school toured two European countries during a summer month.
10. A man flew to a southern city one day.

REVIEW EXERCISE A. The following paragraph contains twenty-five nouns, some common and some proper. List them on your paper, writing the number of the sentence before each. Capitalize all proper nouns. Some nouns will be listed more than once.

1. Many First Ladies in the white house have lobbied for new laws. **2.** eleanor roosevelt urged legislation to assist the poor and the oppressed. **3.** jacqueline kennedy worked for legislation that made the white house a national shrine. **4.** lady bird johnson was interested in the beauty and ecology of america. **5.** her work led to laws which improved the landscape of highways and created many parks. **6.** rosalynn carter spoke before audiences in several states in support of the Equal Rights Amendment.

REVIEW EXERCISE B. Have you a keen imagination? By filling the blanks in the following paragraph with various nouns, you can produce a story. In fact, with different sets of nouns, you could make a number of different stories. Copy the paragraph, filling in the blanks with either common or proper nouns.

We were in the —— when the —— occurred. We were frightened by the —— and the ——. Finally, a —— advised us to try to get to ——. By the time

we reached ——, we were so exhausted that we
headed for the ——. But we could never forget the
—— of the terrifying ——.

THE PRONOUN

Study the following sentences:

> When Sue met Ted, Sue noticed that Ted was
> carrying several books. Sue offered to help
> Ted. Ted thanked Sue.

> When Sue met Ted, **she** noticed that **he** was
> carrying several books. **She** offered to help
> **him.** Ted thanked **her.**

The words in heavy type replace the nouns *Sue* and
Ted. These words are *pronouns. Pro* means "for"; a
pronoun is a word used for, or in place of, a noun.

**2b. A pronoun is a word used in place of one or more
than one noun. It may stand for a person, place, thing,
or idea.**

Can you tell which noun or nouns each pronoun in the
following sentences replaces?

> After Lois borrowed the book, **she** found **it**
> had not been assigned by the teacher.
> Dan, have **you** seen the new skating rink?
> Jo poured a glass of milk and drank **it. She**
> found some cake and ice cream and ate **them.**

Personal Pronouns

There are several kinds of pronouns. The ones you
will be studying in this chapter are *personal* pronouns. These are the personal pronouns:

I, me, my, mine
you, your, yours
he, him, his
she, her, hers
it, its
we, us, our, ours
they, them, their, theirs

Some of the personal pronouns in the preceding list can be combined with *–self* or *–selves:*

Be careful not to cut *yourself.*
I will do it *myself.*

A pronoun combined with *–self* or *–selves* is still a pronoun.

Some other kinds of pronouns, which you will study later, are *indefinite, interrogative,* and *demonstrative.*

INDEFINITE PRONOUNS	INTERROGATIVE PRONOUNS	DEMONSTRATIVE PRONOUNS
anybody	who	this
each	whom	that
either	what	these
none	which	those
someone, one, etc.	whose	

Words like *my* and *her* (possessive forms of the pronouns *I* and *she*) are called pronouns throughout this book. Some teachers, however, prefer to think of possessive pronouns as adjectives. Follow your teacher's direction in labeling these words.

EXERCISE 5. Write the numbers 1–10 on your paper. After each number, copy the pronouns in the sentence, writing after each the noun or nouns that the pronoun stands for.

1. "I can tell you which chapters the quiz will cover," Ms. Halverson told the class.
2. The driver had another cup of coffee before she continued the journey.
3. "I think the bicycle has a flat tire," reported Joe gloomily.
4. The students decorated the gym themselves.
5. Jane asked the students to let her know when they were ready.
6. Bert asked himself how he could have missed so many shots.
7. Jane and Ida decided they would try out for the team.
8. Edward and Ronald are demonstrating their tricks of magic.
9. Mr. Kent said to let him know when Teresa arrives.
10. Grace said she felt the part was not for her.

EXERCISE 6. Read these sentences aloud. Replace the repeated nouns with pronouns.

1. The plane gained speed as the plane taxied down the runway.
2. Christine finished the book and returned the book to the library.
3. When Marilyn met Arthur, Marilyn told Arthur that Marilyn knew Arthur's sister.
4. The parents of the mountain climbers prepared the parents of the mountain climbers for the bad news.
5. Roger doesn't like the city, but Roger commutes to the city every day.
6. Dana asked Barbara, "Will Barbara have a soda with Dana?"
7. Lydia enjoys biology and astronomy because biology and astronomy explain many mysteries to Lydia.

8. The roses had hardly opened before the roses' petals began to drop.
9. Ben confessed, "Ben does not know what the sport of curling is."
10. When the electrician arrived, the electrician found that several power lines had been blown down.

Possessive Pronouns

Among the pronouns listed on page 41 are *his, your, our.* These words and others like them are *possessive pronouns.* They are used to show ownership or relationship.

Possessive Pronouns

my, mine	his	its	their, theirs
your, yours	her, hers	our, ours	

The words in heavy type in the following sentences are possessive pronouns.

All the books that were **theirs** became **mine.**
Your boat goes faster than **ours** does.
Her motor scooter was imported from Italy.

▶ **NOTE** The possessive form of the pronoun *it* is *its.* Do not confuse *its* with the word *it's,* which means "it is" or "it has."

EXERCISE 7. Write the numbers 1–20 on your paper. After each number, write the pronouns that occur in the sentence. Do not overlook the possessive pronouns.

1. Our house is not far from theirs.
2. The baby bruised herself when she fell.
3. They read the false document and approved it.

4. My record player is quite different from hers.
5. We must not allow ourselves to overlook injustice.
6. The record player is his, but the new records are hers.
7. He should have used his skates instead of hers.
8. The professor told us our dog had been burying bones in her garden.
9. You know that a single match can destroy acres of valuable timber.
10. Shall we follow her suggestion?
11. She gave herself a haircut and suggested one for me.
12. "I will act the part left vacant by the missing member of the cast," the director said to us.
13. Marie and Pierre Curie devoted their lives to the discovery of radium and the study of how it affects human beings.
14. We must stop quarreling among ourselves if we are to finish the assignment.
15. "You must give yourselves time to adjust to the new situation," I told them.
16. Will you pick up the laundry for me, please?
17. She thought to herself that they were getting into trouble.
18. Whenever Mr. Nagel gives a talk about "contemporary history," we enjoy it.
19. "Piano lessons are definitely not for me," said Martha.
20. The decision must be ethical if we are to commit ourselves to it.

EXERCISE 8. There are twenty pronouns in the following quotations. Write them on your paper after the number of each quotation.

1. Books think for me. — CHARLES LAMB
2. I never think of the future. It comes soon enough.
— ALBERT EINSTEIN

3. Parents learn a lot from their children about coping with life. — MURIEL SPARK

4. The sea lies all around us. The commerce of all lands must cross it. — RACHEL L. CARSON

5. In the faces of men and women I see God.
— WALT WHITMAN

6. Life is very short, and very uncertain; let us spend it as well as we can. — SAMUEL JOHNSON

7. Who has seen the wind?
— CHRISTINA GEORGINA ROSSETTI

8. War with its iron hand corrupts manners and invades the mind as much as it destroys the body, and all ranks of people are more or less affected by it. . . . — GRACE GROWDON GALLOWAY

9. Never forget any moments; they are too few.
— ELIZABETH BOWEN

10. We have it in our power not only to free ourselves but to subdue our masters.
— ABIGAIL SMITH ADAMS

THE ADJECTIVE

Notice the difference between the following sentences. Which sentence is more interesting?

> A house stood on the hill.
> A **haunted** house stood on the **barren** hill.

The second sentence has additional words, *haunted* and *barren,* which make the house and its location more vivid. These words are called *adjectives.* Adjectives are used to describe nouns and pronouns. The adjective *haunted* describes or modifies the noun *house,* and the adjective *barren* modifies the noun *hill.* These adjectives make more definite your idea of what the house and the hill are like.

2c. An adjective is a word that modifies a noun or pronoun.

Most nouns, like *animal, city,* and *man,* have a very general meaning because they name a whole class of things. To make these words definite and specific, we need the adjective, a word that describes or makes clear the meaning of a noun. As you will see, adjectives are used with some pronouns as well as with nouns. Adjectives are said to *modify* the words they describe.

Adjectives answer the questions *What kind? Which one? How many?* or *How much?* The adjectives in the following phrases are in heavy type.

What kind?	**happy** children
	busy dentist
	sunny day
Which one or *ones?*	**seventh** grade
	these countries
	any book
How many or *How much?*	**full** tank
	five dollars
	no marbles

Adjectives don't always come before the word they modify; sometimes they follow it.

EXAMPLES   The box is **empty.** [The adjective *empty* modifies *box.*]

A woman, **kind** and **wise,** helped us. [The adjectives *kind* and *wise* modify *woman.*]

Study the adjectives in the following sentences. An arrow shows you what word each adjective modifies.

1. **This** drawing was chosen the winner. [*This* tells *which one* was chosen.]

2. I visited San Francisco for **several** days. [*Several* tells *how many* days.]

3. The team was **eager.** [*Eager* tells *what kind* of team.]

4. Fort Laramie was an **important** stop on the way to California. [*Important* tells *what kind* of stop.]

The Article

Three small words — *a, an, the* — are the most commonly used adjectives. They are called *articles*. You use an article almost every time you write a sentence. Because of the number of articles in the exercises in this chapter, you will not be asked to mark them. However, you should remember that they are adjectives.

EXERCISE 9. Copy the following story, filling each blank with an appropriate adjective.

The group explored the __1__ section. They saw __2__ trees and __3__ bushes. Very often they had a __4__ time getting through the __5__ jungle. On __6__ occasions they almost gave up. But they were rewarded for the __7__ effort they put forth. During the __8__ trek through the jungle, the party discovered __9__ kinds of animals. A __10__ parrot particularly amused them. They were admiring the bird when a __11__ jaguar walked out of the undergrowth. Immediately the __12__ animals began to make __13__ noises and wasted __14__ time in getting out of the __15__ cat's way. After a day of __16__ hiking, the __17__ group finally pitched camp in a __18__ clearing. They were __19__ for their __20__ supper.

EXERCISE 10. There are twenty-five adjectives in the following paragraph. Copy each adjective, and before it write the number of the sentence. Then write the word that the adjective modifies. Do not copy the articles *a, an,* or *the*.

EXAMPLE 1. Why don't you take the school bus on cold days?
1. *school, bus*
1. *cold, days*

1. On winter afternoons at dusk, I sometimes take the long walk home after basketball practice instead of the steamy ride on a crowded bus. **2.** Occasionally someone joins me as we leave the nearly deserted building, but usually I take this walk by myself. **3.** I pay little attention to the homeward-bound traffic that streams past me. **4.** The wet sidewalk glistens in the light from the windows of stores and the light from the rows of street lamps. **5.** The traffic lights throw green, yellow, and red splashes on the pavement. **6.** The breath of pedestrians, as they rush toward home, condenses into small wisps of cloud in the crisp air. **7.** After I turn the corner away from the busy avenue, I am on a quiet street, where piles of dirty snow surround the doorways of apartment houses. **8.** Suddenly, before I realize it, I find myself, tired but happy, at home, receiving loud greetings from the other members of the family.

Proper Adjectives

A proper noun, you will recall, is one that names a particular person, place, or thing. A proper adjective is formed from a proper noun.

PROPER NOUNS	PROPER ADJECTIVES
Iceland	**Icelandic** holiday
Spain	**Spanish** dancer
Asia	**Asian** country
the Midwest	the **Midwestern** states

Notice that the proper adjective, like the proper noun, always begins with a capital letter.

EXERCISE 11. There are twenty-five adjectives, common and proper, in the following paragraphs. List them on your paper after the number of the sentence in which they appear. Do not include articles.

EXAMPLE 1. I took a picture of an African antelope.
1. *African*

1. Many animals protect themselves in clever ways. 2. When a cottontail rabbit senses the approach of an enemy, it pounds the ground with powerful hind legs to alert other nearby animals, who can hear the warning sounds that travel along the ground. 3. South American armadillos wear suits of armor that consist of small, close-fitting, bony scales.

4. Asian anteaters wear hard scales that overlap like the shingles on a roof and resemble the coat of iron worn by a medieval knight. 5. The skunk uses chemical warfare. 6. It can shoot a jet of foul odor as far as ten feet. 7. Bats avoid tree branches by means of a highly efficient radar system. 8. The wide hind feet of the snowshoe hare help to support it on winter snows.

EXERCISE 12. Change the following proper nouns into proper adjectives, and write each one in a sentence.

1. Britain	6. Switzerland
2. Canada	7. Shakespeare
3. Paris	8. Aquarius
4. China	9. Bible
5. Mexico	10. Ireland

Diagraming Adjectives

Diagrams show the relationships among words. The patterns on the next page show how an adjective is related to the noun it modifies.

PATTERNS

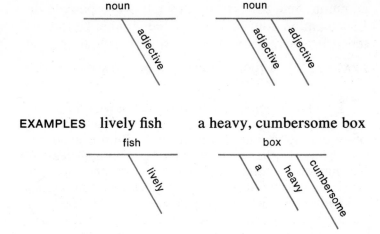

EXAMPLES   lively fish   a heavy, cumbersome box

To diagram adjectives, put them on slanting lines beneath the noun they modify, in the order in which they occur in the sentence. Remember that articles are adjectives.

EXERCISE 13. Using the patterns given above, diagram the following groups of words. For neat work, use a ruler. In each diagram, write the noun first. Leave plenty of space between diagrams.

1. bright morning
2. clear water
3. worn-out sneakers
4. lost pet
5. a blue sweater

6. the mysterious note
7. an impossible feat
8. the three careful hikers
9. a tall, slender woman
10. many mistakes

EXERCISE 14. Diagram the following sentences.

1. Sue Everett sighed.
2. A big orange truck overturned.
3. The package arrived.
4. The new soldier saluted.

5. The two lost children rested.
6. Hot, dusty days have come.
7. An old fort burned.
8. The students attended.
9. A sleek new ship was christened.
10. The tired, hungry pup returned.

THE SAME WORD AS DIFFERENT PARTS OF SPEECH

A word that is a pronoun in one sentence may be an adjective in another. Similarly, a noun may be used as an adjective. You cannot tell what part of speech a word is until you see it in a sentence. Notice how the same word is used in different ways in the pairs of sentences below.

> **That** problem is difficult. [adjective]
> **That** is a surprise. [pronoun]

> The helmet is made of **steel**. [noun]
> It is a **steel** helmet. [adjective]

REVIEW EXERCISE C. Locate all the nouns, pronouns, and adjectives in each sentence in the following paragraph, and write them after the number of the sentence. After each noun, write *n.;* after each pronoun, write *pron.;* and after each adjective, write *adj.* Do not list the articles — *a, an,* and *the.*

EXAMPLE   1. We located the bats in a dark cave.
             1. *We, pron.*
               bats, n.
               dark, adj.
               cave, n.

1. Bats often hang from the roofs of caves during the day and fly out at night. **2.** Although they can fly, they are mammals. **3.** These mysterious creatures have poor eyesight. **4.** People cannot hear their high-pitched sound. **5.** The sound echoes back to the bats like a radar beam. **6.** This beam tells them the location of obstacles, and it also helps them to find food. **7.** Several kinds of bats live in the tropical regions. **8.** Sixty-five varieties are found in the United States. **9.** Many bats feed on insects; other larger kinds eat fruit. **10.** The South American vampire bat feeds on blood.

Chapter **3**

The Parts
of Speech

Verb, Adverb, Preposition,
Conjunction, Interjection

In Chapter 2 you learned about nouns, pronouns, and adjectives. There are five other parts of speech, which you will study in this chapter.

You have already learned to recognize *verbs* from your study of Chapter 1. You know that the verb is the most important word in the predicate of a sentence.

THE VERB

The verb is one of the foundation words of a sentence. Every sentence must contain a verb.

The verb gives the sentence meaning by saying something about the subject. Notice the verbs in these sentences:

> I **like** homemade ice cream.
> The Blakes **drove** through the Ozarks last month.
> **Are** alligators reptiles?

3a. A *verb* **is a word that expresses action or otherwise helps to make a statement.**

Action Verbs

The easiest kind of verb to recognize is one that expresses physical or mental action. Verbs like *walk, speak, write, drive,* and *hope, believe, understand, approve* are *action* verbs.

(1) An *action verb* is a verb that expresses mental or physical action.

EXAMPLES   The owls **hooted** all night.
Gloria **played** with the children.
We **studied** our history at the library.

EXERCISE 1.   Write the numbers 1–20 on your paper. After each number, write the action verb from the sentence.

1. For a science project, Elena built a sundial.
2. Mr. Santos carefully explained the problem again.
3. For my fall sport, I chose soccer.
4. This waterfall drops two hundred feet.
5. Mike's bicycle skidded on the pavement.
6. In Millerville you transfer to another bus.
7. Mix the ingredients slowly.
8. The heavy traffic delayed us.
9. They scored two runs in the first inning.
10. The police arrested two suspects.
11. Planes land here every two minutes.
12. Committee members listened to our complaints.
13. Rick's parrot screams all day.
14. At dawn we hear the motors of fishing boats.
15. Hungry gulls follow the boats on their return.
16. Paula caught the largest fish.
17. In vain we hoped for snow.
18. Everyone ran toward the exits.
19. Who planted these trees?
20. To my surprise, no one believed me.

EXERCISE 2. There are twenty action verbs in the following paragraph. Write them on your paper, with the number of the sentence preceding them.

1. We thought a long time about our vacation. 2. Finally, we decided on the Smoky Mountains. 3. We drove down from Ohio and reached the Smoky Mountain Park about one o'clock in the afternoon. 4. The views from the many mountain peaks thrilled us. 5. The trip to Clingman's Dome particularly excited us. 6. We climbed the ramp to the modern lookout tower. 7. From up there we saw all the mountains around us. 8. We went back the next day. 9. This time clouds floated in on us like great ocean waves. 10. The mist dampened our skin and made us cold. 11. On our way down the mountain we noticed a large group of people. 12. We parked our car and walked over to the group. 13. There, in the middle of the circle of people, stood two large bears. 14. They played happily together. 15. Soon, one came toward us. 16. We quickly jumped back into our car. 17. From the car we watched the antics of the bears for almost twenty minutes.

Linking Verbs

Some verbs do not express mental or physical action. They help make a statement by connecting the subject with a word in the predicate that describes or explains it. These verbs are called *linking* verbs. The most common linking verb is *be*. The following are some forms of the verb *be:*

am	has been	may be
is	have been	would have been
are	had been	can be
was	will be	should be
were	shall be	

Any verb phrase that ends in *be* or *been* is a form of the linking verb *be*.

> I **am** a photographer.
> He **has been** sick.
> We **would have been** early.
> Those berries **were** delicious.

In addition to the forms of *be*, there are other linking verbs. Notice how the linking verbs in heavy type in the following sentences *link* the subject with a word in the predicate.

> The actor **appeared** tired during the play. [The verb *appeared* connects *actor* and *tired*.]
> Sara **stayed** calm in the midst of the clamor. [The verb *stayed* links *Sara* and *calm*.]
> This corn **smells** fresh. [The verb *smells* connects *corn* and *fresh*.]

(2) A *linking verb* is a verb that does not show action but connects the subject with a word in the predicate.

In addition to *be*, the following verbs are commonly used as linking verbs:

taste	look	grow
feel	appear	remain
smell	become	stay
sound	seem	

Some verbs may be either action or linking verbs, depending on how they are used. The meaning of the sentence tells you which kind of verb it is.

Action   Amy **looked** through the telescope.
Linking Amy **looked** pale.

Action   We all **felt** the rough bark of the tree.
Linking We all **felt** excited before the experiment.

Action   Mother **sounded** the bell for dinner.
Linking Mother **sounded** pleased by the news.

EXERCISE 3. There are ten linking verbs in the following paragraph. List them in order on your paper, writing the number of the sentence before each one.

1. Seeds are very strange. **2.** A simple seed becomes a watermelon. **3.** At first the seed remains lifeless in the ground. **4.** Then it becomes larger and larger. **5.** Finally, the plant is large enough to break through the ground. **6.** Later the plant is recognizable. **7.** On the vines the small watermelons first appear green. **8.** After a few weeks the melons sound ripe when thumped. **9.** Then the melon smells and tastes so good that you wish you could buy a watermelon farm.

EXERCISE 4. Pick out the verbs in the following sentences. If the verb is a linking verb, write after it the subject and the word in the predicate to which the subject is linked.

EXAMPLES   1. The pilot flew faster than the speed of sound.
            1. *flew*
           2. A bobcat looks ferocious.
            2. *looks, bobcat—ferocious*

1. He felt bad about his score on the test.
2. The cat's eyes looked green in the dark.
3. The climbers moved slowly along the edge of the cliff.
4. We stayed in Hollywood for the shooting of the film.
5. June Tong felt her way carefully through the dark room.
6. The pavement smells clean after a hard rain.
7. Denver is the capital of Colorado.
8. Sylvia cautiously smelled the strange chemical.
9. The movie previews looked silly.
10. The dancers were natives of Chile.

EXERCISE 5. There are twenty verbs in the following paragraphs. List them in order on your paper, writing the number of the sentence before each one. Write *action* after action verbs and *linking* after linking verbs.

1. I once visited a planetarium. **2.** It was a fascinating place. **3.** Before the lecture, I wandered around the building and looked at the many displays. **4.** One exhibit showed various comets. **5.** Another displayed a meteorite of more than thirty-four tons. **6.** It fell to the earth many years ago and left a crater in the earth's surface. **7.** Meteorites caused the thousands of craters on the moon, also.

8. After a few minutes a group of us went into the large lecture room. **9.** The lecturer was ready for us. **10.** She stood beside a large, strange-looking machine. **11.** It re-created the stars, the moon, and the sun on the great dome-shaped roof of the room. **12.** The lecturer dimmed the lights, and the dome appeared full of stars. **13.** In fact, more stars were visible than on the clearest night. **14.** The lecturer showed us the heavens of centuries ago. **15.** We also got a view of future skies. **16.** At the end of the lecture, we were quiet and awe-struck. **17.** Our universe is full of wonders!

EXERCISE 6. Write ten original sentences, five with action verbs and five with linking verbs.

Helping Verbs

You learned in Chapter 1 that a verb may consist of one word or several words. If it consists of more than one word, it is called a *verb phrase*. A verb phrase contains one *main verb* and one or more *helping verbs*. In the following sentences the verb phrases are underscored, and the helping verbs are in heavy type.

Anita <u>**will** vote</u> in the next Presidential election.
Many Europeans <u>**can** speak</u> a second language.

Kansas <u>**has been** named</u> the Sunflower State.
The lawn <u>**should have been** tended</u> with greater care.

(3) A *helping verb* helps the main verb to express action or make a statement.

Here is a list of words commonly used as helping verbs. Those in the first column are all forms of the verb *be*.

am	has	might
is	have	must
are	had	can
was	do	could
were	does	shall
be	did	should
been	may	will
		would

EXERCISE 7. Read the following verb phrases aloud. Tell which words in each phrase are helping verbs.

1. will be seen
2. can launch
3. has been sighted
4. should have been done
5. will topple
6. may bring
7. have been hammering
8. shall hope
9. would have told
10. had been running

Sometimes the verb phrase is interrupted by another part of speech. A common interrupter is the word *not*. The verb phrase in a question is often interrupted by the subject. Note the separation of the verbs in the following verb phrases.

Ken **does** not **have** a new desk.
Our school **has** always **held** a victory celebration in the fall.
Did you **watch** the launching this morning?
Can you **make** a noise?

EXERCISE 8. Copy the verb phrases from each of the following sentences. Be prepared to tell which words are helping verbs.

1. Have you ever visited the Okefenokee Swamp in Georgia?
2. You would really enjoy a trip through the swamp.
3. The Okefenokee has been called "the land of the trembling earth."
4. Can you find it on a map?
5. Visitors may take boat trips through the swamp.
6. You certainly would not attempt the journey without a guide.
7. The color of the water would surprise you.
8. Its black color is caused by tannic acid.
9. The acid is produced by the thousands of cypress trees in the swamp.
10. The water will reflect your image almost as well as a mirror.

EXERCISE 9. Use each of the following word groups as the subject of a sentence by adding an appropriate verb phrase. Try to use as many different helping verbs as possible. Make some of your sentences questions.

EXAMPLES   1. the long hours of waiting
             1. *The long hours of waiting have ended.*
             2. my younger sister
             2. *Has my younger sister come home?*

1. the research of Charles Drew
2. my letter from the travel agency
3. the bus to Miami
4. our science exam
5. the mother of the child
6. my visitors from Germany
7. valuable mineral deposits
8. a sculpture by Edmonia Lewis
9. a new portable typewriter
10. the dog in the window of the pet shop

REVIEW EXERCISE A. There are twenty verbs in the following paragraph. List them in order on your paper, writing the number of the sentence before each one. Be sure to include helping verbs. Be prepared to tell which are action and which are linking verbs.

1. Ynes Mexia became a famous botanical explorer. **2.** She worked mostly in Latin America and had remarkable experiences there.
3. Ynes Mexia was born in Georgetown, D.C., in 1870. **4.** During her youth, she lived in several states. **5.** In 1921 she started classes at the University of California, where she studied botany. **6.** At the age of fifty-five, she left for a field trip to Mexico, her father's native land. **7.** Although she fell from a cliff and fractured her ribs, she remained active and found 500 species of flowering plants. **8.** Later, she collected thousands of tropical plants in Brazil and Peru, including examples that scientists had rarely seen before. **9.** Once she explored narrow gorges of Peru on a raft. **10.** At other times, she rode on horseback or in canoes.
11. Ynes Mexia felt happiest when she was deep in the wilderness. **12.** In her sixties she faced dangers many younger people would fear.

REVIEW EXERCISE B. Write the numbers 1–20 on your paper. After each number, write the corresponding italicized word or words from the paragraph below. Identify the part of speech of the italicized word or words. Use *n.* for a noun; *pron.* for a pronoun; *adj.* for an adjective; and *v.* for a verb.

There were **(1)** *many* knights during the twelfth and thirteenth centuries. Only sons of the nobility **(2)** *could become* knights. A child **(3)** *began* his education for **(4)** *knighthood* at an early age. First he **(5)** *was taught* the social arts by the lady whom he served as a **(6)** *page.* Then **(7)** *he* became a squire. This was the essential **(8)** *part* of his training. He was taught how to handle **(9)** *arms.* As a squire to a lord, he **(10)** *accompanied* the lord and served him. In return, the lord **(11)** *fed* and **(12)** *housed* his squire. When the lord entered a **(13)** *great* battle, the squire followed his lord and **(14)** *carried* his shield. If the lord was thrown from his **(15)** *horse,* the squire was expected to rescue the lord and help **(16)** *him* back into his saddle. Finally, at the age of twenty or twenty-one the **(17)** *young* man was considered ready for knighthood. By **(18)** *this* time he **(19)** *had received* about **(20)** *fifteen* years of practical education.

THE ADVERB

You have learned that an adjective is a word that modifies a noun or pronoun. An *adverb,* too, is a modifier. By using an adverb you can make a verb, an adjective, or another adverb have a more exact or definite meaning.

A firefighter ran **swiftly** past her.

He was carrying a **very** small child.

The fire blazed **too dangerously** for anyone to enter.

3b. An *adverb* is a word that modifies a verb, an adjective, or another adverb.

Just as an adjective will answer certain questions about a noun or pronoun — What kind? Which one? How many? — so an adverb will answer certain questions about the word it modifies: *Where? When? How? How often? To what extent?*

1. **Yesterday** a fire **completely** destroyed the home of a family on Hill Street. [*Yesterday* and *completely* are adverbs modifying the verb *destroyed*. *Yesterday* tells *when; completely* tells *to what extent.*]

2. A woman who lives **nearby** explained that the fire began **early** in the morning and continued **furiously** until noon. [*Nearby* is an adverb modifying the verb *lived;* it tells *where. Early* is an adverb modifying the verb *began;* it tells *when. Furiously* is an adverb modifying the verb *continued;* it tells *how.*]

3. **Rarely** does a fire last **so long.** [*Rarely,* modifying the verb *does last,* tells *how often. So* modifies the adverb *long,* which modifies the verb *does last.* Together the words *so long* answer the question *to what extent?*]

Here is a list of words that are often used as adverbs.

Where?	here	there	away	up
When?	now	then	later	soon
How?	clearly	easily	quietly	slowly
How often?	never	always	often	seldom
To what extent?	very	too	almost	so really

The word *not* is nearly always used as an adverb to modify a verb. Sometimes *not* is a part of a contraction, as in *hadn't, aren't, didn't.* When it is, the *n't* is an adverb and should not be mistaken for part of the verb.

The Form of Adverbs

Perhaps you have noted that many adverbs end in –*ly*. These adverbs are formed by adding –*ly* to adjectives: *clear — clearly, vigorous — vigorously, quiet — quietly*. But do not think that all words which end in –*ly* are adverbs. Some words ending in –*ly* are adjectives: *friendly* welcome, *timely* remark, *lonely* weekend, *kindly* doctor.

EXERCISE 10. Think of an adverb to modify each of the following verbs. Write both adverb and verb on your paper.

1. works	6. washes
2. are sailing	7. grew
3. sliced	8. can guess
4. sews	9. thought
5. had been yelling	10. scattered

EXERCISE 11. Each sentence below contains one adverb. Write the adverb after the number of the sentence. Then write the word that the adverb modifies. Be prepared to tell what question the adverb answers.

EXAMPLE 1. Many Cherokee Indians still live in the mountains of North Carolina.
1. *still, live*

1. In 1815 a small boy excitedly reported the discovery of gold in Georgia.
2. Many of the white settlers of the area fought greedily for the gold.
3. The Cherokee Indians had been living peacefully in the area of Georgia, North Carolina, Alabama, and Tennessee for many years.
4. The settlers completely forgot about the Indians' right to the land.

5. They quickly asked the government to remove the Indians from the area.
6. In spite of the fact that many Cherokees had fought bravely for the settlers, they were forced to leave their land.
7. Then began the unfortunate "Trail of Tears."
8. The Indians were hardly given a chance to collect their belongings.
9. They were quickly sent to Oklahoma.
10. Many Cherokees can never forget the harsh treatment suffered by their ancestors.

The Position of Adverbs

Adverbs may come before or after the word they modify. Notice the position of the adverbs in these sentences:

> We **often** complain about the cooking.
> We complain **often** about the cooking.

When an adverb modifies a verb phrase, it frequently comes in the middle of the phrase.

> Linda did **not** know the answer to the riddle.
> Falling stars are **often** seen in September.

The adverbs above are close to the words they modify. For variety or emphasis, a writer may begin a sentence with an adverb, separating it from the word it modifies.

> **Suddenly** the door opened.

> **Finally,** after hours of climbing, we came to the end of the trail.

It is an important characteristic of an adverb that it can usually come at more than one place in the sentence. At what other places could *finally* be used in the sentence above? Adverbs often begin questions:

When does your school start? [The adverb *when* modifies the verb *does start*.]

How did you spend your vacation? [The adverb *how* modifies the verb *did spend*.]

EXERCISE 12. Copy the adverbs from the following sentences. After each adverb write the word that the adverb modifies. Remember that adverbs may modify verbs, adjectives, or other adverbs.

1. Squirrels can be seen in almost every park and forest.
2. Most squirrels do not seem to be afraid of people.
3. Often they enjoy human company.
4. They chatter noisily among themselves.
5. They search endlessly for things to eat.
6. People like me, who feed squirrels frequently, find that the squirrels recognize them.
7. Tuft-eared squirrels are the most attractive squirrels.
8. Some of them have completely white tails.
9. How do flying squirrels get their name?
10. They can glide easily from trees to the ground by means of the loose fold of skin between their front and hind legs.

EXERCISE 13. There are twenty adverbs in the following paragraph. Copy them in order, writing the number of the sentence before each adverb. After each one, write the word it modifies. Be prepared to tell what question the adverb answers.

EXAMPLE   1. *Treasure Island* is an extremely exciting story.
    1. *extremely, exciting*

1. A very strange sailor named Bill Bones stalked proudly into the inn owned by Jim Hawkins' father. **2.** Learning that the inn was seldom crowded, Bones quickly decided that it would be an almost perfect hideout for him. **3.** He carefully watched the shore by day and drank heartily in the inn at night. **4.** Jim's father waited patiently for Bill Bones to pay his rent, but Bones never offered him any more money after the first day. **5.** Jim's father was so afraid of Bones that he could not ask his guest for the money. **6.** Somewhat later, Bones received the Black Spot, a very terrible symbol to a pirate. **7.** The Black Spot has always been known as a death notice for pirates. **8.** The Black Spot held such awful terror for Bones that he died of a stroke. **9.** Jim and his mother soon opened the pirate's sea chest to get the money due them. **10.** To their surprise they found there a packet which contained a map locating the treasure of the famous buccaneer, Captain Flint. **11.** Jim later sailed with Long John Silver, an extremely shrewd one-legged sailor, in search of the treasure.

EXERCISE 14. Copy the following paragraph. Fill each blank with an appropriate adverb.

Each fall I __1__ attend the first football game. I can __2__ wait for the gates to open. __3__ I run to my seat and join the __4__ cheering fans. __5__ the cheerleaders come to lead us in the school song. During the kickoff we __6__ stand to encourage the players. If the right halfback receives the ball, we __7__ count on a long run. He dashes __8__ up the field. __9__ he runs the kickoff back for a touchdown. If that happens, we cheer __10__.

Diagraming Adverbs

Adverbs that modify verbs are diagramed in much the same way as adjectives. By using a slanting line for the adverb, you can show the relationship between it and the word it modifies.

1. An adverb modifying a verb:

PATTERN

EXAMPLES   walks briskly   arrived here late

EXERCISE 15. Using the pattern above, diagram the following verbs and adverbs. Use a ruler for lines. In each diagram, write the verb or the verb phrase first; then add the adverb. Leave plenty of space between diagrams.

1. laughed loudly
2. drive slowly
3. did not happen again
4. carefully recorded
5. write legibly

When an adverb modifies an adjective or another adverb, the adverb modifier appears on a slanting line below the word it modifies.

2. An adverb modifying an adjective:

PATTERN

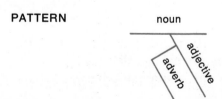

EXAMPLES   badly tarnished silver   very fast boat

3. An adverb modifying another adverb:

PATTERN

EXAMPLES   drove rather care-   could not see
fully   very well

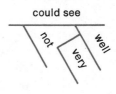

EXERCISE 16. Using the patterns above, diagram the following groups of words. Use a ruler for lines. In each diagram, first write the verb or the noun; then add the modifying word or words. Leave plenty of space between diagrams.

1. almost never find
2. stopped too abruptly
3. extremely fast race
4. very complete report
5. is not swimming well
6. highly skilled carpenter
7. had been practicing often
8. walked too rapidly
9. spoke slowly
10. did not listen carefully

DIAGRAMING SENTENCES

You are now able to diagram more complicated sentences than you have done so far. The long horizontal line supports the subject and the verb. The modifiers, adjectives and adverbs, are suspended below the words they modify. The articles *a, an,* and *the* are, of course, diagramed as adjectives.

PATTERN

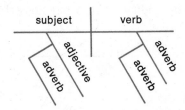

EXAMPLES   The predicted rain came today.

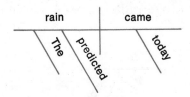

The mare and her colt were looking around rather nervously.

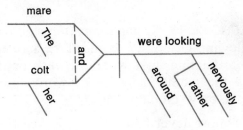

EXERCISE 17. Diagram the following sentences.

1. The judge spoke clearly.
2. The new alarm rings softly.

3. The two dogs ran away quickly.
4. I answered very slowly.
5. Somewhere a rooster crowed loudly.
6. The orange moon shone brightly.
7. Five extremely angry citizens marched in.
8. The young man spoke uncertainly.
9. The whole cast performed especially well.
10. A relatively unknown candidate won easily.

EXERCISE 18.   Diagram the following sentences.

1. The last boat left yesterday.
2. My very good friend moved away recently.
3. Tomorrow I will study more carefully.
4. Jim's guests came early.
5. Never had he laughed so heartily.
6. Suddenly the huge rocket shot upward.
7. The extremely polite usher stood up and nodded graciously.
8. Read rapidly but do not read too rapidly.
9. How is Helen today?
10. When will you be leaving here?

THE PREPOSITION

The preposition is a useful little word. It shows relationship between other words in the sentence. In the sentence, *The plane is on the runway,* the word *on* shows the relation of *plane* to *runway.* The meaning of the sentence would be different if *on* were replaced by *over* or *beside. On, over,* and *beside* are all prepositions.

3c. A *preposition* is a word that shows the relation of a noun or pronoun to some other word in the sentence.

The following words are commonly used as prepositions.

aboard	behind	from	throughout
about	below	in	to
above	beneath	into	toward
across	beside	like	under
after	between	of	underneath
against	beyond	off	until
along	by	on	up
among	down	over	upon
around	during	past	with
at	except	since	within
before	for	through	without

In these sentences the prepositions are in heavy type.

The girl **in** the heavy coat was very hot. [The preposition shows the relation of *girl* to *coat*.]

The plane flew **through** the thick clouds. [The preposition shows the relation of *flew* to *clouds*.]

One **of** my favorite sports is ice hockey. [The preposition shows the relation of *one* to *sports*.]

EXERCISE 19. In each sentence below, a preposition is missing. You are to think of three appropriate prepositions to go in the sentence. (Notice how a change in prepositions changes the relationship between words.) Write the prepositions on your paper after the sentence number. Be sure to use prepositions that make sense in the sentence.

EXAMPLE   1. The girl raced —— the street.
          1. *down, up, across*

1. She saw the cartoons —— dinner.
2. Two friends walked —— the river.
3. My fishing tackle is —— the box.
4. The scout crawled —— the fence.
5. I could hardly see the woman —— the window.

The Prepositional Phrase

The preposition never stands alone in a sentence. It is always used with a noun or pronoun that is called the *object* of the preposition. Usually the noun or pronoun follows the preposition.

> You can press those leaves **under glass.** [The preposition *under* relates its object, *glass,* to *can press.*]

> The quartet sang **in harmony.** [The preposition *in* relates its object, *harmony,* to *sang.*]

A preposition may have more than one object.

> Thelma's telegram **to Nina and Ralph** brought good news.

The objects of prepositions may have modifiers, of course.

> It happened **during the last examination.** [*The* and *last* are adjectives modifying *examination,* the object of the preposition *during.*]

All together the preposition, its object, and the object's modifiers (if there are any) make up a *prepositional phrase.*

EXERCISE 20. Below are several groups of words, each containing a prepositional phrase. Write the numbers 1–10 on your paper. After each number, write the prepositional phrase. Underline the preposition and circle its object.

EXAMPLE   1. the clock in the kitchen
             1. *in the* (*kitchen*)

1. a pad of paper   2. searched at night

3. a friend of mine
4. delighted by the good news
5. a bird outside my window
6. a cottage on the lake
7. one of you
8. flying far above the clouds
9. the display of books and artwork
10. two among the many

EXERCISE 21. Write the numbers 1–10 on your paper. Find the prepositional phrases in the following sentences. Copy each preposition and its object.

EXAMPLE 1. There are many historic landmarks in the West.
       1. *in, West*

1. Donner Pass is located in northwestern California.
2. A great tragedy happened there during 1846 and 1847.
3. Eighty-two settlers from Illinois became snowbound.
4. The party was led by George and Jacob Donner.
5. They knew that without help they could not escape.
6. When their food supply was gone, they killed their horses for meat.
7. Seven settlers made it through the pass and sent back help.
8. But the rescuers could not reach the settlers until spring.
9. When help finally arrived, thirty-five members of the party had died.
10. Do you think such a tragedy could happen to modern travelers?

Prepositions and Adverbs

You remember from your study of Chapter 2 that the part of speech a word is depends on its use in the sentence. Some words may be used as prepositions or as adverbs.

> The woman got **off** her horse. [*Off* is used as a preposition. Its object is *horse*.]
>
> The woman rode **off**. [*Off* is used as an adverb. It tells *where* the woman rode.]

A preposition always has an object. An adverb never does. If you are in doubt about whether a word is used as an adverb or a preposition, look for an object.

> The bear walked **around** and then went **inside**. [*Around* and *inside* are used as adverbs. They modify the verbs *walked* and *went*.]
>
> The bear walked **around the yard** and then went **inside the cabin**. [*Around* and *inside* are used as prepositions. Their objects are *yard* and *cabin*.]

EXERCISE 22. The italicized words in the sentences below are adverbs or prepositions. Decide which each is, and write *adverb* or *prep.* on your paper after the number. Be prepared to explain your answer.

1. In the story "The Most Dangerous Game," a famous hunter, Rainsford, fell *overboard* and was washed ashore on a strange island.
2. Rainsford knew that the island was greatly feared *by* all sailors who passed by.
3. *Among* sailors the place was known as "Ship-Trap Island."
4. After he had looked *around* for several hours, Rainsford found a house on a high bluff.
5. A man with a revolver *in* his hand answered Rainsford's knock.
6. He introduced himself *to* his guest as General Zaroff, a man who, like Rainsford, was a hunter.

7. Rainsford went *inside* and was amazed by the richness of Zaroff's home.
8. That evening Rainsford learned *about* the kind of hunting Zaroff liked.
9. Rainsford soon wished that he could get *out* and never see Zaroff again.
10. Zaroff had tired of ordinary hunting and had cast about *for* a new kind of game — human beings.

THE CONJUNCTION

The next part of speech that you will study is the conjunction. The term *conjunction* comes from two Latin words: *con,* which means "together," and *jungere,* which means "join." A *conjunction* joins things together.

3d. A *conjunction* is a word that joins words or groups of words.

The most common conjunctions, or connecting words, are *and, but, or, nor,* and *for.*

CONJUNCTIONS JOINING WORDS
> Jill **and** Peggy
> pretty **but** useless
> rain **or** snow

CONJUNCTIONS JOINING GROUPS OF WORDS
> listened to the code **and** reported it accurately
> all alone **but** not bored
> in the newspaper **or** on the radio

CONJUNCTIONS JOINING PARTS OF COMPOUND SENTENCES
> Melba is waiting for the mail, **and** Mother is expecting a telephone call.

Rabbits are born blind, **but** hares can see at birth.

These peaches should be used at once, **for** they are overripe.

The tiny bird could not fly, **nor** could it feed itself.

EXERCISE 23. Write sentences using conjunctions as directed.

EXAMPLE   1. Use *and* to join two verbs.
         1. *Geraldine talked and laughed excitedly.*

1. Use *or* to join two adjectives.
2. Use *but* to join the parts of a compound sentence.
3. Use *and* to join two adverbs.
4. Use *or* to join two prepositional phrases.
5. Use *for* to join the parts of a compound sentence.
6. Use *and* to join the parts of a compound subject.
7. Use *or* to join two pronouns.
8. Use *or* to join two proper nouns.
9. Use *but* to join two linking verbs.
10. Use *or* in an imperative sentence.

THE INTERJECTION

You already know that an exclamatory sentence is one which expresses strong feeling. One part of speech has the same purpose as an exclamatory sentence: the *interjection*. Like an exclamatory sentence, the interjection is usually followed by an exclamation point.

3e. An *interjection* is an exclamatory word that expresses strong emotion. An interjection has no grammatical relationship to the rest of the sentence.

Ouch! That hurts!
Goodness! What a haircut!
Wow! The moon is full.

Aha! I know the trick.
Oops! The glass slipped out of my hand.

Sometimes the interjection is followed by a comma:

Oh, I made the same mistake again!
The weather here, **alas,** is worse than I expected.

EXERCISE 24. Copy the following sentences on your paper, supplying an appropriate interjection for each blank. Try to use a different interjection in each.

1. ——! I stubbed my toe!
2. ——! I dropped the eggs.
3. ——! What a touchdown!
4. ——! What a pretty dress!
5. ——! Did you see it?
6. "——!" I exclaimed.
7. The time, ——, had come.
8. ——! It's hot!
9. "——!" I shouted.
10. ——! It's about time!

► **NOTE** In the next chapter you will learn more about the prepositional phrase, including how to diagram it. You already know how to diagram conjunctions in compound subjects or verbs and compound sentences. (See page 25.) The interjection is usually not diagramed, since it has no grammatical relation to the rest of the sentence.

In this chapter and in Chapter 2, you have been studying the eight parts of speech. At this point, you should review what you have learned about them. If you are not sure that you understand each part of speech and can identify each one in sentences, take time now to go back and study them further.

Remember that you cannot tell what part of speech a word is until you know how it is used in a sentence. The same word may be used in different ways.

EXAMPLES The **storm** ended by midnight. [*Storm* names something; it is a noun.]

The soldiers will **storm** the enemy camp. [*Storm* shows action; it is a verb.]

Play **outside** for a while. [*Outside* is an adverb modifying *play*. It tells *where*.]

The **outside** of the house needs paint. [*Outside* is a noun.]

I saw the birds' nest **outside** my window. [*Outside* is a preposition. Its object is *window*.]

SUMMARY

Rule	Part of Speech	Use	Example
2a	noun	names	**Marie** had an **idea** about the **dress.**
2b	pronoun	takes the place of a noun	**This** is **mine,** but **I** will give **it** to **you.**
2c	adjective	modifies a noun or pronoun	We have **two attractive Danish** bowls.
3a	verb	shows action, makes a statement	Ada **had** the right of way, and she **drove** through the intersection.
3b	adverb	modifies a verb, an adjective, or another adverb	We were **so** tired that we watched the game **very quietly.**
3c	preposition	relates a noun or pronoun to another word	**After** the ball game the players got **into** a discussion **about** the umpire's decision.
3d	conjunction	joins words or groups of words	**and, but, or, nor, for**
3e	interjection	shows strong feeling	**Ouch! Help!**

REVIEW EXERCISE C. In each of the following sentences one word is in italics. Write the numbers 1–10 on your paper. After the proper number write the part of speech of the italicized word. Be prepared to give a reason for your answer.

EXAMPLE   1. *Sheep* are raised in Australia.
           1. *noun*

1. The sun set *in* the west.
2. Matthew Henson *reached* the North Pole in 1909.
3. *Oh!* What a brilliant diamond!
4. The teacher *carefully* prepared the science exhibit.
5. The *message* was confidential.
6. Call Maria *or* Sue to the phone.
7. Who discovered *electricity?*
8. A family of nine lives *across* the street.
9. Judith told *me* what had happened.
10. My new *woolen* socks are very warm.

REVIEW EXERCISE D. Write ten sentences, using the following words as directed. Underline the given word in each sentence.

EXAMPLE   1. *dance* as a noun
           1. *Are you going to the <u>dance</u>?*

1. *hike* as a verb
2. *beyond* as a preposition
3. *motor* as a noun
4. *study* as a verb
5. *under* as a preposition
6. *outdoors* as an adverb
7. *slow* as an adjective
8. *spring* as a verb
9. *down* as an adverb
10. *one* as an adjective

REVIEW EXERCISE E. Diagram the following sentences.

1. The audience applauded.
2. We have been warned.
3. The large balloon was released.
4. The old train stopped abruptly.
5. Our yellow kite floated gracefully upward.
6. The lecturer has traveled widely and has spoken often.
7. Bill and Dana live here.
8. The new submarine proceeded very cautiously.
9. Emily Dickinson wrote well.
10. Where are my books?

REVIEW EXERCISE F. Diagram the following sentences.

1. Silently the lion waited.
2. Then it sprang forward noiselessly.
3. A small animal had been trapped.
4. The lion roared and attacked.
5. The prey was quickly eaten.
6. Lions and other wild animals do not kill needlessly.
7. Wild animals are often killed unnecessarily.
8. They must be protected, or they will disappear entirely.
9. Some species are endangered now.
10. They can never be replaced.

REVIEW EXERCISE G. In each of the following sentences one word is in italics. Write the numbers 1–10 on your paper. After the proper number, write the part of speech of the italicized word. Be prepared to give a reason for your answer.

1. Where did she find *this* extremely well-shaped starfish?

2. I seldom miss a *summer* at the seashore.
3. There I pick up shells, starfish, *and,* occasionally, a sea horse.
4. Once I wandered down *to* the beach alone.
5. On the shore I *found* several extremely large fish.
6. "*Wow!*" I exclaimed to a lifeguard who was nearby. "How did these creatures get here?"
7. *She* explained that they were pilot whales, or blackfish.
8. They always travel in *schools.*
9. They follow their leader so closely that they *may be stranded* on the shore by a mistake on the part of the leader.
10. I frequently think about the unfortunate school of fish which followed the leader *too* well.

REVIEW EXERCISE H. Write a paragraph of ten sentences. Underline adjectives, adverbs, and prepositions. You may wish to write about a story you have read, a trip you have taken, or a movie you have seen.

Chapter **4**

The Prepositional Phrase

Adjective and Adverb Uses

In Chapters 2 and 3 you learned how individual words function as parts of speech. A group of words may also be used as a single part of speech — as a noun, adjective, or adverb. One such word group is called a *phrase*.

4a. A *phrase* is a group of related words that does not contain a subject and verb and that is used as a single part of speech.

It is important to remember that a phrase never has a subject and a verb. Phrases cannot stand alone — they must be part of a sentence.

4b. A *prepositional phrase* is a phrase that begins with a preposition and ends with a noun or pronoun. A prepositional phrase may be used as an adjective or an adverb.

Prepositions are words like *at, by, of,* and *with* that show the relation of a noun or pronoun — called the object of the preposition — to another word in the sentence. The preposition and the object and whatever modifiers it may have make up a prepositional phrase.

The groups of words printed in heavy type in the following sentences are all prepositional phrases.

> Sandra has a collection **of shells.**
>
> She started it **in Maine,** but she has gathered shells **from tropical waters,** too.
>
> Her trip **to Puerto Rico** doubled the size **of her collection.**

EXERCISE 1. Find the prepositional phrases in the following sentences and write them on your paper. Underline each preposition and circle its object(s).

1. The whole world watched the flight into space.
2. A bouquet of roses was the centerpiece.
3. The water in the cellar is getting deeper!
4. The view from the mountain is spectacular.
5. Grandma brought a gift for Sandy.
6. This morning she had a dish of cereal and strawberries.
7. Who bought the house across the way?
8. Did you see the lightning during the storm?
9. The baby left her fingerprints along the wall.
10. Betty Myers read with expression and feeling.
11. We're having a party with some friends tonight.
12. You don't know any people like them.
13. The girls told ghost stories before the campfire.
14. There is a leak underneath the sink.
15. The picture over the mantle is crooked.
16. Shhh — I'm leaving without permission.
17. They hacked a trail through the very dense jungle.
18. This is a secret between you and me.
19. We were riding across unusually flat plains.
20. Carmen hid a surprise behind the sofa.

EXERCISE 2. Copy the following sentences, filling in each blank with an appropriate prepositional phrase.

EXAMPLE 1. The hornet stung Ms. Simpson ——.
     1. *The hornet stung Ms. Simpson without any warning.*

1. The lady —— is the wife ——.
2. —— residents were evacuated from the area ——.
3. We planted tulips —— and rose bushes ——.
4. When we peered ——, we saw cobwebs and dust ——.
5. —— we discovered a sword that once belonged ——.

EXERCISE 3. There are twenty prepositional phrases in the following paragraph. Write them in order on your paper, putting the number of the sentence before each phrase. In each phrase, underline the preposition and circle the object(s).

1. King Arthur was a hero during the days of chivalry. **2.** Through his strength he proved his right to the throne of Britain. **3.** He removed a great sword from a solid rock. **4.** Later, Arthur was given a sword with magical strength. **5.** The knights who gathered around King Arthur were known throughout the land for their courage and goodness. **6.** They were dedicated to the service of those in need of help. **7.** Under King Arthur's rule they met and feasted at Camelot. **8.** When someone was in trouble, one of the knights rode to the rescue. **9.** The Knights of the Round Table led adventurous lives and fought many strong opponents.

ADJECTIVE PHRASES

Like an adjective, a prepositional phrase can be used to modify a noun or a pronoun. Such a prepositional phrase is called an *adjective phrase*. The adjective phrase answers the same questions that a single-word adjective answers—*What kind? Which one? How many?* (or *How much?*)

Adjective Karen learned an **important** lesson.

Adjective Phrase Karen learned a lesson **of importance.**

Adjective Lucy chose the **striped** one.

Adjective Phrase Lucy chose the one **with stripes.**

4c. An *adjective phrase* **modifies a noun or a pronoun.**

EXERCISE 4. Write the numbers 1–20 on your paper. Each of the following sentences contains an adjective phrase. Write the phrase and the noun or pronoun it modifies after the proper number.

EXAMPLE 1. The work of Marie and Pierre Curie was invaluable.
    1. *of Marie and Pierre Curie, work*

1. Marie was an unknown student with little money when she met Pierre Curie.
2. Pierre was already a scientist of great ability.
3. Marie was a bright, eager young girl from Poland.
4. Her life at the university was unbelievably hard.
5. Her meals of tea and bread were hardly nourishing.
6. But her love of science kept her going.
7. The marriage of the two scientists was a true partnership.
8. Marie's years with Pierre were happy ones.
9. Long hours of laboratory work filled their days and nights.
10. Finally, their theories about a new element were proved true.
11. Their research on pitchblende uncovered the new element, radium.

12. Radium, with its powerful rays, is used to fight diseases.
13. Suddenly people around the world knew the Curies.
14. The Curies disliked publicity about their discovery.
15. The laboratory near their home did not change.
16. Their dedication to their work continued.
17. The end of their long partnership came when Pierre was killed crossing a street.
18. Marie continued the work on radium.
19. Once again her devotion to science kept her going.
20. Her experiments with radium won her many honors.

An adjective phrase frequently follows another adjective phrase in a sentence. Sometimes both adjective phrases modify the same noun or pronoun.

> The portrait **of George Washington by Gilbert Stuart** is familiar to all Americans. [The two phrases, *of George Washington* and *by Gilbert Stuart*, both modify the noun *portrait*.]

Sometimes an adjective phrase modifies a noun or pronoun in another adjective phrase.

> A majority **of the mammals in the world** sleep during the day. [The adjective phrase *of the mammals* modifies the noun *majority*, and the adjective phrase *in the world* modifies the noun *mammals*, which is the object of the preposition in the first phrase.]

EXERCISE 5. The following sentences contain twenty adjective phrases. List the phrases in order on your paper, writing the number of the sentence before each phrase. After each phrase, write the noun or pronoun it modifies. Most sentences contain more than one adjective phrase.

EXAMPLE   1. Recent legislation by Congress has legalized the use of the metric system.
1. *by Congress, legislation*
of the metric system, use

1. One of the advantages of the metric system is its simplicity.
2. It is a system with obvious benefits for the United States.
3. Trade with other nations would increase, and tourists to the United States would also benefit.
4. The major drawback to a sudden changeover is that adults, like children, do not master new systems immediately.
5. Their knowledge about our present system required a lifetime of practice and experience.
6. The schools in this country and the students in the classroom must show the way.
7. Perhaps you already know some terminology from the metric system.
8. The size of an engine on a motorcycle is a metric measurement, and the distances of Olympic races are metric too.
9. When we begin "thinking metric," distances in kilometers will be easily understandable, and 25° Celsius will become a normal temperature for a summer day.
10. Maybe someday we will even be taught that "28.3 grams of prevention is worth .45 kilograms of cure."

EXERCISE 6. Think of an appropriate adjective phrase to fill the blank in each of the following sentences. Write the phrase on your paper after the number. Remember that an adjective phrase must modify a noun or a pronoun.

EXAMPLE   1. The dachshund —— is very amusing to watch.

1. *with its short legs and long body*

1. A scream —— awakened us.
2. The shopping center —— is seldom crowded.
3. The comic strips —— are funny.
4. Her painting —— won the grand prize.
5. The trip —— was exciting.
6. I found a clue to the location ——.
7. On a table —— she piled the heavy bundles.
8. The girl —— is staring at the necklace.
9. My tree house is in the oak tree ——.
10. Finally someone —— threw her a life raft.

ADVERB PHRASES

When a prepositional phrase modifies a verb, an adjective, or an adverb, it is called an *adverb phrase*. An adverb phrase usually modifies the verb in the sentence. Like a single-word adverb, an adverb phrase qualifies or limits the meaning of the word it modifies. It answers the questions that an adverb does: *Where? When? How? How often? To what extent?*

Adverb   The soldier reported **there** first.

Adverb phrase   The soldier reported **to the fort** first.

Adverb   The cavalry **soon** reached the fort.

Adverb phrase   **By noon** the cavalry reached the fort.

4d. An *adverb phrase* modifies a verb, an adjective, or another adverb.

EXAMPLES   **For the first few weeks,** the education of a puppy may be difficult. [The adverb phrase *for the first few weeks* modifies the verb *may be*.]

A puppy is always ready **for a game.** [The adverb phrase *for a game* modifies the adjective *ready*.]

Early **in the morning** our puppy awakens us. [The adverb phrase *in the morning* modifies the adverb *early*.]

EXERCISE 7. Each of the following sentences contains an adverb phrase. After the proper number on your paper, write the phrase and the verb, adjective, or adverb it modifies. Be sure not to select any adjective phrases.

EXAMPLE   1. Pecos Bill will live forever in the many legends about him.
                1. *in the many legends, will live*

1. When he was a baby, Pecos Bill was dropped from a covered wagon.
2. He fell into the Pecos River.
3. There were several other children in the wagon.
4. His parents did not miss him for a long time.
5. Pecos Bill was reared by coyotes.
6. He thought for many years that he was a coyote.
7. After a long argument a cowboy convinced him that he was not a coyote.
8. At last, Bill became a cowboy himself.
9. He was soon known throughout the West.
10. Hunting gold, he dug the Grand Canyon in a week's time.
11. During a drought he dug the bed of the Rio Grande.
12. On one occasion Bill rode a cyclone.
13. He rode the bucking wind without a saddle.

14. On another occasion, a ten-foot rattlesnake attacked him.
15. After that a mountain lion startled Bill.
16. The lion leaped from a ledge above Bill's head.
17. Bill had it tamed soon after the leap.
18. He even put a saddle on the lion and rode it.
19. You can see that Pecos Bill was always in difficulty.
20. Stories like these about Pecos Bill are common in the West.

Two or more adverb phrases may occur in succession.

> She drove **for hours through the storm.** [Both adverb phrases, *for hours* and *through the storm,* modify the verb *drove.*]
>
> The library opens **on weekdays at eight o'clock.** [Both adverb phrases, *on weekdays* and *at eight o'clock,* modify the verb *opens.*]

Sometimes an adverb phrase is followed by an adjective phrase modifying the object of the preposition in the adverb phrase.

> The boat landed **on an island** [adverb] **near the coast** [adjective].

Many adverb phrases may be moved from one part of the sentence to another. In this they are unlike adjective phrases, which usually follow the word they modify. Adverb phrases can often be placed in different parts of the sentence without changing the meaning.

> She planted spruce seedlings **along the driveway.**
>
> **Along the driveway** she planted spruce seedlings.

At our house we have dinner early.
We have dinner early **at our house.**

EXERCISE 8. The following paragraphs contain twenty adverb phrases. List the phrases in order on your paper, writing the number of the sentence before each phrase. After each phrase, write the word it modifies. Many sentences contain more than one adverb phrase. Be sure not to select any adjective phrases.

EXAMPLE   1. In the clearing she saw three deer.
                      1. *In the clearing, saw*

1. In the spring she hiked through a national park. **2.** Around her were many kinds of animals. **3.** On several occasions she spotted some deer. **4.** She found a doe and its spotted fawn in a little glade. **5.** When they saw her, they ran quickly into the forest. **6.** She was glad that they were protected by law. **7.** At one time the Key deer, approximately the size of large collies, were hunted without restrictions. **8.** Almost all of them were killed by hunters. **9.** Now the population of Key deer is increasing in the Big Pine Key of southern Florida. **10.** During colonial times game laws protected the white-tailed deer from hunters.

11. For many hours she wandered among the scores of animals. **12.** At her approach, she could hear animals as they scurried through the trees in alarm. **13.** Soon after sundown she returned to her car.

EXERCISE 9. Write original sentences using the following word groups as adverb phrases. Underline the phrase and draw an arrow to the word or words that each phrase modifies.

EXAMPLE   1. to the tower

1. *They sent radio signals to the tower.*

1. under the stone
2. near the seashore
3. around 1:00 A.M.
4. up the hill
5. on the chalkboard
6. during the winter
7. without her cane
8. by some coincidence
9. in the meantime
10. toward the west

REVIEW EXERCISE A. The following paragraph contains eight adjective phrases and twelve adverb phrases. List the phrases in order on your paper, writing the number of the sentence before each phrase. After each phrase, write *adj.* for an adjective phrase or *adv.* for an adverb phrase. Remember that adjective phrases modify nouns or pronouns and that adverb phrases modify verbs, adjectives, or adverbs.

EXAMPLE   1. To many people Spain is the most beautiful country in Europe.
1. *To many people, adv.*
1. *in Europe, adj.*

1. Spain is located in the southwest corner of Europe. 2. Several centuries ago it was a country with great power. 3. Columbus sailed under the Spanish flag, and Mexico was conquered by Cortés of Spain. 4. Spain was an empire in the days of the early explorers. 5. After the defeat of the Spanish Armada, Spain's power declined. 6. For a while Napoleon ruled the country. 7. Since Napoleon's time Spain has had many forms of government. 8. In 1975, Juan Carlos became king of Spain. 9. During his reign, King Juan Carlos has brought democratic reforms to this European country. 10. Of course, the people of Spain are grateful for his strong leadership.

DIAGRAMING ADJECTIVE AND ADVERB PHRASES

To diagram a prepositional phrase — either adjective or adverb — place the preposition on a slanting line below the word modified. Then put the object of the preposition on a horizontal line connected with the slanting line. Let the slanting line extend slightly beyond the line for the object.

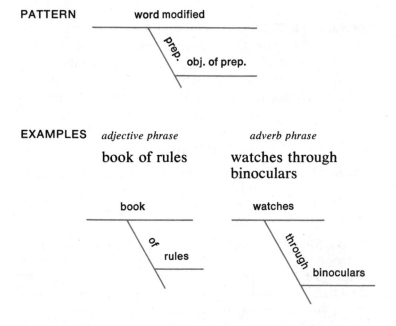

PATTERN   word modified

prep.
obj. of prep.

EXAMPLES   *adjective phrase*   *adverb phrase*
book of rules   watches through binoculars

book   watches

of   through
rules   binoculars

If the preposition has two objects, draw two horizontal lines and connect them with a broken line on which you write the conjunction. Modifiers of the objects are diagramed in the usual way. They are placed on slanting lines below the words they modify.

EXAMPLES   *adjective phrase*

a plane with ten passengers and two
pilots

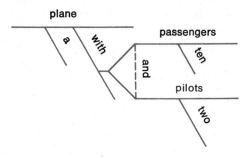

adverb phrase

landed in rain and fog

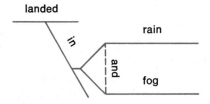

EXERCISE 10.   Using the patterns above, diagram the
following groups of words.

1. rain against the window
2. some weeds in the garden
3. dashed after the ball
4. hats with bright feathers
5. was well hidden among the bushes
6. games for older boys
7. looked in the attic or the basement
8. cars for sale
9. lighted by a small candle and a very dim lamp
10. houses with green shutters and tile roofs

Here is a complete sentence containing adjective and adverb phrases. Study the diagram until you are sure that you understand the position of every word.

The family down the street is moving to Canada in the fall.

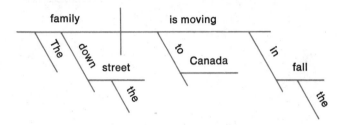

EXERCISE 11. Diagram the following sentences. Each sentence contains an adjective phrase or an adverb phrase or both.

1. Our car is parked across the street.
2. Sit in the front row.
3. The visitor from Ireland has left.
4. A movie with my favorite actor is showing.
5. A dog with long ears trotted behind its owner.
6. The old wagon was stuck in the mud.
7. A play about Cleopatra will be given tonight.
8. Years of study and hard work were finally rewarded.
9. We painted with oils and watercolors.
10. The plane with only one engine landed on a slippery runway.

REVIEW EXERCISE B. The following paragraph contains eight adjective phrases and twelve adverb phrases. List the phrases in order on your paper, writing the number of the sentence before each phrase. After each phrase write adjective (*adj.*) or adverb (*adv.*). Then write the word or words the phrase modifies.

EXAMPLE 1. In the seventeenth century a famous story about knighthood was published.
1. *In the seventeenth century, adv., was published*
1. *about knighthood, adj., story*

1. Don Quixote is a comical figure of literature. **2.** Although knighthood had not existed for many generations, Don Quixote became a knight. **3.** With some difficulty he mounted his bony old nag and began his search for adventure. **4.** He was dressed in armor from his great-grandfather's time, and at his side hung a very dull sword. **5.** Soon he encountered his first adventure. **6.** In his path stood twenty windmills. **7.** But in Don Quixote's eyes the windmills were giants. **8.** Like a knight in a tournament he charged at the windmills. **9.** A vane in a windmill caught his armor. **10.** It lifted him and threw him into the air. **11.** Don Quixote had an explanation for the situation. **12.** During his charge on the giants, a magician had changed them into windmills. **13.** Adventures like the windmill fight occur often in *Don Quixote.*

REVIEW EXERCISE C. For each of the following words, write one original sentence containing an adjective phrase and one containing an adverb phrase. Remember that an adjective phrase must modify a noun or pronoun and that an adverb phrase must modify a verb, adjective, or adverb.

EXAMPLE 1. girl
1. *She saw a girl with a knapsack.*
The girl hiked in the hills.

1. pie 2. turkey 3. climbed 4. appeared 5. parade

Chapter 5

Complements

**Direct and Indirect Objects;
Predicate Nominatives,
Predicate Adjectives**

Every sentence, long or short, is built upon a foundation called the *sentence base*. The sentence base always contains a subject and verb. For some sentences another element essential to the meaning of the sentence appears in the complete predicate with the verb. This word is a *complement* ("completer"). It completes the meaning begun by the subject and verb.

COMPLEMENTS WITH ACTION VERBS

Some verbs express action by themselves: *Children play; Work began.* Many verbs, however, call for another word to indicate the person or thing that the action of the subject is directed toward. A complement that indicates the receiver of an action is called an *object*. There are two kinds of objects: *direct objects* and *indirect objects*.

The Direct Object

The complements in the following sentences are direct objects of the verb. Notice that they are all nouns or pronouns.

Edith met **Dolores** after class.
Edith helped **her.**
The girls led the **meeting.**

5a. The *direct object* receives the action of the verb or shows the result of that action. It answers the questions "What?" or "Whom?" after an action verb.

EXAMPLES   She eats **berries.** [*Berries* receives the action of the verb *eats.*]

That shop manufactures small **parts** for jet engines. [*Parts* is the result of the action of the verb *manufactures.*]

A direct object can never follow a linking verb, since a linking verb does not express action. You should notice, also, that a direct object is never in a prepositional phrase.

EXAMPLES   Augusta Savage was a sculptor during the Harlem Renaissance. [The verb *was* does not express action; therefore, it has no direct object.]

She learned a **lesson** in safety. [*Lesson* is the direct object of the verb; *safety* is the object of the preposition *in.*]

Direct objects may be compound:

We bought **ribbon, wrapping paper,** and **tape.** [The compound direct object of the verb *bought* is *ribbon, wrapping paper,* and *tape.*]

EXERCISE 1.   Each of the following sentences contains a direct object. Copy the direct object after the proper number. Remember that you can find a direct object by asking "What?" or "Whom?" after an action verb.

EXAMPLE   1. Laura Waring painted portraits.
            1. *portraits*

1. Bill redecorated his room.
2. She studied wildlife at camp.
3. Mrs. Gibson read a story to her class.
4. José recited a poem for the talent show.
5. Her neighbors drive her to school every day.
6. On her last fishing trip my mother caught a marlin.
7. Ms. Thrasher raises Irish setters and boxers.
8. Suddenly she found herself alone in the museum.
9. During the winter we often attend concerts.
10. The Christmas parade delighted her.

EXERCISE 2.   All of the following sentences contain one or more direct objects. Write the numbers 1–10 on your paper. After each number, write the object or objects in the sentence.

1. Long-distance, or marathon, swimming requires strength and courage from an athlete.
2. Diana Nyad eats five or six raw eggs before swimming in a marathon.
3. She smears grease on her legs and arms for protection against the cold water.
4. During the marathon, Diana might lose seventeen pounds, but she continues to swim.
5. Fatigue, pain, and huge waves challenge marathon swimmers like Diana Nyad.
6. As she swims, she endures extreme isolation from the rest of the world.
7. Toward the end of the race, Diana Nyad hears the loud clapping and screaming of her many fans along the shore.
8. Spectators at a marathon can watch only the finish of the long swim.
9. Nevertheless, they know the long distance that Diana has traveled.

10. Emerging from the water, Diana has successfully completed the race.

EXERCISE 3. There are ten direct objects in the following paragraph. Copy each one after the number of its sentence. Some sentences do not contain direct objects. Remember that objects follow action verbs only.

1. Adventurous people are enjoying the new sport of hang gliding. **2.** A hang glider, which is like a large kite, can carry a person hanging from it. **3.** A hang glider has a lightweight sail with a triangular control bar underneath. **4.** To become airborne, the pilot grasps the sides of the triangle, lifts the glider to the shoulders, and runs hard down a slope into the wind. **5.** The wind lifts the glider and the pilot off the ground. **6.** Takeoffs from a hilltop or a cliff are the easiest. **7.** The airborne pilot controls the path of flight. **8.** To slow down, the pilot pushes the control bar. **9.** To increase speed, the pilot pulls it. **10.** When ready to land, the pilot stalls near the ground and lands softly.

The Indirect Object

The next kind of complement you will study is the *indirect object*. Some verbs have both direct and indirect objects. When they do, the sentence base consists of subject, verb, indirect object, and direct object. Like all complements, the indirect object helps to complete the meaning begun by the subject and verb.

You have learned that a direct object answers the questions "What?" or "Whom?" after an action verb. An indirect object answers the questions "To what?" or "To whom?" or "For what?" or "For whom?" after an action verb. The indirect object always comes before the direct object in the sentence.

Pam left the **waiter** a tip. [*Waiter* is the indirect object of the verb *left*. It answers the question, "For whom did she leave a tip?"]

Despite her nervousness, Lynn gave the **audience** a quick glance. [To what did she give a quick glance? *Audience* is the indirect object of the verb *gave.*]

5b. The *indirect object* of the verb precedes the direct object and tells to whom or what or for whom or what the action of the verb is done.

Linking verbs do not have indirect objects, of course, since they do not show action. Indirect objects have two characteristics in common with direct objects: (1) They are never in prepositional phrases, and (2) they may be compound.

EXAMPLES   The travel bureau sent the necessary information to her. [*Information* is the direct object of the verb *sent. Her* is the object of the preposition *to.*]

The travel bureau sent **her** the necessary information. [*Her* is the indirect object of the verb *sent.* It precedes the direct object, *information,* and answers the question "To whom?"]

Helen threw **Jane** and **Paula** slow curve balls for the first time. [*Curve balls* is the direct object of the verb *threw; Jane* and *Paula* is the compound indirect object of the verb.]

EXERCISE 4. Each of the following sentences contains a direct object and an indirect object. After the sentence number, copy the indirect object and then the direct object on your paper. Underline the indirect objects.

EXAMPLE   1. History has given us an idea of Roman sporting games.
           1. <u>us,</u> idea

1. Gladiators gave the Roman people many thrilling moments of sport.
2. The government sent the gladiator schools thousands of slaves and convicts.
3. Instructors gave their students training in the art of combat.
4. In the arena, gladiators showed the crowd a fight to the death.
5. Roman historians have told us the details of these gruesome battles.
6. Each gladiator promised the emperor the death of his opponent.
7. The emperor awarded the winning gladiator palm branches and money.
8. Some emperors gave victorious gladiators their freedom.
9. Often the crowd at the arena showed the emperor its support for a courageous gladiator.
10. Do today's sports give you a similar feeling of combat?

EXERCISE 5. All of the following sentences contain direct objects, and some contain indirect objects, too. Write the numbers 1–10 on your paper. After each number, write the object or objects in the sentence. Underline the indirect objects.

1. More than a hundred years ago, A. G. Spalding began his career in professional sports.
2. He played baseball for the Boston, Massachusetts, club.
3. In those days, baseball players did not wear gloves.
4. The manager of the Boston team put Spalding on the pitcher's mound in every game.

5. A pitcher catches the ball many times in a game.
6. The hard ball gave Spalding many bruises on his hand.
7. In 1875 Spalding first saw a baseball glove.
8. Charles Waite, another player, showed Spalding the glove.
9. Waite told him the advantages of baseball gloves for players.
10. Soon Spalding and many other players used gloves in every game.

EXERCISE 6. There are twenty objects of verbs, direct and indirect, in the following paragraph. List them on your paper, writing the number of the sentence before each one. Underline the indirect objects.

1. Tina's parents took her to an aquarium. 2. The guide at the entrance gave them some information about exhibits. 3. They walked around the main building and studied the fish in the glass tanks. 4. One large tank contained porpoises, sea turtles, sharks, and many small fish. 5. A woman in diving equipment gave them a scare. 6. She entered the tank! 7. The fish swarmed around her and she fed them smaller fish from a basket on her arm. 8. Next Tina and her parents moved upstairs; there the porpoises performed for them, leaping high into the air. 9. They snatched fish from the attendant's hand. 10. At the sharks' pool, an attendant was giving the sharks their dinner. 11. She tied a rope around a fish and lowered it to the surface of the water. 12. In a few seconds the sharks stripped the fish of its flesh. 13. Finally, around closing time, Tina and her parents left the aquarium.

SUBJECT COMPLEMENTS

In addition to direct objects and indirect objects, there are two other kinds of complements: the *predicate nominative* and the *predicate adjective*. These two complements are both called *subject complements*, since they refer to the subject of a sentence. The words in heavy type in the following sentences are subject complements. Notice that they all follow linking verbs.

> Julio has been **president** of his class for three years. [*President* refers to the subject *Julio*.]
> Tomorrow will be too **late**. [*Late* refers to the subject *tomorrow*.]
> Was it **you**? [*You* refers to the subject *it*.]
> Barbara looks **sleepy** this morning. [*Sleepy* refers to the subject *Barbara*.]

5c. A *subject complement* is a complement that refers to (describes or explains) the subject.

Subject complements always follow linking verbs, never action verbs. In order to recognize subject complements, you should review your knowledge of linking verbs.

Common Linking Verbs

be (all forms)	smell	appear	grow
taste	sound	become	remain
feel	look	seem	stay

There are two kinds of subject complements: the predicate nominative and the predicate adjective. Both occur in the predicate of a sentence, and both refer to the subject.

The Predicate Nominative

The words in heavy type in the following sentences are predicate nominatives:

This piece of stone may be an old **arrowhead.**
By night the sleet had become **snow.**
Porpoises are **members** of the whale family.

(1) A *predicate nominative* **is one kind of subject complement. It is a noun or pronoun that explains or identifies the subject of the sentence. It follows a linking verb.**

EXAMPLES A good dictionary is a valuable **tool** for homework assignments. [*Tool* is a predicate nominative following the linking verb *is*. It refers to the subject *dictionary*.]

That unlucky swimmer might have been **you!** [*You* is a predicate nominative following the linking verb *might have been*. It identifies the subject *swimmer*.]

You must be careful not to confuse a predicate nominative with a direct object. Remember that a direct object must follow an action verb; a predicate nominative must follow a linking verb. Like other kinds of complements, predicate nominatives are never in prepositional phrases.

EXAMPLES This slice is the **end** of the loaf. [*End* is a predicate nominative referring to the subject *slice*. *Of the loaf* is a prepositional phrase used as an adjective to modify *end*.]

Last year the delegates were **Joan Atkins** and **Marcia Philipo** from Carbondale School. [The compound predicate nominative is *Joan Atkins* and *Marcia Philipo*.]

EXERCISE 7. Each of the following sentences contains a predicate nominative. After the proper number on your paper, copy the linking verb and predicate nominative from each sentence.

EXAMPLE 1. Siam became modern Thailand.
1. *became, Thailand*

1. Whales are mammals.
2. The real winner is the little girl down the street.
3. Karen will soon be a dentist.
4. Helene may become a good actress.
5. Rhode Island is the smallest state in the Union.
6. The old green convertible is hers.
7. Will a woman be the next President?
8. Jo may be the most likely choice for the office.
9. Our present enemies were once our friends.
10. U Thant was the Secretary General of the United Nations for over eight years.

EXERCISE 8. The sentences below contain predicate nominatives. After each number, write the verb and the predicate nominative.

1. Sea cows are part of ancient legends.
2. They became mermaids in the sailors' stories.
3. Armadillos are our oddest animals.
4. Their outer covering is a series of bony plates.
5. Television is an important tool of education.
6. Space travel has become a subject for complex research.
7. Many stars are brighter objects than our sun.
8. The origin of comets has long been a mystery to us.
9. Halley's Comet should be the next bright comet to appear.
10. The Hebrides are a group of about five hundred islands off the coast of Scotland.

The Predicate Adjective

Like the predicate nominative, the *predicate adjective* is a subject complement that is found in the predicate and refers to the subject.

The girls were **hoarse** from cheering. [*Hoarse* is a predicate adjective modifying the subject *girls*.]

Iced tea tastes **good** on a hot day. [*Good* is a predicate adjective modifying the subject *iced tea*.]

The cake was **light** and **delicious.** [*Light* and *delicious* are predicate adjectives modifying the subject *cake*.]

Like predicate nominatives, predicate adjectives always follow linking verbs.

(2) A *predicate adjective* is one kind of subject complement. It is an adjective that modifies the subject of the sentence. It follows a linking verb.

EXERCISE 9. Each of the following sentences contains a predicate adjective. After the proper number on your paper, copy first the linking verb and then the predicate adjective.

EXAMPLE   1. Both girls are very sociable.
             1. *are, sociable*

1. The homework was easy tonight.
2. That pitcher of lemonade tasted sour.
3. Her rug is too small for her living room.
4. After a cold shower she felt good.
5. The audience remained silent for a few seconds after the performance.
6. The water looked dark green because of the chemicals in it.
7. During the interrogation the detective became angry.
8. She grew tired of his complaints.
9. From her seat the drums sound too loud.
10. In the midst of the panic, Sue stayed calm.

EXERCISE 10. Think of an appropriate predicate adjective for each blank in the following sentences. Write the predicate adjective on your paper after the sentence number.

1. The pie at dinner tasted ——.
2. Even from a distance of five miles, the cannons sounded ——.
3. To the station attendant the lady seemed —— beyond belief.
4. The sword felt —— in her hand.
5. Emily was —— about the change in plans.
6. Most holidays seem —— to her.
7. My date for the prom is —— and ——.
8. Our football team looks ——, while the opposing team looks ——.
9. The last time she saw them they were ——.
10. The manager of the park becomes —— when people litter the park with paper and food.

REVIEW EXERCISE A. There are twenty complements of all kinds in the following paragraph. Copy each complement after the number of the sentence. Then identify it as a direct object (*d.o.*), an indirect object (*i.o.*), a predicate nominative (*p.n.*), or a predicate adjective (*p.a.*).

EXAMPLE   1. Shall I tell you the old story of Barbara Allen?
      1. *you, i.o.*
        story, d.o.

1. A mountaineer sang us the ballad of Barbara Allen. **2.** It is a beautiful ballad about a cruel girl. **3.** Ballad hunters have found ninety-two versions of "Barbara Allen" in Virginia alone. **4.** The stories of all versions are similar. **5.** A young man was ill with a broken heart. **6.** His servant brought the young man's sweetheart to his master's bed. **7.** The sweetheart was Barbara Allen. **8.** The young man told Barbara Allen his tale of love for her. **9.** But the young man had once slighted her, and now she was cruel to him. **10.** She left his house; soon after, she heard the death bell. **11.** Every knell was terrible to her. **12.** It warned her of doom, and she became repentant. **13.** She had killed her lover this day, and she would be the victim of love tomorrow. **14.** So fate punished the cruel Barbara Allen.

Diagraming Complements

Except for the indirect object, the parts of a sentence base always go on the main horizontal line. You have already learned how to diagram a sentence base consisting of a subject and verb. Now you will learn to diagram a sentence base which contains a complement also.

Direct Objects

The direct object is placed on the horizontal line with the subject and verb. A short vertical line separates it from the verb.

PATTERN

subject	action verb	direct object

EXAMPLES 1. We made pizza. [d.o.]

We	made	pizza

2. Lizards eat flies and earthworms. [compound d.o.]

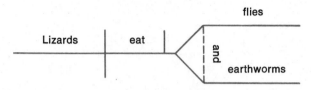

Notice that the vertical line between the verb and the direct object stops at the horizontal line.

Predicate Nominatives and Predicate Adjectives

The diagram for a predicate nominative and a predicate adjective is similar to the diagram for the direct object. Instead of a vertical line separating the complement from the verb, use a diagonal line slanting back toward the subject and verb.

PATTERN

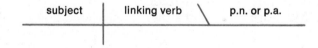

EXAMPLES 1. The sun is a star. [p.n.]

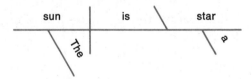

2. Peaches are delicious. [p.a.]

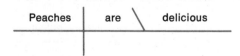

3. The Indigo snake is large and shiny.
[compound p.a.]

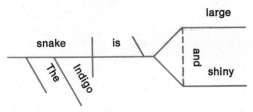

EXERCISE 11. Diagram the following sentences.

1. Turtles are reptiles.
2. Turtles have no teeth.
3. Their tough bills tear their food.
4. Turtles may grow very old.
5. The alligator snapper is the largest freshwater turtle.
6. Its mouth is huge.
7. Its jaws are very powerful.
8. The snapper can maim a hand or foot.
9. Few turtles are dangerous.
10. Most are quiet and slow.

Indirect Objects

To diagram an indirect object, write it on a short horizontal line below the verb, with a slanting line joining it to the verb.

PATTERN

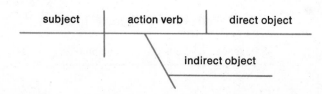

EXAMPLES   1. The veterinarian gave us a dog. [i.o.]

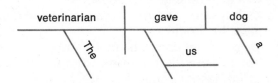

2. The guide showed my cousin and me the falls. [compound i.o.]

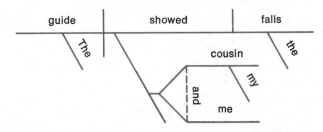

EXERCISE 12. Diagram the following sentences.

1. I handed the clerk a dollar.
2. Several businesses gave our school a check.
3. Her aunt left her a fortune.
4. The teacher assigned her a project.
5. Send them your extra clothes.
6. My aunt knitted Violet and me sweaters.
7. The students gave him their attention.
8. The store offered Ann and Dottie good salaries.
9. The carpenter built herself a desk.
10. My neighbor lent me her camera.

REVIEW EXERCISE B. Each of the following sentences contains one or more complements. Copy the complements on your paper, putting the number of the sentence before each one. Then tell whether the complement is a direct object (*d.o.*), indirect object (*i.o.*), predicate nominative (*p.n.*), or predicate adjective (*p.a.*).

1. Rip Van Winkle was a lazy man.
2. He was also a henpecked husband.
3. He took his gun and his dog and climbed a mountain near his home.
4. On top of the mountain he met a strange little man.
5. The man offered him a drink from his jug.
6. The drink tasted good.
7. Rip became tired and lay down.
8. He was soon asleep.
9. Later he opened his eyes with a start.
10. His gun had become rusty, and his dog did not answer.
11. The people of the village looked strange.
12. He asked advice from the people around him.
13. Finally he located his home.
14. It was hardly recognizable.
15. Rip had been asleep for twenty years.
16. His wife was dead.
17. Rip had become an old man.
18. He told visitors his strange story.
19. Would you enjoy a twenty-year sleep?
20. Life would be very different when you woke up.

Usage

PART TWO

Chapter **6**

Agreement of Subject and Verb

Singular and Plural Number

Some of the most common mistakes in speaking and writing are made when verb and subject do not agree. Perhaps you have overheard a conversation like this one:

> Ken: How many is in your club?
> Tom: We was hoping for twenty, but there's only fifteen of us so far.

Do you see the three errors in agreement in that passage? The verbs and their subjects do not agree in number. This chapter will help you to avoid such errors.

NUMBER

All nouns and pronouns have number. They are singular in number if they refer to one thing. They are plural in number if they refer to more than one thing.

6a. When a word refers to one person or thing, it is *singular* in number. When a word refers to more than one, it is *plural* in number.

EXAMPLES   hat, I, sky, principle [singular]
              hats, we, skies, principles [plural]

EXERCISE 1. Write the numbers 1–20 on your paper. If a word is singular, write *S* after its number. If it is plural, write *P*.

1. morning	8. heights	15. leaves
2. calves	9. geese	16. chief
3. women	10. it	17. men
4. she	11. mosquitoes	18. babies
5. pencils	12. actress	19. Congress
6. shelf	13. cave	20. mice
7. they	14. we	

6b. **A verb agrees with its subject in number.**

Two words *agree* when they have the same number. The number of the verb must always agree with the number of its subject.

EXAMPLES   He fights. [singular subject and singular verb]

Animals fight. [plural subject and plural verb]

(1) Singular subjects take singular verbs.

EXAMPLES   The **lightning fills** the sky. [The verb *fills* is singular to agree with the singular subject *lightning*.]

Linda begins her vacation today. [The verb *begins* is singular to agree with the singular subject *Linda*.]

(2) Plural subjects take plural verbs.

EXAMPLES   **Cheetahs run** faster than most other animals. [The verb *run* is plural to agree with the plural subject *cheetahs*.]

New **families move** into our neighborhood frequently. [The verb *move* is plural to agree with the plural subject *families*.]

Notice that an –*s* ending is often a sign of the singular in the verb and a sign of the plural in the subject.

► **NOTE**   When a sentence contains a verb phrase, it is the helping verb that agrees with the subject.

EXAMPLES   The **motor is** running. The **motors are** running.
The **girl has** been delayed. The **girls have** been delayed.

EXERCISE 2. The subjects and verbs that follow are in agreement. If an item is singular, write *S* after its number. If it is plural, write *P*.

1. people think	11. night arrives
2. wind howls	12. gates open
3. owls hoot	13. she tries
4. we practice	14. actor rehearses
5. days pass	15. girls study
6. monkeys chatter	16. leaf falls
7. Karen writes	17. thieves steal
8. it seems	18. boy giggles
9. snakes hiss	19. they watch
10. glasses break	20. lion lurks

EXERCISE 3. The subjects and verbs in the following sentences agree in number. Write each subject and verb on your paper, changing them to the opposite number. If the verb consists of more than one word, write the whole verb phrase.

EXAMPLES   1. Many exhibits are housed in the Smithsonian Institution.
1. *exhibit is housed*
2. The museum is located in Washington, D.C.
2. *museums are located*

1. The museum was built in 1846.

2. Several million persons visit the Smithsonian Institution each year.
3. They see there a 2,573-pound meteorite.
4. A two-story colonial farmhouse is also on exhibit.
5. Visitors always marvel at the Wright brothers' original plane.
6. Five halls have a magnificent collection of American Indian material.
7. Tourists are taken through the various branches of the museum.
8. Many private citizens have donated gifts to the Smithsonian.
9. Many people especially like the displays of dresses of the First Ladies.
10. Washington's uniform appeals to the children as well as to the adults.

EXERCISE 4. In each of the following sentences, two verbs are written in parentheses. Choose the one which agrees with the subject. Write the subject and verb after the proper number.

EXAMPLE 1. Cherry trees (lines, line) the Potomac.
1. *trees line*

1. An electric computer (solves, solve) difficult problems quickly.
2. Many colleges (has, have) computers.
3. Over one hundred thousand forest fires (is, are) reported each year.
4. Lightning sometimes (causes, cause) fires.
5. Careless people (is, are) often at fault.
6. Forest rangers (says, say) that we can prevent forest fires.
7. Some Polynesian divers (descends, descend) almost forty-five feet without special equipment.
8. The owl's eyes (makes, make) it look wise.
9. Actually, the owl (sees, see) poorly during the day.
10. Every year scientists (discovers, discover) new drugs to fight diseases.

PROBLEMS IN AGREEMENT

In the exercises so far, it has been easy to make the subjects and verbs agree because the verbs have followed their subjects closely and the number of the subject has been clear. However, a phrase may come between the subject and verb, creating an agreement problem. Or, the subject may be a pronoun, the number of which is hard to determine.

Phrases Between Subject and Verb

Sometimes a prepositional phrase comes between the subject and verb in a sentence. If the object of the preposition is different in number from the subject of the sentence, you must be especially careful to make the verb agree with the subject in number.

NONSTANDARD[1] The special effects in the movie was particularly original. [The verb should agree with the plural subject *effects,* not with the singular noun *movie,* which is the object of the preposition *in.*]

STANDARD[1] The special **effects** in the movie **were** particularly original.

NONSTANDARD The lights in the stadium has been turned on. [The verb should agree with the plural subject *lights,* not with the singular noun *stadium,* the object of the preposition *in.*]

STANDARD The **lights** in the stadium **have** been turned on.

[1] *Standard* and *nonstandard* are the terms used in this book to describe kinds of usage. This book teaches standard English. The word *standard* suggests a model with which things can be compared. In this case, the model—standard English—is the set of usage conventions most widely accepted by English-speaking people. All other kinds of usage are called nonstandard English. These are variations in usage that are not acceptable in formal writing and formal speaking.

6c. The number of a subject is not changed by a phrase following the subject.

EXAMPLES **Seats** for the concert **are** reserved.

One of us **is** guilty.

The successful **candidate,** with two of her aides, **has** entered the auditorium.

Scientists from all over the world **have** gathered in Geneva.

EXERCISE 5. Copy the subject from each of the following sentences. Then choose the correct verb from the two in parentheses and write it after the subject.

1. The heart, although weighing less than 12 ounces, (is, are) a muscle about the size of a person's fist.
2. This muscle in both children and adults (beats, beat) more than 100,000 times each day.
3. The walls of the heart (contracts, contract), forcing blood to rush out.
4. The lungs on either side of the heart (takes, take) oxygen from the air and add it to the blood.
5. A network of tubes (connects, connect) the heart to all the organs in the body.
6. The veins in this network (brings, bring) blood to the heart.
7. Arteries, on the other hand, (carries, carry) the blood away.
8. A system of valves (controls, control) the flow of blood throughout the heart itself.
9. The heart, along with the 100,000 miles of arteries and veins, (supplies, supply) the oxygen needed by all parts of the body.
10. This hollow muscle inside all people (is, are) one of the most efficient and durable pumps ever created.

EXERCISE 6. Choose the correct verbs from the

following paragraph and write them on your paper. Before each verb, write the number of its sentence. Be prepared to identify the subjects.

1. *Moby Dick,* an exciting story about Captain Ahab and a great white whale, (interests, interest) readers of all ages. **2.** The men on Ahab's ship, the *Pequod,* (fears, fear) him because of his desire to destroy the great whale named Moby Dick. **3.** Many signs of bad luck (occurs, occur) during the voyage. **4.** But Ahab, with the crew, (continues, continue) to look for Moby Dick. **5.** Finally, above the waves (appears, appear) a seeming mountain of white. **6.** Then the sailors of the *Pequod* (knows, know) that they have found Moby Dick. **7.** Ahab, together with some of the crew, (gives, give) chase. **8.** Two of the small boats (is, are) finally destroyed. **9.** The whale, plunging through the waves, (throws, throw) Ahab's boat high in the air. **10.** The *Pequod* picks up most of the men, but one of the sailors (is, are) not found.

Indefinite Pronouns

In Chapter 2 you saw that one kind of pronoun is the *indefinite* pronoun. It is so called because the person or thing to which it refers is not named. Like all pronouns, indefinite pronouns take the place of nouns. Unlike personal pronouns, however, indefinite pronouns replace or refer to nouns that are usually not named. Here are some examples of personal and indefinite pronouns:

PERSONAL	INDEFINITE
we	anybody
you	both
she	either
them	everyone

When indefinite pronouns are used as subjects of sentences, their verbs must agree with them.

6d. The following common words are singular: *each, either, neither, one, everyone, everybody, no one, nobody, anyone, anybody, someone, somebody.*

EXAMPLES   **Anyone** without tickets **is** asked to see Mrs. Harris.

Each of the newcomers **was** welcomed to the city.

No one understands a person who mumbles.

EXERCISE 7. Find the subject of each sentence below and write it on your paper after the number. Then choose the correct verb from the two in parentheses and write it after the subject. Remember that the number of the verb is not affected by a word in a prepositional phrase.

EXAMPLE   1. One of the dogs (is, are) mine.
              1. *One is*

1. Neither of the languages (is, are) widely spoken today.
2. Everybody in those classes (wants, want) to learn a foreign language.
3. Someone among the local distributors (supplies, supply) us with tapes.
4. Each of us (records, record) attendance each day.
5. No one in either of the two schools (was, were) ever in a language laboratory before.
6. Everyone with an interest in foreign languages (is, are) glad to have the chance to use the laboratory.
7. Anybody with earphones (feels, feel) rather important.
8. Everybody in Mr. Woodring's and Mrs. Oliver's classes (files, file) quietly down to the lab.
9. There one of the laboratory instructors (helps, help) us adjust our machines.

10. Of all those thirty-seven students, no one (likes, like) to miss a session in the lab.

6e. The following common words are plural: *both, few, many, several.*

EXAMPLES **Few** of my neighbors **have** parakeets.
Many of them **keep** dogs as pets.

EXERCISE 8. After the number of each sentence, copy the subject. Then choose the correct verb from the two in parentheses and write it after the subject.

1. Many of our group (has, have) had flu shots.
2. Everyone in the surrounding towns (was, were) warned about the epidemic.
3. Of the new cases, few (is, are) serious.
4. Neither of those paths (leads, lead) home.
5. Few (knows, know) how to write a good business letter.
6. Each of the stores (gives, give) gifts to our graduates.
7. Several of the tests for iron ore (has, have) been tried.
8. No one in that whole group of doctors (knows, know) an easy cure for the common cold.
9. Several in the group (doubts, doubt) the existence of intelligent life on other planets.
10. Many of them (suspects, suspect) that intelligent life exists somewhere else.
11. (Has, Have) either of you seen an ice hockey game?
12. In the corner (stands, stand) one of the suspects.
13. Many of the critics of America (thinks, think) we are too concerned with material goods.
14. Someone up in the trees (is, are) signaling us.
15. Several from the seventh grade (is, are) needed to form a debate team.
16. Many of the schools in our area (sends, send) delegates to the state convention.

17. Both of the coaches of the varsity team (works, work) with the students every afternoon.
18. Several of the days last week (was, were) uncomfortably hot.
19. Many of the good players in the junior orchestra (hopes, hope) to be promoted to the senior orchestra.
20. (Has, Have) both of you seen the art exhibit?

6f. The words *all, any, most, none,* and *some* may be either singular or plural.

In order to know whether to use a singular or plural verb with the pronouns *all, any, most, none,* and *some,* you must observe the sense of the sentence. If the pronoun refers to one person or thing, it is singular and takes a singular verb. If it refers to more than one person or thing, it is plural and takes a plural verb. Study the following examples and note how the number of the pronoun changes as its meaning changes.

EXAMPLES   **All** of the nation's interest **centers** on politics during a political convention. [The subject *all* is singular because it refers to one thing—*interest.* The verb *centers* is singular to agree with it.]

All of the states **send** delegates to national political conventions. [The subject *all* is plural because it refers to more than one thing—fifty *states.* The verb *send* is plural to agree with it.]

Some of the excitement of such a convention **is** conveyed by television coverage. [The subject *some* is singular because it means "a part" of the excitement. The helping verb *is* is singular to agree with it.]

Some of the delegates **are** disappointed

in the candidate who was chosen. [The subject *some* is plural because it refers to more than one delegate. The verb *are* is plural to agree with it.]

EXERCISE 9. Write ten original sentences using the words below as subjects. Make sure that the verbs agree with the subjects in number.

1. either	6. none
2. one	7. several
3. many	8. some
4. any	9. most
5. everybody	10. few

Compound Subjects

A compound subject, you will recall, consists of two or more connected subjects having the same verb. When two subjects are connected by *and*, even if they are both singular, they are followed by a plural verb.

6g. Subjects joined by *and* take a plural verb.

EXAMPLES **A dictionary and** a one-volume **encyclopedia make** a good beginning for a reference library.

Mr. Duffy and his daughter have gone fishing.

EXCEPTION A compound subject that refers to a single person or to two or more things considered as a unit (one thing) takes a singular verb.

A sweater and skirt makes a good outfit for school. [*Sweater and skirt* is considered one outfit.]

A mother and homemaker has a challenging job. [One person is meant.]

EXERCISE 10. Some of the following sentences have compound subjects and some do not. Copy each subject after the proper number, then choose the correct verb from the parentheses. If you choose a singular verb with a compound subject, be prepared to explain why.

1. (Is, Are) New York and Chicago the two largest cities in the United States?
2. Sleet with some snow (is, are) predicted for tomorrow.
3. My guide and companion for the tour (was, were) Pilar.
4. New words and new meanings for old words (is, are) included in all modern dictionaries.
5. Your fingernail and a piece of glass (is, are) two means for testing hardness in minerals.
6. Both talc and gypsum (shows, show) a fingernail scratch.
7. The leader with her group (has, have) just left for the summit.
8. The opossum and the kangaroo (is, are) members of the same family of mammals.
9. Rattlesnakes, copperheads, coral snakes, and cottonmouths (is, are) four kinds of poisonous snakes found in the United States.
10. A horse and buggy (seems, seem) an unusual method of travel today.

6h. Singular subjects joined by *or* or *nor* take a singular verb.

EXAMPLES   The chief **geologist or** her **assistant is** due to arrive tonight.

A large **station wagon or** a small **truck has** enough room for the bicycles.

Neither a **rabbit nor** a **raccoon does** that kind of damage in a garden.

6i. When a singular subject and a plural subject are joined by *or* or *nor*, the verb agrees with the nearer subject.

EXAMPLES   Neither the **air conditioner nor** the **lights work.** [The verb *work* is plural to agree with *lights,* the part of the compound subject that is nearer to it.]

          Flowers or a **book** usually **makes** an appropriate gift. [The verb *makes* is singular to agree with the part of the compound subject that is nearer to it, *book.*]

Compound subjects having both singular and plural parts often sound awkward even if they are correct. It is usually better to rephrase a sentence to avoid such constructions.

AWKWARD   Two girls from Argentina or a girl from Chile is to speak to our class today.

BETTER   Today our class will hear two girls from Argentina or a girl from Chile.

Plural subjects joined by *or* or *nor,* of course, take a plural verb.

EXAMPLE   Neither the senators nor the representatives want the bill to be vetoed by the President. [The plural verb *want* agrees with either *senators* or *representatives.*]

EXERCISE 11. Choose the correct verb from the two in parentheses and write it on your paper. Be able to explain the reason for your choice.

1. Either a loan or a scholarship (is, are) available to selected applicants.
2. A desk or a bookcase (goes, go) into that corner.
3. Neither sheets nor towels (is, are) furnished at camp.

4. (Has, Have) the books or other supplies come?
5. A vocabulary notebook or vocabulary flashcards (is, are) helpful for review.
6. Either the clock on the town hall or my watch (is, are) wrong.
7. Another boy or girl (takes, take) the part of the narrator.
8. A map or a guidebook (has, have) been my constant companion in this city.
9. Enthusiasm for the proposal or excitement about it (is, are) not the same as solid support.
10. A course in ceramics or a course in woodworking (is, are) recommended.

Other Problems in Agreement

There are a few other constructions that may pose special problems in agreement of subject and verb. This section will cover some of these.

Some nouns that are singular in form name a group of people or things: *class, family, team, group, flock,* for example. These nouns are called *collective nouns.* They are singular when they are used to mean the group as one unit. They are plural when they are used to mean the individual members of the group.

6j. Collective nouns may be either singular or plural.

EXAMPLES   The **class were** divided in their opinions of the play. [Here *class* means several individuals; it is plural and takes a plural verb.]

The **class has** decided to have a science table in the room. [Here *class* is thought of as one unit; it is singular and takes a singular verb.]

The **family are** coming from all over the state for the reunion. [*Family* is plural because it suggests several members acting as individuals.]

The **family plans** to attend Beth's graduation. [*Family* is singular because it is acting as one unit.]

6k. When the subject follows the verb, as in sentences beginning with *there* and *here,* be careful to determine the subject and make sure that the verb agrees with it.

In sentences that begin with *there* or *here,* you may have difficulty in finding the subject. Until you are sure what the subject is, you cannot make the verb agree with it. In analyzing such sentences, you should remember that the subject is the word about which something is said. Look for the verb first, and then find the word about which the verb makes a statement.

EXAMPLES   There **are** three sparrow's **eggs** in that nest. [*Are* is the verb. What are? The subject must be *eggs.*]

Here **begins** the **chapter** on Asia. [*Begins* is the verb. What begins? The *chapter* begins. *Chapter* must be the subject.]

In conversation as well as in writing be especially careful not to use the contractions *here's* and *there's* with plural subjects. They are singular and must have singular subjects. If a plural verb is called for, you must use *here are* or *there are.*

EXERCISE 12. Copy the subject from each of the following sentences. Then choose the correct verb from the two in parentheses, and write it after the subject.

1. There (is, are) at least two ways to find this answer.
2. The group (was, were) all going to different camps.

3. Here (is, are) fifteen members of the Little League, all hungry.
4. (Is, Are) both of the twins graduating this year?
5. Here (is, are) some sandwiches and milk.
6. Here (is, are) the shells from Old Orchard Beach.
7. (Here's, Here are) the answers to the test.
8. On the steps of the Capitol there (is, are) several senators and representatives.
9. That flock of geese (makes, make) a beautiful pattern in the sky.
10. There (is, are) neither time nor money enough.

6l. Words stating amounts are usually singular.

Some words that are plural in form may be singular in meaning if they mean an amount of something.

EXAMPLES   Thirty-five **cents is** enough for lunch today. [Although *thirty-five cents* is plural in form, it means a single amount of money. It takes a singular verb, *is*.]

Two **weeks** never **seems** long enough for vacation. [Although *two weeks* is plural, it is thought of here as a single unit of time. It takes a singular verb, *seems*.]

6m. The title of a book, organization, or country, even when plural in form, usually takes a singular verb.

EXAMPLE   *Lost Pony Tracks* **is** a book about an Easterner who moved to a ranch in the West.

EXERCISE 13. Write the numbers 1–10 on your paper. Choose the correct one of the two verbs in parentheses and write it after the number.

1. "The Hundred Dresses" (is, are) a story about a lonely girl.

2. Two cups of flour (seems, seem) too much for that recipe.
3. Three days (was, were) all the time I missed from school last year.
4. Morgan and Company (advertises, advertise) beach bags for a dollar.
5. The Veterans of Foreign Wars (is, are) holding its convention in Chicago this year.
6. Five pounds of sugar (is, are) a lot to carry with all the other groceries.
7. Two hours of homework in one subject (is, are) unfair.
8. *The Women* (was, were) written by Clare Boothe Luce.
9. Three weeks of rehearsal time usually (proves, prove) to be sufficient.
10. Fifty cents (is, are) all I have been able to save this month.

6n. *Don't* and *doesn't* **must agree with their subjects.**

The words *don't* and *doesn't* (contractions of *do not* and *does not*) must, like all other verbs, agree with their subjects. Mistakes are often made with these forms. Be careful, when you use them, to use *don't* with all plural subjects and the pronouns *I* and *you*. Use *doesn't* with all singular subjects except *I* and *you*.

NONSTANDARD   Lena don't exercise enough.
   STANDARD   Lena **doesn't** exercise enough.

NONSTANDARD   That answer don't make sense.
   STANDARD   That answer **doesn't** make sense.

If you are in doubt as to whether to use *don't* or *doesn't* in a sentence, substitute *do not* or *does not*. Your ear will usually tell you which is standard. In the sentences above, for example, if you substitute *do not* for *don't* in the first and third sentences, you realize that they are nonstandard.

EXERCISE 14. *Oral Drill.* Read the following sentences aloud, supplying *don't* or *doesn't* as needed. Saying the correct form several times will help you to write the verb correctly.

1. The girl —— understand the problem.
2. —— she want the prize?
3. The lettuce —— look fresh.
4. That school —— have a stage.
5. It —— matter at all.
6. He —— see the rainbow.
7. The boxer and the poodle —— get along.
8. The curtains in the room —— match the color of the walls.
9. Mary —— need to go with me.
10. This bar of candy —— taste good.

EXERCISE 15. Using the subjects below, write ten original sentences with *don't* or *doesn't* for verbs.

1. the senators from Oklahoma
2. an eclipse of the sun
3. algebra
4. our music teacher
5. apple
6. this typewriter
7. that old bicycle
8. your new idea
9. movie stars
10. piano lessons

6o. A few nouns, though plural in form, take a singular verb.

EXAMPLES   **Mathematics seems** easy this year.
Civics is being taught by Ms. Rodgers while Mrs. Emerson is away.
Mumps is certainly an uncomfortable disease.
The **news was** not encouraging.

REVIEW EXERCISE A. This exercise covers all the rules in this chapter. Write the numbers 1–20 on your paper. After each number, write the correct verb from the parentheses.

1. Unfortunately, my mother (doesn't, don't) get a vacation this year.
2. Many of the people in her shop (gets, get) only a few days.
3. The safety commissioner or the radio announcer (suggests, suggest) that we drive especially carefully on holidays.
4. Each of us (knows, know) that many accidents are caused by carelessness.
5. Our car (doesn't, don't) have any antifreeze yet.
6. There (is, are) several islands in the state of Hawaii.
7. Several of the place-names in our country (comes, come) from Spanish words.
8. Five hours (is, are) all you need to fly across the Atlantic.
9. Anyone on the tennis courts today (is, are) liable to get a sunburn.
10. The architects (wasn't, weren't) sure what kind of building to plan for the new hotel.
11. Some of the many kinds of seaweed (is, are) edible.
12. One of the wheels (wasn't, weren't) functioning properly.
13. Both Janet and Hilda (hopes, hope) to get summer jobs.
14. The plane and its pilot (wasn't, weren't) hurt.
15. (Is, Are) there enough copies of the music to go around?
16. I hope it (doesn't, don't) rain tomorrow.
17. Economics (is, are) a complex but fascinating subject.
18. Either the leader or his followers (doesn't, don't) understand the instructions.

19. A herd of cattle (was, were) grazing on the hill.
20. The news (has, have) surprised all of us.

REVIEW EXERCISE B. Write the numbers 1–20 on your paper. Choose the correct verb for each sentence and write it after the number. Be able to cite the rule for each choice that you make.

1. *Great Expectations* (is, are) the first novel by Charles Dickens that I have read.
2. Several of the novels by this author (is, are) interesting to young people.
3. A few of his titles (is, are) *Oliver Twist, David Copperfield,* and *A Tale of Two Cities.*
4. New readers in every generation (discovers, discover) Dickens' charm for themselves.
5. Every one of Dickens' novels (was, were) read eagerly in America.
6. A writer in England or a writer in America (knows, know) that books written in English are read all over the world.
7. One of the advantages of learning a foreign language (is, are) the ability to read the literature of that language.
8. Translations of literature (is, are) generally inferior to the original works.
9. There (is, are) simple books for beginning students in all languages.
10. Two years (is, are) usually long enough to acquire a fairly good knowledge of a foreign tongue.
11. French and Spanish probably (is, are) the most popular languages to study.
12. A language class at any level (requires, require) repeated drill on pronunciation.
13. Accurate pronunciation (doesn't, don't) come easily to some students.
14. None of the sounds in English (is, are) quite like the sounds of some of the French vowels.

15. Everybody (is, are) quite likely to have some trouble with accents, too.
16. Knowledge of foreign languages (is, are) important for scientists.
17. Reports of research (is, are) published in many different languages.
18. Anyone in a certain field of knowledge (is, are) expected to keep informed in that field.
19. The exchange of ideas among scientists (is, are) a vital kind of communication.
20. Many (finds, find) German a useful language to know.

Chapter 7

Using Verbs Correctly

Principal Parts; Regular and Irregular Verbs

A verb has many forms, which you must know if you are to speak and to write correctly. A verb has several different forms because it expresses different times (present, past, and future). The time expressed by a verb is called its *tense:* present tense, past tense, future tense.

PRINCIPAL PARTS

Every verb has four basic parts, which are called its principal parts. You must know all of these in order to form the different tenses correctly. Two of the principal parts are called *participles.*

The *present participle* of a verb always ends in *–ing:*

> calling   hoping   riding   going

The *past participle* is the form used with *have, has,* or *had:*

> (have) called   (has) hoped   (had) ridden

7a. The four basic forms of a verb are the *infinitive,* the *present participle,* the *past,* and the *past participle.* These basic forms are called the *principal parts.*

INFINITIVE	PRESENT PARTICIPLE	PAST	PAST PARTICIPLE
talk	talking	talked	(have) talked
draw	drawing	drew	(have) drawn

The following sentences show how each form is used to express time.

1. They **draw** excellent pictures. [*present time*]
2. Susan **is drawing** one now. [*present time*]
3. Last week she **drew** two maps. [*past time*]
4. She **has** often **drawn** cartoons. [*past time*]
5. Perhaps she **will draw** one for you. [*future time*]

The following list gives the six tense (time) forms of a verb. A list of all the forms of a verb is called its *conjugation.*

Conjugation of See

INFINITIVE	PRESENT PARTICIPLE	PAST	PAST PARTICIPLE
see	seeing	saw	(have) seen

Present Tense

Singular	Plural
I see	we see
you see	you see
he sees	they see

Past Tense

Singular	Plural
I saw	we saw
you saw	you saw
he saw	they saw

Future Tense

Singular	*Plural*
I will (shall) see	we will (shall) see
you will see	you will see
he will see	they will see

Present Perfect Tense

Singular	*Plural*
I have seen	we have seen
you have seen	you have seen
he has seen	they have seen

Past Perfect Tense

Singular	*Plural*
I had seen	we had seen
you had seen	you had seen
he had seen	they had seen

Future Perfect Tense

Singular	*Plural*
I will (shall) have seen	we will (shall) have seen
you will have seen	you will have seen
he will have seen	they will have seen

Regular Verbs

7b. A *regular verb* forms its past and past participle by adding –ed or –d to the infinitive form.[1]

INFINITIVE	PRESENT PARTICIPLE	PAST	PAST PARTICIPLE
clean	cleaning	cleaned	(have) cleaned
inspect	inspecting	inspected	(have) inspected

[1] The addition of –ed sometimes means that the final consonant must be doubled, as in *hop, hopped* and *skip, skipped*.

Irregular Verbs

Many verbs, as you know, do not follow the regular way of forming principal parts. These *irregular verbs* are the troublesome ones. To avoid errors, you must learn the principal parts of common irregular verbs. You will find that you know many of them already.

7c. An *irregular verb* is one that forms its past and past participle in some other way than a regular verb.

Irregular verbs form their past and past participles in several ways:

(1) by changing a vowel

ring	rang	(have) rung
come	came	(have) come
shrink	shrank	(have) shrunk

(2) by changing a vowel and consonants

do	did	(have) done
go	went	(have) gone
see	saw	(have) seen

(3) by making no change

hurt	hurt	(have) hurt
put	put	(have) put
burst	burst	(have) burst

Memorize the principal parts of the following irregular verbs if you do not already know them. Study them ten at a time, until you have mastered them all. When you are practicing these verbs, always use *have* before the past participle. The past participle can never be used alone.

Common Irregular Verbs

INFINITIVE	PRESENT PARTICIPLE	PAST	PAST PARTICIPLE
begin	beginning	began	(have) begun
blow	blowing	blew	(have) blown
break	breaking	broke	(have) broken
bring	bringing	brought	(have) brought
burst	bursting	burst	(have) burst
choose	choosing	chose	(have) chosen
come	coming	came	(have) come
do	doing	did	(have) done
drink	drinking	drank	(have) drunk
drive	driving	drove	(have) driven
eat	eating	ate	(have) eaten
fall	falling	fell	(have) fallen
freeze	freezing	froze	(have) frozen
give	giving	gave	(have) given
go	going	went	(have) gone
know	knowing	knew	(have) known
ride	riding	rode	(have) ridden
ring	ringing	rang	(have) rung
run	running	ran	(have) run
see	seeing	saw	(have) seen
shrink	shrinking	shrank	(have) shrunk
sing	singing	sang	(have) sung
sink	sinking	sank	(have) sunk
speak	speaking	spoke	(have) spoken
steal	stealing	stole	(have) stolen
swim	swimming	swam	(have) swum
take	taking	took	(have) taken
throw	throwing	threw	(have) thrown
wear	wearing	wore	(have) worn
write	writing	wrote	(have) written

EXERCISE 1. *Oral Drill.* Here is an exercise for the whole class to do together. Let one student choose

a verb from the list of irregular verbs and begin a pattern like this: Today we *go* to the store. Then let another student give the other three sentences: Now we are *going* to the store. Yesterday we *went* to the store. Twice we have *gone* to the store. Do the same with the other irregular verbs in the list.

EXERCISE 2. The following exercise covers the first ten irregular verbs on page 142. Write the numbers 1–20 on your paper. For the blank in each sentence, write the correct form of the verb given before the sentence.

1. *come* Porpoises have often —— to the rescue of shipwrecked sailors.

2. *burst* When the dike ——, the people fled to higher ground.

3. *break* The four-minute mile has been —— many times.

4. *drive* After reading an article on Cape Hatteras, North Carolina, my parents —— there for a vacation.

5. *begin* I have —— my assignment for tomorrow.

6. *break* Because her glasses were ——, she had trouble reading the book.

7. *blow* Finally we —— air into the large balloons that we had bought at the fair.

8. *burst* When one ——, we were surprised at the loud noise it made.

9. *do* Do you remember what we —— then?

10. *come* Finally the time —— to go home.

11. *bring* What has your mother —— you from Mexico?

12. *choose* Mimi and Julia have —— to stay in the glee club.

13. *drink* Every morning fresh footprints showed that the moose had —— from the brook.

14. *bring* Paul —— a turtle egg to school today.

15. *begin*   It —— to rain about an hour ago.
16. *choose*   After days of indecision, Rae —— to keep the smallest puppy in the litter.
17. *do*   Shirley —— everything possible to make the patient comfortable.
18. *drive*   Dad has —— our car almost fifty thousand miles.
19. *blow*   The wind has —— down a large branch of the old oak.
20. *drink*   Sue —— the milk at one gulp and then put the glass down.

EXERCISE 3. The following exercise covers the next ten verbs on page 142. Write the numbers 1–20 on your paper. For the blank in each sentence, write the correct form of the verb given before the sentence.

1. *eat*   We have —— a bushel of peaches this summer.
2. *see*   When mother —— us, she brought us some cold lemonade.
3. *freeze* Parts of the body are sometimes —— during operations.
4. *give*   I should have been —— a better grade in geography.
5. *ring*   After the bell has —— today, let's go down to the beach.
6. *ride*   We wished we could have —— longer on the Ferris wheel.
7. *know*   We have —— for several centuries that the earth is round.
8. *go*   Last Sunday we could have —— with our parents on a picnic.
9. *eat*   After we had —— all the hot dogs that we could hold, we roasted marshmallows.
10. *fall*   The temperature has —— thirty degrees in the last twenty-four hours.
11. *freeze* I am afraid that the tomato plants have ——.

12. *run* In 1954 Roger Bannister —— a mile in less than four minutes.

13. *know* Ann —— that she had lost some of her science notes.

14. *give* Sarah and Nellie —— their book reports yesterday.

15. *ride* Molly has —— in two horse shows.

16. *fall* That skier must have —— more than once.

17. *run* While we waited in the bleachers, Joe —— down to the dugout.

18. *go* Since Juan doesn't answer, I guess he has —— to the pool.

19. *ring* The phone has —— at least ten times today.

20. *see* I wish I had —— the movie before I started the book.

EXERCISE 4. The following exercise covers the last ten verbs on page 142. Write the numbers 1–20 on your paper. For the blank in each sentence, write the correct form of the verb given before the sentence.

1. *swim* Florence Chadwick —— the English Channel in 1950.

2. *write* A friend of my parents has —— a novel about our town.

3. *throw* The fullback was —— for a loss.

4. *steal* Mom's car was —— during the night!

5. *sink* In the fourteenth century pirates —— many ships.

6. *speak* Until the energy crisis many people had —— of solar energy as impractical.

7. *take* People have always —— an interest in the unknown.

8. *sing* I wish the glee club had —— more popular songs in its concert.

9. *take* I should have —— more time to find a book in the library.

10. *sing*   My sister said she hadn't —— that song for a long time.

11. *swim*   The children watched two ducks as they —— across a pond.

12. *sink*   They —— their heads in the water looking for food.

13. *shrink*   This sweater has —— to a baby's size!

14. *wear*   I had only —— it a few times.

15. *steal*   Two players have —— bases while you weren't paying attention.

16. *throw*   If you had —— the ball straight, I might have caught it.

17. *speak*   The visitors have —— a few words in Spanish to the delighted audience.

18. *write*   Helen has —— to her congresswoman about the natural resources bill.

19. *shrink*   The time it takes to travel across the continent has —— almost unbelievably in the last decade.

20. *wear*   This old jacket has certainly —— well.

REVIEW EXERCISE A. The following exercise covers several irregular verbs from the list on page 142. Write the numbers 1–20 on your paper. After each number, write the form of the verb that will fit correctly in the blank.

1. *blow*   Last night the wind —— the garbage pail into the neighbor's yard.

2. *break*   Because she has —— so many promises, I no longer trust her.

3. *bring*   It was an open-book test, but I —— the wrong book.

4. *burst*   On Christmas Eve, the children almost —— with excitement.

5. *choose*   The coach has already —— the first-string players.

6. *come*   My sister's friend —— to dinner last night.

7. *do*   Just because you have always —— it that way doesn't mean that it is right.

8. *drink* At Teresa's party, six of us ate two chocolate cakes and —— four quarts of punch.

9. *fall*   He would have made another touchdown if he had not —— on the five-yard line.

10. *freeze* The look she gave me would have —— water.

11. *go*   The whole troop wished they had not —— on the overnight hike.

12. *know* Had I —— that, I would have refused the invitation.

13. *ring* Who —— the fire alarm?

14. *run*   Even though she lost, she —— a good race.

15. *see*   Fortunately, Jan —— where the arrow landed.

16. *shrink* Either John has grown, or his trousers have ——.

17. *speak* He stopped suddenly after he had —— only a few words.

18. *throw* The shortstop should have —— to first base.

19. *write* I wish she had —— to me about it.

20. *swim* Before we had lunch we —— out to the island.

SIX TROUBLESOME VERBS

There are three pairs of verbs that seem to be particularly troublesome for students. You should be especially careful not to misuse them. Study the following explanations of how to use *sit* and *set, rise* and *raise, lie* and *lay.*

Sit and *Set*

The verb *sit* means "to sit down" or "to rest," as in a chair. Its principal parts are *sit, sitting, sat,* (have) *sat.*

EXAMPLES   Bob **sits** in that seat.
Three girls **sat** on the platform.
I **had sat** there for a long time.

The verb *set* means "to place" or "to put." Its principal parts are *set, setting, set,* (have) *set.*

EXAMPLES   **Set** those tomato plants in a sunny place.
Paula **set** the toolbox on top of the motor.
Have you **set** a day for the meeting?
Hunters sometimes **set** traps for fur-bearing animals.

If you keep in mind the meaning of the sentence, you should be able to choose the correct verb. If the meaning is "to rest," use the verb *sit.* If the meaning is "to put" or "to place," use the verb *set.*

It may help you to know that *set* takes an object and that *sit* does not.

I **will sit** here for a while. [no object]

I **will set** your dinner on the table. [object: *dinner*]

If the verb has an object, you should use *set.*

EXERCISE 5. *Oral Drill.* In the following sentences the verbs *sit* and *set* are correctly used. Read the sentences aloud several times to become familiar with the correct usage.

1. We *set* up the card table in the den.
2. Then we *sat* down to play a game of Monopoly.
3. We *set* our pieces on the board and began to play.
4. After we had been *sitting* there for an hour, we decided to make some fudge.
5. We *set* the pan on the stove.
6. After *setting* out all the ingredients, we mixed them and returned to our game.
7. We could not *sit* still for long.

8. We had to *set* the stove at the right temperature.
9. Once we almost *sat* too long.
10. The pan had been *set* on the wrong burner, and the fudge was beginning to burn.

EXERCISE 6. Write the numbers 1–10 on your paper. For each blank, write the correct form of *sit* or *set*.

1. On the train to Boston I —— next to an aloof woman. **2.** She —— a large briefcase down by her seat. **3.** When the conductor asked her if she would like to —— it in the baggage rack, she refused. **4.** She insisted that the briefcase must —— by her side. **5.** As I —— beside her, I wondered about the contents of the briefcase. **6.** Her strange behavior —— my imagination working. **7.** I thought that I might be —— next to a secret service agent or a spy. **8.** Perhaps she had —— a time bomb to go off at a certain time. **9.** As the woman —— her other packages down, I watched the briefcase carefully. **10.** A sudden movement of the train caused the briefcase to open, and there beside the woman —— a small black and white puppy.

EXERCISE 7. Write ten sentences. In five of them, use a form of the verb *sit*. In the other five, use a form of the verb *set*.

Rise and *Raise*

The verb *rise* means "to arise," "to get up," or "to go up." Its principal parts are *rise, rising, rose,* (have) *risen.*

EXAMPLES   Like the sun, the stars **rise** in the east.
The director **rose** to speak.
He **had** already **risen** from the bench.

The verb *raise* means "to lift up" or "force up." Its principal parts are *raise, raising, raised,* (have) *raised.*

EXAMPLES   **Raise** your arms above your head.
My mother **raised** the curtain.
We **raise** many of our own vegetables.

The verb *rise* never has an object; *raise* does.

Clouds of smoke **were rising** above the school. [no object]

Passing cars **were raising** clouds of dust. [object: *clouds*]

Errors in the use of *rise* and *raise* almost always occur because a form of *raise* has been used where a form of *rise* is required.

EXERCISE 8. *Oral Drill.* Read the following sentences aloud. Note the uses of the verbs *rise* and *raise,* which are correct.

1. One of the peaks in the Alps *rises* over fifteen thousand feet in the air.
2. The American flag was *raised* on the moon.
3. The student *raised* an important question.
4. The speaker *rose* from her seat.
5. By midnight the Big Dipper had *risen* high in the heavens.
6. We have *raised* tulips for several years.
7. Look to see if the cake is *rising.*
8. When the starter *raises* his hand, be ready to run.
9. Your voice *rises* at the end of a question.
10. In the movie a gigantic sea monster *rose* up out of the ocean.

EXERCISE 9. Choose the correct form of *raise* or *rise* to fill each blank below; then write it after the proper number on your paper.

1. The audience had —— a great clamor to see Sarah Caldwell conduct the opera.

2. We all —— from our seats when she stood on the podium.
3. A hush quickly fell over the audience when she —— her baton to begin conducting.
4. I shut my eyes and listened to the melodious music that —— from the orchestra.
5. Then the curtain was —— and an elaborate stage set was revealed.
6. During one scene the chorus on stage —— their shields and swords.
7. At the end of the opera, the music —— to a fevered pitch.
8. When Caldwell turned around, she saw that the audience had —— to applaud her conducting.
9. She asked the members of the orchestra to —— for their applause.
10. After seeing Sarah Caldwell conduct, it was clear to us why she has —— to such prominence.

EXERCISE 10. Write ten sentences, using each one of the following verb forms. Try for interest and variety in your sentences.

1. rising
2. raising
3. rose
4. have risen
5. raised
6. rises
7. had raised
8. had risen
9. will rise
10. raise

Lie and Lay

The verb *lie* means "to recline" or "to remain lying down."[1] Its principal parts are *lie, lying, lay,* (have) *lain.*

EXAMPLES   Rocky Ridge **lies** twenty miles east of here.

[1] The verb *lie* meaning to "tell a falsehood" is another word.

The dictionary **is lying** face down on the window seat.

Mrs. Miller **lay** down for a short nap.

Pam's bicycle **has lain** in the ditch all morning.

The verb *lay* means "to put down," "to place something." Its principal parts are *lay, laying, laid,* (have) *laid.*

EXAMPLES   **Lay** that puzzle aside and come help me, please.

Mom **is laying** tile in the kitchen.

Who **laid** the first telephone cable across the Atlantic?

Father **has laid** your clean shirts and socks on the bed.

The verb *lie* never has an object; the verb *lay* may have an object. If the verb has an object, use a form of *lay.*

Errors in the use of *lie* and *lay* almost always occur because a form of *lay* has been used where a form of *lie* is required.

NONSTANDARD   Rose was laying down.
STANDARD   Rose **was lying** down.

NONSTANDARD   He laid in wait for us.
STANDARD   He **lay** in wait for us.

EXERCISE 11. *Oral Drill.* Read the following sentences aloud. Pay attention to the use of the verbs *lie* and *lay,* which in these sentences are used correctly.

1. If you are tired, *lie* down for a while.
2. We *laid* our tools on the table an hour ago.
3. The two dogs *lay* down beside each other.
4. After *lying* there for a few minutes, they were ready to play again.

5. Vivian *laid* out her winter clothes.
6. Sometimes snow *lies* on the ground into late spring.
7. Do not *lay* the blame on someone else.
8. After Mrs. Peterson had *lain* down for a few hours, she was ready to travel again.
9. The sheriff has *laid* a trap for the bank robber.
10. The animal is *lying* in wait for its prey.

EXERCISE 12. Write the numbers 1–10 on your paper. After each number, copy the correct verb from the parentheses. Remember that only a form of *lay* can have an object.

1. A book of stories by Edgar Allan Poe is (lying, laying) on the table.
2. Horror (lies, lays) in wait for the reader of Poe's stories.
3. Some of his characters (lay, laid) under the spell of strange diseases.
4. Few people have (lain, laid) down a story by Poe until it was finished.
5. Many have (lain, laid) awake at night after reading a Poe story.
6. In one of Poe's most lyrical poems, a lover grieves for Annabel Lee, who (lies, lays) "in a tomb by the sounding sea."
7. In "The Tell-Tale Heart," a man (lying, laying) in bed thinks the tick of a watch is a heartbeat.
8. The appeal of Poe's poem "The Bells" (lies, lays) in its musical sounds.
9. In "The Raven," a man's midnight encounter with a raven (lies, lays) a deep sorrow over his spirit.
10. "The Pit and the Pendulum" is a story of the tortures a man undergoes while he is (lying, laying) at the bottom of a dark pit.

REVIEW EXERCISE B. Write the numbers 1–10 on your paper. In the parentheses, you will find various forms of *sit, set, rise, raise, lie,* and *lay.* Choose the form that will make each sentence correct, and write it after the number.

1. Many minerals have (lain, laid) untouched in the earth for years.
2. Can't you (sit, set) still during class?
3. The old sailor (lay, laid) his hand on the tiller.
4. The cat was (lying, laying) peacefully on the rug.
5. The queen and her advisers (sat, set) down at the table together.
6. After the celebration everyone (lay, laid) down to sleep.
7. A tiny cloud of black smoke (rose, raised) from a distant hill.
8. The painters (sat, set) their ladders against the walls of the barn.
9. Have you been (sitting, setting) in the library all day?
10. The sun had already (risen, raised) before we woke.

REVIEW EXERCISE C. Write the numbers 1–20 on your paper. If a sentence contains a verb error, write the correct form of the verb on your paper after the number. If the sentence is correct, write *C* after its number.

1. Because I laid in bed too long, I was late getting to school.
2. Hughie threw the ball toward third base.
3. I have wore out my old green sweater.
4. The men set talking until early morning.
5. At the reception Diane chose to serve the cake.
6. Have you spoke to Ms. Thatcher yet?
7. When I heard my name called late last night, I raised up to see what was happening.

8. After the car turned over, it busted into flames.
9. Ted knows a woman who has wrote a play.
10. Have you saw *Hamlet* performed on the stage?
11. Our drama group raised enough money to build a small theater.
12. My bicycle was stole while I was in the library.
13. The police have went looking for it.
14. The pitcher and the catcher throwed the ball back and forth.
15. We went to the game and set in the bleachers.
16. After the flag was raised and the national anthem was sung, the game began.
17. The water in the pond had froze during the night.
18. Have we drunk a whole quart of milk?
19. The water level has continued to raise, even though the rain has stopped.
20. Halloween come on Friday last year.

REVIEW EXERCISE D. Write the numbers 1–25 on your paper. For each sentence below, choose the correct form of the verb preceding it to fit into the blank. Then write that form on your paper after the sentence number.

1. *lie*   Deep-sea divers sometimes find treasure that has —— at the bottom of the ocean for centuries.
2. *eat*   Have you ever —— a mango?
3. *sing*   She couldn't have —— such a difficult piece without lots of practice.
4. *drive*   My mother has —— me to school every day this week.
5. *give*   Who —— the main talk in assembly yesterday?
6. *run*   Some candidates have —— for President again and again.
7. *break*   This heat wave has —— all records.
8. *ring*   I think the doorbell —— a minute ago.

9. *swim* Gail —— out to the raft before supper.

10. *rise* If the oven isn't hot enough, the cake won't —— properly.

11. *sit* Nine justices —— on the Supreme Court.

12. *sink* The big submarine —— beneath the surface with hardly a ripple.

13. *lay* Consulting his charts, the skipper —— a course to Cape Fear.

14. *blow* The wind must have —— forty miles an hour last night.

15. *take* Kim has —— a course in electrical engineering.

16. *ride* The Robbinses have —— over in their pickup truck.

17. *know* Margie —— her answer wasn't right.

18. *do* Some of the early settlers —— their best to make friends with the natives.

19. *fall* The barometer has —— during the day.

20. *choose* Would you have —— differently if you had known the consequences?

21. *bring* Miriam and Ruth —— a new spirit of enthusiasm to the meeting.

22. *sit* Is it all right for those seedlings to be —— in the sun all this time?

23. *rise* A shout —— from the bleachers.

24. *shrink* Either I have grown or this shirt —— in the wash.

25. *go* The Coopers have —— to Mexico for a month.

Chapter 8

Using Pronouns Correctly

Nominative and Objective Case Forms

In the following sentences, notice the different forms of the pronouns:

> **She** and **I** work for the school newspaper. The editor assigns stories to **her** and **me.**

If you examine these sentences, you will notice that *she* and *I* are subjects of the first sentence, and that *her* and *me,* in the second sentence, are objects of a preposition. A pronoun may have one form when it is a subject and a different form when it is an object.

Some pronouns change their form according to the way they are used in sentences. This difference in forms is called *case.* There are three cases. Pronouns used as subjects and as predicate nominatives are in the *nominative* case. Pronouns used as objects are in the *objective* case. Pronouns that show ownership (*my, his, hers, their,* and so on) are in the *possessive* case. In this chapter, you will study the nominative and objective forms of pronouns.

Memorize the nominative and objective case forms of the following personal pronouns.

NOMINATIVE		OBJECTIVE	
Singular	*Plural*	*Singular*	*Plural*
I	we	me	us
you	you	you	you
he	they	him	them
she		her	
it		it	

Notice that the pronouns *you* and *it* are the same in the nominative and objective forms.

THE NOMINATIVE CASE

When you use a pronoun as a subject or after a linking verb, always use a nominative form.

8a. The subject of a verb is in the nominative case.

A pronoun used as the subject must always be one of these forms: *I, you, he, she, it, we, they.*

EXAMPLES   **They** made candles from antique molds. [*They* is the subject of the verb *made*.]

He and **I** mowed lawns on Saturday afternoon. [*He* and *I* are the subjects of the verb *mowed*.]

EXERCISE 1. *Oral Drill.* Read aloud the following sentences to accustom your ear to the correct pronoun form.

1. Elena and I are looking forward to a wonderful vacation.
2. She and I are sailing for Europe.
3. We students are taking a tour of several countries.
4. Elena and I agree about most of the places we want to see.
5. She and I went on deck just before the ship sailed.

6. We and the other students crowded toward the railing.
7. She and I spotted our parents on the dock.
8. We on the boat and they on the shore waved and shouted.
9. Then she and I waved a final good-by.
10. As the ship was towed out into deep water, we and they suddenly felt very lonely.

Errors in the case of pronouns usually occur when the subject is compound, that is, when it consists of two subjects joined by *and* or *or*. For example, no one is likely to say, "*Me* had lunch." But many people make a similar mistake by saying something like, "*Helen* and *me* had lunch."

You can select the correct pronoun in a compound subject by trying each part of the subject alone with the verb.

NONSTANDARD   Her and me looked for tracks. [*Her looked for tracks* and *me looked for tracks* are clearly wrong.]

STANDARD   **She** and **I** looked for tracks. [*She looked for tracks* and *I looked for tracks* are correct.]

When a pronoun is immediately followed by a noun — *we girls, us girls* — you can determine the correct pronoun by dropping the noun.

EXAMPLE   (We, Us) girls voted together.
We [not us] voted together.
We girls voted together.

EXERCISE 2. In the following sentences, choose the correct one of the two pronouns in parentheses, and write it after the proper number on your paper.

1. He and (me, I) pretended to be Tom Sawyer and Huck Finn.

2. (We, Us) boys have lively imaginations.
3. Once he and (I, me) were supposed to paint a fence.
4. Neither (he, him) nor I wanted to do it.
5. Jack and (I, me) decided to trick some friends.
6. When they came down the street, my friend and (I, me) pretended to be enjoying painting the fence.
7. (We, Us) two finally agreed to let the other boys help us.
8. Barbara and (they, them) were happy.
9. My friend and (me, I) enjoyed watching them work.
10. Later at the clubhouse (us, we) members had a good laugh.

EXERCISE 3. *Oral Drill.* Use each of the groups of words below as the subject of a sentence, choosing the correct pronoun from the pair in parentheses.

EXAMPLE   1. My mother and (I, me) ——
           1. *My mother and I are going on a camp-ing trip.*

1. The scientists and (them, they) ——
2. The coach and (us, we) ——
3. (Him, He) and (I, me) ——
4. My neighbors and (them, they) ——
5. You and (me, I) ——
6. (We, Us) players ——
7. Chris and (she, her) ——
8. (Them, They) and (we, us) ——
9. (Her, She) and I ——
10. The police officer and (he, him) ——
11. The James children and (them, they) ——
12. Last night (her, she) and (they, them) ——
13. (We, Us) citizens ——
14. The firefighters and (they, them) ——
15. Suddenly, you and (her, she) ——

16. For five years you and (me, I) ——
17. (Him, He) and his followers ——
18. (She, Her) and (I, me) ——
19. Both you and (him, he) ——
20. You spectators and (we, us) players ——

8b. **A predicate nominative is in the nominative case.**

A predicate nominative, as you learned on page 106, always refers to the subject. It follows a linking verb. A pronoun used as a predicate nominative must be in the nominative case: *I, he, she, we, they.*

EXAMPLES The candidates for class president were **he** and **she.**

The members of the debating team are **we** three.

► NOTE This rule is often ignored in the usage *It is me* or *It's me.* Although *me* is the objective form, it is acceptable as a predicate nominative. *It is her, him, us, them* are usually acceptable in spoken English, but not in writing. In doing the following exercises, follow the usage of written English.

EXERCISE 4. After each number on your paper, write the correct pronoun from the parentheses.

1. See if it is (she, her).
2. Who are (they, them)?
3. The witness claimed that the thief was (him, he).
4. The next contestant will be (she, her).
5. The ones invited to the party are you and (them, they).
6. They were sure that it was (her, she) behind the mask.
7. The committee members are Jean, Andy, and (I, me).
8. Could the fortuneteller possibly be (her, she)?

9. The next batter should be (him, he).
10. Our closest neighbors are you and (them, they).

EXERCISE 5. *Oral Drill.* Choosing the correct pronoun from the pair in the parentheses, use each word group as the predicate nominative in a sentence. Be sure to use a linking verb.

EXAMPLE   1. —— Mr. Lane and (he, him)
                  1. *It could have been Mr. Lane and he.*

1. —— you and (they, them)
2. —— Angie and (her, she)
3. —— my mother and (she, her)
4. —— you and (us, we)
5. —— the neighbors and (them, they)
6. —— Cal, Pat, and (I, me)
7. —— her partner and (her, she)
8. —— the pilot and (he, him)
9. —— she and (them, they)
10. —— they and (us, we)

THE OBJECTIVE CASE

When you use a pronoun as an object of a verb or a preposition, always use the objective case form.

8c. The direct and indirect objects of a verb are in the objective case.

A pronoun used as the direct object or indirect object of a verb must always be one of these forms: *me, you, him, her, it, us, them.*

EXAMPLES   Mother called **me** to the phone. [*Me* is the direct object of the verb *called.*]
                  The hostess handed **her** a piece of cake. [*Her* is the indirect object of the verb *handed.*]

Difficulties in choosing the correct form of the pronoun usually arise when the object is compound. You can make sure the pronoun in a compound object is correct by trying it alone in the sentence. Study this example.

PROBLEM   The teacher chose (she, her) and (I, me).

AWKWARD   The teacher chose she.
The teacher chose I.

SOLUTION   The teacher chose **her.**
The teacher chose **me.**
The teacher chose **her** and **me.**

EXERCISE 6. *Oral Drill.* The following sentences are all correct. Read them aloud, and explain the form and use of each italicized pronoun.

1. I took Jim and *her* to the rodeo with me.
2. The attendants gave *us* newcomers programs.
3. Then a guide showed them and *me* to our seats.
4. The bucking broncos frightened Jim and *her.*
5. But they delighted the crowd and *me.*
6. The wild bulls gave *us* spectators a real scare.
7. We watched the riders and *them.*
8. The rope tricks pleased Alice and *me* most.
9. But the tricks did not impress the others and *him* as much as the roping contest.
10. When the rodeo was over, I asked *him* and *her* if they were glad they went.

EXERCISE 7. Write the numbers 1–20 on your paper. After each number, write a pronoun or pronouns that will correctly complete the sentence.

1. The man hired Suzie and —— to run errands.
2. Lisa sent —— and —— Christmas presents.
3. We gave Bill and —— our old magazines and newspapers.

4. The lifeguard rescued —— and ——.
5. The magician showed my sister and —— a magic hat.
6. The show pleased my sister and ——.
7. The host passed —— and —— generous helpings of chicken and dumplings.
8. The class chose —— and —— as its delegates to the convention.
9. The convention nominated Rhoda and —— on the first ballot.
10. The clerk charged Allen and —— ten dollars for the pants.
11. The ski lift carried —— and —— to the top.
12. The mayor gave —— and —— the keys to the city.
13. I handed Mrs. Barnes and —— my resignation.
14. A neighbor drove —— and —— to the fair.
15. We raced —— and —— to the top of the hill.
16. The pitcher threw —— and —— a fast ball.
17. The police turned —— and —— over to the FBI.
18. Rosa lent —— and —— some books about ships.
19. The judge gave the prize to —— and ——.
20. The audience gave —— a standing ovation.

REVIEW EXERCISE A. The following sentences require pronouns in either the nominative or objective case. Choose the correct pronoun for each sentence, and write it on your paper after the number.

1. (We, Us) students in History 201 gave our reports yesterday.
2. Mr. Ortega, our teacher, had assigned Paul and (I, me) the topic of Amelia Earhart.
3. Some of the students and (he, him) thought that more reports should be on women in American history.
4. According to Bonnie and Francine, their achievements and (they, them) are overlooked by historians.

5. Actually, the only ones who complained were (they, them).
6. Paul and (I, me) researched the topic thoroughly.
7. The rest of the students and (we, us) were amazed at our findings.
8. Amelia Earhart's place in the history of aviation surprised (he, him) and (I, me).
9. We learned that it was (she, her) who made the first solo flight by a woman across the Atlantic.
10. The fact that Amelia Earhart was the first pilot to fly from Hawaii to California astounded the class and (we, us).
11. Bonnie and Francine had told Paul and (I, me) that we might learn a lot from our research.
12. The other girls and (they, them) enjoyed hearing our report.
13. Mr. Ortega told the girls and (we, us) to research Amelia Earhart's death.
14. The mystery we found astounded Bonnie, Francine, and (we, us) as well.
15. In 1937, her navigator and (she, her) took off in a twin-engine plane.
16. Supposedly, the journey was taking Fred Noonan and (she, her) around the world.
17. After completing two-thirds of the trip, the navigator and (she, her) could not be contacted by radio.
18. The plane and (they, them) were never sighted again.
19. Apparently, the Pacific Ocean had claimed both (she, her) and (he, him).
20. The rest of our history class and (we, us) are among the many people still puzzling over this tragedy.

8d. The object of a preposition is in the objective case.

As you know, prepositions are always followed by objects. (If you need to review prepositions, see the list on page 72.) When a pronoun is used as the object of a preposition, it is in the objective case. The objective forms of pronouns, you recall, are *me, you, him, her, it, us, them.*

EXAMPLES   The secret is between **you** and **me.** [*You* and *me* are the objects of the preposition *between.*]

We waited for Ed and **them** to arrive. [*Them* is one of the objects of the preposition *for.*]

EXERCISE 8. *Oral Drill.* The pronouns in these sentences are all objects of prepositions and are in the objective case. Read the sentences aloud and identify the pronouns and the prepositions.

1. My father divided the money among the younger children and us.
2. We walked behind our parents and them.
3. I sat down beside him and her.
4. She turned her head toward Annie and me.
5. The boy walked between us girls.
6. I bought two hot dogs for Gwen and her.
7. The Steinbergs will have a new house near the McHughs and them.
8. Look at him and me when you talk.
9. Vivian's mother is keeping the surprise party a secret from her and the twins.
10. Suddenly frogs were leaping around Herb and me.

EXERCISE 9. Write the numbers 1–10 on your paper. Copy the correct one of the two pronouns in parentheses.

1. near Ken and (I, me)
2. for you and (she, her)
3. upon the fire fighters and (them, they)
4. with Dr. Thomas and (he, him)

5. behind Joe and (we, us)
6. by you and (they, them)
7. against Joyce and (me, I)
8. from his cousin and (he, him)
9. about Anita and (she, her)
10. except the Greens and (we, us)

EXERCISE 10. Write ten short sentences, using each of the following prepositions. Follow the prepositions with compound objects. Make at least one of the objects in each sentence a pronoun.

EXAMPLE   1. toward
             1. *The dog ran toward Nina and her.*

1. before   6. around
2. for   7. beside
3. between   8. at
4. to   9. except
5. from   10. behind

REVIEW EXERCISE B. The following sentences contain pronouns used as subjects, predicate nominatives, direct and indirect objects of verbs, and objects of prepositions. Write the numbers 1–10 on your paper. After each number, write the correct pronoun from the parentheses. Be prepared to tell how the pronoun is used in the sentence.

1. Elizabeth Blackwell was the first woman to graduate from medical school, and (she, her) later became a famous teacher of doctors.
2. Geneva College gave (she, her) a medical degree in 1849.
3. At first, other male doctors would not offer a job to (she, her) because she was a woman.
4. A fighter, not a quitter, was (she, her).
5. Elizabeth Blackwell wanted to help the poor and opened her own clinic for (they, them).

6. Soon, wealthy citizens supported (she, her) and the clinic with donations.
7. Elizabeth's work among the poor won for (she, her) the respect of many other doctors.
8. To help train other women doctors, (she, her) opened the first medical school for women.
9. Elizabeth set high standards for her students and expected (they, them) to work very hard.
10. Elizabeth's teaching helped (they, them) to become excellent doctors, and Elizabeth was proud of their success.

► **NOTE** Some students make serious errors by using *hisself* or *theirselfs* in the place of the correct objective case forms *himself* and *themselves*. You should remember that *hisself* and *theirselfs* are not acceptable words.

NONSTANDARD   The secretary voted for hisself in the last election.

STANDARD   The secretary voted for **himself** in the last election.

NONSTANDARD   The cooks served theirselfs some of the cake.

STANDARD   The cooks served **themselves** some of the cake.

REVIEW EXERCISE C. Write the numbers 1–20 on your paper. Select the correct one of the two pronouns in parentheses, and write it after the proper number.

1. The cocaptains for this game will be Dick and (he, him).
2. We have heard many stories about you and (he, him).
3. We were told by my parents and (they, them).
4. They and (we, us) belong to the same club.
5. "Who are (they, them)?" he asked.

6. "Don't hide behind the coach and (they, them)," she said.
7. "What do you think about him and (I, me)?" he asked.
8. "You and (he, him) are both excellent players," we replied.
9. My parents gave their parents and (they, them) a farewell party.
10. They did not remember my sister and (I, me).
11. The members are Raúl, Pam, and (I, me).
12. The teacher spoke to (we, us) officers before the meeting.
13. Are you and (she, her) ready?
14. The unexpected guests surprised my mother and (I, me).
15. When the door was opened, (she, her) and her aunt were standing there.
16. Both (he, him) and (she, her) had written us, but we had not received their letters.
17. We had to serve (he, him) and (she, her) leftovers.
18. Luckily the group did not leave without (he, him) and (I, me).
19. (We, Us) hikers saw many beautiful scenes.
20. Will you call Karen and (I, me) in the morning?

REVIEW EXERCISE D. Use the following expressions correctly in sentences of your own.

1. my brother and me
2. us scouts
3. you and I
4. herself
5. he and she
6. the Jacksons and us
7. the principal and them
8. you and they
9. him and me
10. her husband and she

Chapter 9

Using Modifiers Correctly

Comparison of Adjectives and Adverbs; Double Negatives

If you had a peanut-butter sandwich for lunch on Monday, a hamburger on Tuesday, and roast chicken on Wednesday, you might say, "Monday's lunch was *good,* Tuesday's was *better,* and Wednesday's was *best* of all."

In comparing the meals, you used different forms of the adjective *good.* Each of the forms expresses a slightly different meaning. The contrast expressed by these different forms is called *comparison.*

COMPARISON OF ADJECTIVES AND ADVERBS

9a. The three degrees of comparison of modifiers are the *positive,* the *comparative,* and the *superlative.*

Positive	San Francisco is a **large** city.
Comparative	Chicago is **larger** than San Francisco.
Superlative	New York is the **largest** of the three.

(1) The positive degree is used when only one thing is being described.

This suitcase is **heavy.**

An **old** statue stood in the garden.

Luis began the job **cheerfully.**

Bernice wrote **fast** when she came to the last question.

(2) The comparative degree is used when two things are being compared.

My suitcase is **heavier** than yours.

That statue is **older** than my grandmother.

She began to talk **more cheerfully** about her plans.

Hank wrote **faster.**

(3) The superlative degree is used when three or more things are being compared.

Sylvia's suitcase is the **heaviest** of all.

It is the **oldest** statue I have ever seen.

Of all the girls, Debbie accepted the situation **most cheerfully.**

Donald wrote the **fastest** of all.

► **NOTE** The superlative is often used for emphasis when it clearly refers to one of two: "Put your best foot forward." However, in your writing you will do well to observe rule (3).

Study the comparison of the following adjectives and adverbs.

POSITIVE	COMPARATIVE	SUPERLATIVE
happy	happier	happiest
short	shorter	shortest
anxious	more anxious	most anxious
slowly	more slowly	most slowly

You will observe that there are two ways of forming

the comparative and superlative degrees. To form the comparative, the ending –er may be added to the end of the word itself (and sometimes the final letter is changed, as in *happy — happier*), or the word *more* may precede the word. To form the superlative degree, the ending –*est* is added to the end of the word, or the word *most* is put before it. These are the two regular methods of comparing adjectives and adverbs.

The rules telling you which method of comparing to use with a particular word are complicated and difficult to remember. Most of the time, you can tell which is correct by judging which sounds right. You can hear that *more quick* sounds wrong; therefore, you would say *quicker* or *more quickly*. Your ear tells you that *excitingest* is incorrect; you would say *most exciting*. When you are in doubt about the correct comparative or superlative form of a modifier, look the word up in a dictionary or ask your teacher for help.

The comparative and superlative degrees of a few words are formed in irregular ways. You should memorize the ones given here.

POSITIVE	COMPARATIVE	SUPERLATIVE
good	better	best
well	better	best
bad	worse	worst

EXERCISE 1. Write the numbers 1–10 on your paper. After each number, write the form of the italicized adjective or adverb that will correctly fill the blank in the sentence. If you are in doubt about the correct way to form the comparative or superlative degree of a modifier, look it up in your dictionary.

EXAMPLE　1. *good*　This is the —— show I have ever seen.
　　　　　　1. *best*

1. *smart*   Is she —— than her sister?
2. *calm*   The lake was —— than usual after the storm.
3. *difficult* This is one of the —— tests I have ever taken.
4. *bright*   Many distant stars are actually —— than some that are closer to our planet.
5. *slow*   The closer she got to the dentist's office, the —— she walked.
6. *well*   The patient feels —— than he did last night.
7. *clear*   This is the —— night we have had in a long time.
8. *good*   Jennifer's is the —— of the two papers.
9. *early*   June's guests arrived —— than she expected.
10. *bad*   I played my —— game yesterday.

9b. Distinguish between *good* and *well* as modifiers.

Many errors with modifiers are made by students who confuse *good* and *well*. You should learn to use all the forms of these words correctly.

(1) Use *good* to modify nouns or pronouns.

The outcome was **good**.

We expect a **good** crop this fall.

She is **good** at badminton.

(2) Use *well* to modify verbs.

The game started **well**.

The trees are producing **well** this fall.

She plays badminton **well**.

EXCEPTION When *well* means "in good health," it may be used after a linking verb to modify a noun or pronoun.

Mother feels quite **well** today.

9c. Use an adjective, not an adverb, after linking verbs.

Linking verbs (forms of *be,* and such words as *feel, taste, seem, appear,* etc.) are often followed by predicate adjectives modifying the subject. You must be careful not to use an adverb when an adjective is called for.

EXAMPLES Ingrid looks **sleepy.** [The predicate adjective *sleepy* modifies the subject *Ingrid. Looks* is a linking verb.]

Ingrid looked **sleepily** at the clock. [The adverb *sleepily* modifies the action verb *looked.*]

Bill feels **uncertain** about the race. [The predicate adjective *uncertain* modifies the subject *Bill. Feels* is a linking verb.]

Bill felt his way **uncertainly** along the hall. [The adverb *uncertainly* modifies the action verb *felt.*]

EXERCISE 2. Write the numbers 1–10 on your paper. After each number, write the one of the two words in parentheses that will make the sentence correct.

1. The fire feels (good, well) on this cold wintry day.
2. The wind is howling so (fierce, fiercely) I can hardly hear you.
3. At camp we always eat (good, well).
4. We moved as (slow, slowly) as a horse and buggy.
5. The stars look (beautiful, beautifully) on a clear night.

6. She did her work (good, well).
7. We (sure, surely) enjoyed our visit to San Diego.
8. We examined the bookbag (careful, carefully) before we bought it.
9. Hot chocolate tastes (good, well) on a winter evening.
10. The ball dropped (easy, easily) into the basket.

9d. Avoid double comparisons.

Comparison is expressed in either of two ways: by changing the form of the modifier (as with *pretty, prettier; small, smallest*) or by adding *more* or *most* to the modifier. Using both ways at once is not correct.

NONSTANDARD   This is the **most finest** performance he has given.

STANDARD   This is the **finest** performance he has given.

NONSTANDARD   Her hair is **more curlier** than her sister's.

STANDARD   Her hair is **curlier** than her sister's.

DOUBLE NEGATIVES

A common mistake with modifiers is using more than one negative word where only one is required. Words like the following are called negatives: *no, not, none, never, no one, nothing, hardly.* (Notice that many negatives begin with the letter *n*.) When such a word is used in a sentence it makes an important change in the meaning.

> I have been to Denver.
> I have **never** been to Denver.

Notice that one negative is enough to make the meaning clear. Using two negatives together is incorrect.

> *Positive* She said something.
> *Negative* She said nothing.
> *Double negative* She did*n't* say *nothing*.

9e. Avoid the use of double negatives.

Study the following examples until you are sure that you will not make mistakes in the use of negatives. (The word *not* when it is contracted to *n't* and attached to a verb is, of course, still a negative.)

NONSTANDARD We can't hardly wait for the opening of the fair.

STANDARD We can **hardly** wait for the opening of the fair.

NONSTANDARD I never told no one about our secret hideout.

STANDARD I told **no one** about our secret hideout.

STANDARD I **never** told anyone about our secret hideout.

EXERCISE 3. Each of the following sentences contains a double negative or an error in comparison. Rewrite each sentence correctly.

1. There wasn't no ball game played today.
2. I can't hardly understand the speaker.
3. These olives are more saltier than the others.
4. When I looked for the cookies, I found that there weren't none left.
5. During intermission I couldn't find no one that I knew.
6. Maria is more happier since she came back from Puerto Rico.
7. The football team didn't try nothing new in this game.
8. The book was more sadder than the movie.

9. We searched for hours for hidden caves, but we didn't find none.
10. Double negatives don't have no place in good English.

REVIEW EXERCISE A. Some of the following sentences are correct. Others contain double negatives or errors in adjective or adverb usage. If the sentence is correct, write a *C* after its number on your paper. If the sentence contains an error, rewrite it correctly.

1. She is the more intelligent of the two women.
2. The hare ran more faster than the tortoise.
3. The tortoise was more persistent.
4. No one plays tennis as good as Alice Wu.
5. Time goes too slow when there's nothing to do.
6. You can't hardly find leather-bound books any more.
7. Rae reported that the fish are biting good today.
8. With the May Day Pageant approaching, we are more busier than ever.
9. After a swim in the cold water, she felt fine.
10. I wasn't hardly able to hear her.
11. We can't decide which of the Adams twins is the best looking.
12. Mr. Hyde didn't have no control over himself.
13. Killing didn't mean nothing to him.
14. He hardly considered his victims.
15. He was sure troubled when he changed into his normal self, Dr. Jekyll.
16. Dr. Jekyll wanted to be more wiser than he was.
17. He wanted to experiment with the most strangest of all formulas.
18. The formula was one which would quite easy change him from one personality to another.
19. This story by Robert Louis Stevenson is one of the excitingest tales in literature.
20. Do you know anyone who changes personality as quick as Dr. Jekyll and Mr. Hyde?

REVIEW EXERCISE B. Write ten original sentences, using the constructions described below.

1. the superlative of *bright*
2. a single negative
3. the comparative of *useful*
4. the comparative of *good*
5. a linking verb and a predicate adjective
6. the superlative of *often*
7. the positive of *well*
8. the comparative of *joyful*
9. the superlative of *angry*
10. the comparative of *sharp*

Mechanics

PART THREE

Chapter **10**

Capital Letters

Rules for Capitalization

You already know a great deal about the use of capital letters. For example, you have learned that proper nouns and proper adjectives are capitalized. You are accustomed to beginning sentences with capital letters. In this chapter you will review what you know and learn some more rules for using capitals.

10a. Capitalize the first word in every sentence.

If you have difficulty recognizing the beginning of sentences, the section on run-on sentences (pages 247–51) will help you.

INCORRECT	my dog knows several tricks. it will shake hands or play dead when I tell it to.
CORRECT	My dog knows several tricks. It will shake hands or play dead when I tell it to.

The first word of a direct quotation should begin with a capital whether or not it starts the sentence. For more on writing quotations, see pages 218–26.

▶ **NOTE** Traditionally, the first word of every line of poetry begins with a capital letter. Some modern poets do not follow this style. If you are copying a poem, be sure to follow the capitalization that the poet used.

10b. Capitalize the pronoun *I*.

EXAMPLE   This week **I** have to write two papers and give a book report.

10c. Capitalize proper nouns.

A proper noun, as you learned on page 37, names a particular person, place, or thing. Such a word is always capitalized. A common noun names a kind or type of person, place, or thing. The common noun is not capitalized unless it begins a sentence or is part of a title.

PROPER NOUNS	COMMON NOUNS
Central High School	high school
Saturday	day
Ethel Kennedy	woman
Sweden	country
Lassie	collie

Memorize the following rules about proper nouns, and study the examples that are given.

(1) Capitalize the names of persons.

EXAMPLES   Hello, Aunt Celia.
Monica Sone wrote *Nisei Daughter*.
Ginny's broken leg was set by **Dr.** Buxton.
Frank **B.** Gilbreth, **Jr.**, is one of the authors of *Cheaper by the Dozen*.

(2) Capitalize geographical names.

| *Cities, Towns* | Miami, Jackson, Indianapolis |
| *States* | Tennessee, Wyoming, Delaware |

Countries	Australia, Finland, Egypt
Islands	Aleutian Islands, Long Island, Crete
Bodies of Water	Mississippi River, Lake Ontario, Chesapeake Bay, Jackson's Pond, Suez Canal, Indian Ocean
Streets, Highways	Main Street, White Avenue, Kingsbridge Road, Daniel Drive, Highway 14, Route 66, Sunset Boulevard, Park Plaza, Forty-eighth Street [In a hyphenated number, the second word begins with a small letter.]
Parks	Yosemite Park, Grand Canyon, Carlsbad Caverns
Mountains	Catskills, Alps, Mount Everest
Continents	Europe, Asia, South America, Antarctica
Sections of the Country	the West, the Southeast

▶ **NOTE** Do *not* capitalize *east, west, north, south,* or any combinations of these, such as *northeast,* when the words merely indicate *direction,* as in these examples: two blocks *south,* headed *east,* a *north* wind.

EXAMPLES A green truck was going south on Oak Street. [direction]

The South has produced some of America's great writers. [section of the country]

(3) Capitalize names of organizations, business firms, institutions, and government bodies.

EXAMPLES Dramatic Club
Mary's Sporting Goods
United Fund

> Girl Scouts
> Rice University
> Carnegie Foundation
> Federal Bureau of Investigation
> City Planning Commission
> the Senate

► **NOTE** Do not capitalize such words as *hotel,*
theater, or *high school* unless they are part of the
name of a particular building or institution.

EXAMPLES | Bijou Theater | a theater
| Lane Hotel | the hotel
| Taft High School | this high school

(4) Capitalize special events and calendar items.

EXAMPLES | Dogwood Festival | February
| Easter | Independence Day
| Monday

► **NOTE** Do *not* capitalize the names of seasons:
spring, summer, fall, winter.

(5) Capitalize historical events and periods.

EXAMPLES | Revolutionary War
| Battle of Gettysburg
| Bronze Age

**(6) Capitalize the names of nationalities, races, and
religions.**

EXAMPLES | Mexican, English, Iroquois, Caucasian,
| Indian, Presbyterian

(7) Capitalize the brand names of business products.

EXAMPLES | Lux soap, General Electric stove, Pepsi
| Cola bottle [Notice that only the brand

name of a product is capitalized; the common noun following it is not.]

(8) Capitalize the names of ships, planets, monuments, awards, and any other particular places, things, or events.

EXAMPLES Jefferson Memorial   the *Orient Limited*
Golden Gate Bridge Voyager 2
Merchandise Mart   the Bill of Rights
the *Mayflower*   Junior Achievement
Mars   Award

EXERCISE 1. Write the numbers 1–10 on your paper. In each of the following items, you are to choose the correct one of the two forms given. After each number on your paper, write the letter of the correct form (*a* or *b*). Be prepared to explain your answer.

1. a. My sister attends Columbia university.
   b. My sister attends Columbia University.
2. a. The fishing is good at Oconee Lake.
   b. The fishing is good at Oconee lake.
3. a. The House of Representatives passed the bill, but the senate did not.
   b. The House of Representatives passed the bill, but the Senate did not.
4. a. We drove through the Pocono mountains last Spring.
   b. We drove through the Pocono Mountains last spring.
5. a. Have you bought your Halloween costume?
   b. Have you bought your halloween costume?
6. a. My cousin from the south is visiting me.
   b. My cousin from the South is visiting me.
7. a. On her return from Africa, Rhea James had a number of stories to tell.

    b. On her return from africa, Rhea James had a
       number of stories to tell.

8. a. The Delo Gum Commercial uses cartoons.
   b. The Delo gum commercial uses cartoons.

9. a. Near the Washington Monument is a long re-
     flecting pool.
   b. Near the Washington monument is a long re-
     flecting pool.

10. a. We have some reproductions from the museum
      of Modern Art.
    b. We have some reproductions from the Museum
      of Modern Art.

EXERCISE 2. Each of the following sentences contains at least one uncapitalized proper noun. Copy all
the proper nouns after the number of the sentence,
beginning each with a capital letter.

EXAMPLE   1. On may day the seniors at anderson
             high school present a pageant.
             1. *May Day, Anderson High School*

1. The George Washington bridge, which spans the
   Hudson river, is one of the largest suspension
   bridges in the world.
2. Glacier national park, in montana, is noted for its
   sixty glaciers.
3. Before the building of dams by the tennessee
   valley authority, much of the land in the south
   was flooded during heavy rains.
4. Thousands of cherokee indians live in the smoky
   mountains in and around cherokee, north carolina.
5. The peace corps became an agency of the government by an act of congress.
6. On september 6, 1979, a total eclipse of the moon
   was viewed by people in ships traveling across the
   pacific ocean.

7. The last two states to be admitted to the united states were alaska and hawaii.
8. On new year's day many fans crowded into football stadiums for the annual bowl games.
9. The rose bowl is the oldest of the bowls.
10. The oldest institution of higher learning in america is harvard college.

EXERCISE 3. In the following paragraph all capital letters have been omitted. Copy the paragraph, using capitals wherever they are needed.

the branford shopping center is the largest in melville county. it is on jefferson parkway two miles north of duck lake state park and the big bridge that crosses duck lake. across the parkway from the shopping center is the new branford high school with its parking lots, playing fields, and stadium, the home of the branford panthers. the shopping center has two supermarkets, nicholson's department store, the palace cinema, and thirty-five other businesses. they range from small stationery stores to the finest restaurant in the midwest. the restaurant larue is run by marie and jean larue, who are from france. also in the center is the american paper box company, which supplies boxes for armstrong cereals and styleform shoes. a branch factory of northwestern motors of chicago makes gears for ford cars. within the boundaries of the center are the american legion hall, bowlerama, and the king rink.

10d. Capitalize proper adjectives.

A proper adjective, which is formed from a proper noun, is always capitalized.

PROPER NOUN	PROPER ADJECTIVE
Greece	Greek theater
Mars	Martian moons

PROPER NOUN	PROPER ADJECTIVE
Congress	Congressional hearing
England	English literature
Orient	Oriental custom

10e. Do *not* capitalize the names of school subjects, except languages and course names followed by a number.

EXAMPLES history, typing, mathematics, English, German, Latin, History 101, Music III, Art Appreciation I

EXERCISE 4. Write the numbers 1–10 on your paper. In each of the following sentences, find the words that should be capitalized but are not. Write those words correctly after the sentence numbers.

EXAMPLE 1. Helga assured us that we were eating real german cooking.
          1. *German*

1. The european Common Market helps to improve trade.
2. We ordered swiss cheese and ham sandwiches on rye bread.
3. There are many students of french and spanish in this country, but few are learning russian or chinese.
4. The scandinavian countries have a high standard of living.
5. Jan said that she enjoyed listening to someone with an australian accent.
6. During the elizabethan age there were many great dramatists in England.
7. As one of his electives, Marvin chose typing II.
8. The floor of the bedroom was covered by a huge oriental rug.
9. England, France, Scotland, Russia, and the

United States play important roles in canadian history.

10. The profile shot called attention to the actor's roman nose.

10f. Capitalize titles.

(1) Capitalize the title of a person when it comes before a name.

EXAMPLES   President Lincoln   Mrs. Wendell
Mayor Lyons   Commissioner Jones

(2) Capitalize a title used alone or following a person's name if it refers to a high official or to someone to whom you wish to show special respect.

EXAMPLES   In a few hours we will know who has been elected President of the United States.

That is Mr. Hendricks, president of the Rotary Club.

March Fong was elected California's Secretary of State.

The Senator from South Dakota has the floor.

She is one of the senators who were elected this year.

The Mayor is conferring with the City Council.

Eunice Brabston is our new mayor.

The Superintendent is visiting classes today.

When a title is used instead of a name in direct address, it should be capitalized.

EXAMPLES   Is it very serious, Doctor?
Good morning, Judge.

(3) Capitalize words showing family relationship when used with a person's name but *not* when preceded by a possessive.

EXAMPLES   We expect Uncle Fred and Aunt Helen to arrive tonight.
We always go to Grandma Lowery's for a few weeks in the summer.
Jim's father is a miner.
That hat belongs to her sister Eva.
Angela's mother made some delicious brownies.

Words showing family relationship followed by a name and preceded by a possessive may be capitalized if they are considered part of the name.

EXAMPLES   Helen, this is my Aunt Liz.
We'll stay overnight with our cousin Ralph.

Words of family relationship may be capitalized or not when they are used without a name. Either way is acceptable.

Let's go with Mom. *or* Let's go with mom.

(4) Capitalize the first word and all important words in titles of books, periodicals, poems, stories, movies, paintings, and other works of art.

Unimportant words in a title are *a, an, the,* and prepositions and conjunctions of fewer than five letters. Do not capitalize the word *the* before the title of a magazine or newspaper unless it begins a sentence.

Book	*The Mask of Apollo*
Magazine	***Popular Mechanics***
Newspaper	the ***Miami Herald***
Poem	"Season at the Shore"
Story	"The Night the Bed Fell"
Movie	***Star Wars***
Painting	the ***Mona Lisa***
Musical piece	"September Song"

(5) Capitalize words referring to the Deity.

God, the Creator, the Almighty

▶ **NOTE** The word *god* is not capitalized when it refers to the gods of ancient mythology.

EXAMPLE The Vikings had many gods.

EXERCISE 5. Copy the following sentences, inserting capitals wherever they are needed.

1. Have you read edna st. vincent millay's "the courage that my mother had"?
2. While waiting to see dr. hoskins, I read the *chattanooga times* and *newsweek.*
3. *The thinker* is one of rodin's best-known pieces of sculpture.
4. We watched an old movie called *mildred pierce* on television last night.
5. Today the voters will elect a new president and new members of Congress.
6. Uncle nick bought me a copy of *sonnets from the portuguese,* a work by elizabeth barrett browning.
7. At our last meeting we elected a new secretary and listened to a speech by senator jane fong.
8. The principal speaker was dr. andrew holt, the former president of the university of tennessee.
9. Besides uncle ted, there are aunt ella and aunt sara, my grandmother, and my great-grandfather.

10. Before the president's broadcast begins, an announcer always says, "Ladies and gentlemen, the president of the united states."

REVIEW EXERCISE A. Some of the following sentences are correct as they are; some are not. Write the numbers 1–20 on your paper. For correct sentences, write *C* after the proper number. For the others, copy the words that require capitals.

EXAMPLE 1. everyone was cheered on that gloomy monday by the thought that tuesday, columbus day, was a holiday.

1. *Everyone, Monday, Tuesday, Columbus Day*

1. In the fall everyone looks forward to the football season.
2. Football fans can see their favorite high school or college team play on saturday and their favorite professional team on sunday.
3. Last weekend i saw ohio state play michigan.
4. Kay's aunt introduced her to the captain of one of the world's largest passenger ships, the *queen elizabeth 2*.
5. The greeks believed that zeus, the king of the gods, lived on mount olympus.
6. Ann likes geography and history, but she makes her best grades in english and french.
7. The chief justice explained the ruling of the supreme court.
8. On july 4 miller's department store puts on a spectacular display of fireworks.
9. The *titanic* sank after hitting an iceberg off the coast of newfoundland.
10. My aunt went to amsterdam to see rembrandt's *the night watch*.

11. Fresh water is now being produced from salt water at a plant in freeport, texas.
12. Tod has registered for astronomy 212, which is taught by professor anna streifus.
13. Nan's brother has won several medals since he became a volunteer firefighter.
14. At the auto show we saw the fords and chevrolets of the future.
15. The first american to make a flight into space was commander alan b. shepard, jr.
16. In *roots,* alex haley, a famous journalist, traces the history of his family.
17. The President is expected to veto the bill passed by Congress.
18. The city planning commission has several proposals for improving tourist trade in our town.
19. Mrs. McCloud, our mayor, has set aside the month of april for the arts festival.
20. Iceland is an island located in the atlantic ocean near the arctic circle.

REVIEW EXERCISE B. Copy the following sentences, inserting capitals wherever needed.

1. Mail the letter to the republic of south africa and the package to genoa, italy.
2. This year palm sunday is the last sunday in march.
3. Among the early settlers were roman catholics and congregationalists.
4. The ancient greeks and romans believed in many gods.
5. The department of agriculture publishes many pamphlets that are useful to the home gardener.
6. Did aunt josie send you that mexican straw hat?
7. The *windy jane* is a small white sailboat.
8. Last winter Carrie had an iceboat at greenwood lake.

9. In history and in spanish, we are studying the same historical period.
10. One woman is an armenian, the other a greek.

REVIEW EXERCISE C. Of the following sentences, some are correct as they stand. In the others certain words need capitals. For correct sentences, write *C* after the proper number. For the others, write in order the words that require capitals.

1. nan and I are spending the summer at camp medomak in washington, maine.
2. Tommy has a new English bicycle, a gift from his aunt.
3. Suddenly i saw the boeing 747 darting across the sky.
4. Here is a new series of Norwegian airmail stamps.
5. The waters of the Mediterranean are very blue.
6. The table is made of asian teakwood.
7. The Ohio Tractor Company is looking for a qualified treasurer.
8. Have you ever seen a Mexican jumping bean?
9. We heard a performance of jazz music.
10. My sister is taking english, math II, social studies, biology, and french.
11. Just then i noticed her new persian rug.
12. Is the altoona bus company on strike?
13. Silk is an important Japanese export.
14. Jerry lives on the west side of oak street.
15. sometimes the boys went fishing at Lake Shasta.
16. At Aspen, Colorado, I learned to ride a horse.
17. She is traveling by northeast airlines.
18. My favorite program is sponsored by gold crisp cereal.
19. Lever brothers has introduced a new soap.
20. Octopuses lurk in the mediterranean sea.

SUMMARY STYLE SHEET

The following list may be used as a style sheet for quick reference. Be sure that you know and understand all of the rules represented.

10a. **C**umulus clouds are often seen before a storm.

10b. Next month **I** will be thirteen years old.

10c. (1) **B**ert and **A**lice once heard **M**arianne **M**oore reading her poems.
   (2) We moved from **A**mes, **I**owa, in the **M**iddle **W**est, to **N**ew **E**ngland that year.
   (3) The new president of the **C**hamber of **C**ommerce is Wallace Gates, who owns **G**ates **A**uto **S**upply **C**enter.
   (4) The **P**resque **I**sle **F**air, which used to be held in the fall, opens on **A**ugust 10 this year.
   (5) The effects of the **I**ndustrial **R**evolution in England were felt throughout the British Empire.
   (6) Many **I**ndians, **C**hinese, and **J**apanese are **B**uddhists.
   (7) Try this new **P**epperidge **F**arm **b**read.
   (8) The **G**olden **G**ate **B**ridge and **F**ishermen's **W**harf are two of the attractions of San Francisco.

10d. My brother is the family's champion in playing **C**hinese checkers.

10e. Next year we will have Mr. Tall for **m**ath and Mrs. Huddersfield for **E**nglish.

10f. (1) I asked **M**rs. Cook to introduce the **R**everend Mr. Perkins.
   (2) Do you plan to run for reelection next year, **G**overnor?
      Inés Torres, who is the **s**ecretary of our class, likes to compare her duties with those of the **S**ecretary of **S**tate.
   (3) My **c**ousin **E**mily is **U**ncle **F**rank's oldest daughter.
   (4) There were some superb shots of sailing ships in **M**utiny on the **B**ounty.
   (5) May the **L**ord bless us and keep us.

Chapter 11

Punctuation

End Marks, Commas, and Semicolons

In spoken language, your voice tells where thoughts are interrupted or completed, but in written language you must depend upon punctuation to indicate pauses and to make your meaning clear. To punctuate written papers so that your reader will readily understand what you are trying to say, learn the rules for punctuation in this chapter and in Chapter 12. Follow them whenever you write.

END MARKS

The term *end marks* refers to punctuation which appears at the end of sentences. Periods, question marks, and exclamation points are end marks.

11a. A statement is followed by a period.

EXAMPLES   The chess player considered his next move.
Tea is grown in Ceylon.

11b. A question is followed by a question mark.

EXAMPLES   Who has lost the book?
What time is it?

11c. An exclamation is followed by an exclamation point.

EXAMPLES   What a high bridge!
How big the moon is!

11d. A request or an order is followed by either a period or an exclamation point.

EXAMPLES   Please call the dog. [a request — no strong feeling is expressed]
Stay where you are! [The exclamation point shows strong feeling.]

To determine which end mark to use, consider whether the sentence expresses excitement or strong feeling. If it does, use an exclamation point; if it does not, use a period.

EXERCISE 1. Read the following sentences and decide which end mark is needed for each one. Then write the last word of the sentence and the correct end mark. (Do not write in this book.)

1. Can you name a play by William Shakespeare
2. Look for a copy of *Romeo and Juliet* in your library
3. Shakespeare wrote many comedies, tragedies, and histories
4. Do you know how much formal schooling he had
5. Shakespeare had only an elementary school education, but he studied all his life
6. Of course, few people in Shakespeare's time went to college
7. Even in elementary school the students learned Latin and Greek
8. How strange Shakespeare's school would seem to us
9. Would you have preferred Shakespeare's school to your own

10. Perhaps there is someone in your classroom who will be a great writer

EXERCISE 2. In the following paragraph, all initial capital letters and end marks of punctuation have been omitted. You must decide where the sentences begin and end. Copy the paragraph, providing capital letters and marks of punctuation as needed.

who invented the phonograph who invented the electric light who patented in his lifetime 1,097 inventions the answer to all three of these questions is the American inventor Thomas Alva Edison what a great achievement fame came to Edison first in 1877, when he invented the phonograph like all inventors, Edison built on the work of others who came before him the phonograph, however, was entirely his own other inventors had worked before him on the electric light, but he made the first practical light bulb in 1878 and 1879, Edison worked himself and his five assistants twenty hours a day perfecting the bulb what a tireless worker he was he had learned to get along with very little sleep Edison built a research laboratory in Menlo Park, New Jersey

11e. An abbreviation is followed by a period.

EXAMPLES	Ave.	Oct.
	Calif.	lb.
	Fri.	P.M.

Make it a practice to look up abbreviations in a dictionary if you are not sure of their spelling.

COMMAS

An end mark calls for a full stop, but a comma means a pause. It is like a traffic sign that tells a motorist to slow down and proceed with caution. A comma makes writing easier to understand, since it helps to convey the writer's meaning. You already know some uses for the comma; for example, you put a comma after your last name when you write it before your first name. You use a comma in writing a number of more than three digits (4,500). To make your writing clear, you ought to be familiar with several other important uses of the comma.

11f. Use commas to separate items in a series.

A series is three or more items written one after another. The items may be single words or groups of words.

EXAMPLES   December, January, and February are summer months in the Southern Hemisphere. [single words in a series]

For my lunch I had a sandwich, some milk, and an orange. [groups of words in a series]

The delegates nominated one candidate, voted, and installed her in office. [verbs in a series]

There were spots at the top, at the sides, and on the bottom. [phrases in a series]

► NOTE Some writers omit the comma before the *and* between the last two items of a series. Nevertheless, you should form the habit of including this comma, since it is sometimes necessary to make your meaning clear. Notice how the comma affects the meaning in the following example.

EXAMPLE The samples of soil in the exhibit included clay, loam, coarse sand and gravel. [No comma is used. Is "coarse sand and gravel" one sample or two?]

The samples of soil in the exhibit included clay, loam, coarse sand, and gravel. [Comma is used. It is clear that ". . . coarse sand, and gravel" are two samples.]

Always be sure that there are at least three items in the series before you insert commas. Two items do not need a comma between them.

INCORRECT   You will need a pencil, and plenty of paper.

CORRECT   You will need a pencil and plenty of paper.

When the items in the series are separated by conjunctions, there is no need for commas.

INCORRECT   Take water, and food, and matches with you.

CORRECT   Take water and food and matches with you.

EXERCISE 3. Some of the sentences below need commas; others do not. If a sentence is correct, write *C* after the proper number. If a sentence needs commas, copy the word preceding the comma, and write the comma after it.

EXAMPLE   1. Open the window look up the street tell me what you see.
        1. *window, street,*

1. Crabs and lobsters are both on the restaurant's menu this evening.
2. Cleveland Toledo and Dayton are three cities in Ohio.
3. The pilot boarded the plane checked her instruments and prepared for takeoff.
4. Denise has guppies and goldfish and mollies in her home aquarium.

5. The writer opened her book and began to read one of her short stories to the audience.
6. Our dog will play dead roll over and stand on its hind feet for a piece of meat.
7. The police shone their spotlights down the street along the walls and into the yards.
8. Abraham Lincoln was a rail-splitter an attorney and finally the President of the United States.
9. Eleanor Roosevelt's courage her humanity and her service to her country will always be remembered.
10. The tornado took a heavy toll in lives and property.

11g. **Use a comma to separate two or more adjectives preceding a noun.**

EXAMPLES   Jupiter is a large, strange planet.
Althea Gibson played a powerful, brilliant game.

Do not place a comma between an adjective and the noun immediately following it.

INCORRECT   Pyrite is a pale, golden-colored, mineral. [The last comma is incorrect.]

CORRECT   Pyrite is a pale, golden-colored mineral.

▶ NOTE   Some adjectives are so closely connected in meaning to the nouns they modify that no comma is needed to separate them from another adjective. *Horned owl, oak chest,* and *electric light* are examples of such pairs of adjectives and nouns. Notice how the following sentences are punctuated:

A huge horned owl lives in those woods. [not huge, horned owl]
The girls are refinishing an old oak chest. [not old, oak chest]

> An unshaded electric light hung from the ceiling. [not unshaded, electric light]

You can test to see whether or not a comma is needed by inserting an *and* between the adjectives (*unshaded and electric,* for example). If the *and* sounds awkward, the comma is unnecessary.

EXERCISE 4. Some of the following sentences need commas; others do not. If a sentence does not need additional punctuation, write *C* after its number on your paper. If it needs punctuation, copy the word preceding the needed comma, and write the comma after it.

1. Among Thomas Edison's 1,100 inventions were the phonograph the incandescent light and the motion picture camera.
2. Washington Irving's "The Legend of Sleepy Hollow" is an exciting humorous short story.
3. Smoking has been shown to be a costly dangerous habit.
4. The hammer anvil and stirrup are three tiny bones which carry sound waves to the brain.
5. Before becoming a peace officer, Wyatt Earp had been a surveyor a stagecoach driver and a buffalo hunter.
6. According to Greek mythology, three Fates spin the thread of life measure it and finally cut it.
7. Shakespeare created such famous characters as Falstaff Juliet and Lady Macbeth.
8. Falstaff was a fat jolly fellow who liked to brag.
9. He pretended to be wise loyal and brave.
10. When he faced two men in battle, he begged for mercy ran away from the fight and later bragged about his bravery.

11h. Use a comma before *and, but, or, nor, for,* **and** *yet* **when they join the parts of a compound sentence.**

If you are not sure that you can recognize a compound sentence, you should review pages 26–27.

EXAMPLES   Betty offered to get the tickets, and I accepted gratefully.

They had been working very hard, but they didn't seem especially tired.

The twins will see their favorite baby-sitter, for their parents are going out.

A very short compound sentence is sometimes written without a comma.

EXAMPLE It rained and it rained.

► NOTE Do not confuse a compound sentence and a compound verb; do not place a comma between the parts of a compound verb.

COMPOUND SENTENCE   Usually we study in the morning, and we play tennis in the afternoon.

COMPOUND VERB   Usually we **study** in the morning and **play** tennis in the afternoon.

EXERCISE 5. Among the following sentences are compound sentences, simple sentences with single verbs, and simple sentences with compound verbs. If the sentence is correctly punctuated, write *C* after the number. If it needs additional punctuation, copy the word preceding the needed comma, and write the comma after it.

1. According to Greek mythology, Paris, a young Trojan, tried to settle an argument among three of the goddesses.
2. Each of the goddesses wanted to be chosen the most beautiful and each of them offered Paris a gift.

3. Paris considered the three gifts and finally chose Venus, the goddess of love, as the most beautiful of the three.
4. Venus had promised Paris that he could have the most beautiful woman in the world as his wife and she did not forget her promise.
5. Helen was the most beautiful woman in the world but she was already married to Menelaus, a Greek king.
6. Nevertheless, Helen was taken from Menelaus and was given to Paris.
7. Menelaus called together all the Greek kings and warriors and they set sail for Troy to reclaim Helen.
8. The Greeks attacked Troy for ten years but the Trojans did not yield.
9. Finally, the Greeks built the famous Trojan horse and presented it to the Trojans.
10. In accepting the gift, the Trojans sealed their doom for hidden within the wooden horse were several Greek warriors.

11i. Use commas to set off expressions that interrupt the sentence.

Two commas are needed if the expression to be set off comes in the middle of the sentence. One comma is needed if the expression comes first or last.

EXAMPLES   Our neighbor, Ann Myers, is a fine golfer.
Naturally, we expect to win.
My answer is correct, I think.

There are several kinds of expressions that may interrupt a sentence. One kind of interrupter is the *appositive,* a word that means the same thing as the word it follows. An appositive phrase is an appositive with its modifiers.

(1) Appositives and appositive phrases are usually set off by commas.

EXAMPLES   Carrie, my cousin, is here today. [*Cousin* is an appositive, meaning the same person as Carrie.]

Mrs. French, the secretary of our school, is in Florida. [*The secretary of our school* is an appositive phrase meaning the same person as Mrs. French.]

Occasionally when the appositive is a single word closely related to the preceding word, the comma is not needed.

EXAMPLES   our friend Alicia
William the Conqueror

EXERCISE 6. Copy each appositive or appositive phrase and the word which precedes it. Supply commas where needed. Not all of the appositives require commas.

EXAMPLE   1. Mars one of the closest planets can be seen without a telescope.
1. *Mars, one of the closest planets,*

1. Shana Alexander one-time editor of *McCall's* was the main speaker.
2. We have a figurine made of clay from Kilimanjaro the highest mountain in Africa.
3. The whole class read the book *Kidnapped.*
4. Saint Augustine the oldest city in the United States has many very narrow streets.
5. Sugar cane an important Florida crop may be shipped raw or refined.
6. Do you own a thesaurus a dictionary of synonyms and antonyms?
7. At North Cape the northernmost point of Europe

the sun does not set from the middle of May until the end of July.

8. The American mastodon an extinct, elephantlike animal was hunted by primitive people.
9. John F. Kennedy's brother Robert was assassinated during a Presidential campaign.
10. At Gettysburg a town in Pennsylvania General Meade and the Union forces defeated General Lee and the Confederate forces.

EXERCISE 7. Write ten sentences containing the following groups of words as appositives. Insert commas wherever needed.

EXAMPLE 1. her twelfth birthday
1. *She is having a party on Tuesday, her twelfth birthday.*

1. an Eagle Scout
2. the club's president
3. Carmen
4. the Big Dipper
5. his best friend
6. a popular game
7. the umpire
8. the day of the picnic
9. a famous author
10. Mrs. Kimball

(2) Words used in direct address are set off by commas.

People often address by name others to whom they are talking. In written conversation, a name used in *direct address* is set off by commas.[1]

EXAMPLES Ben, please answer the doorbell.
Your tickets, Mrs. Blake, are in this envelope.
Mother needs you, Franny.
Stop, you fool!

EXERCISE 8. Copy the words in direct address from

[1] For rules governing the use of commas in quotations, see pages 220–22.

the following sentences. Insert commas either before or after the words, as needed.

1. Sandra why did you name your cat Cleopatra?
2. Stop this talking now class.
3. We my fellow students are going to win the game tomorrow.
4. Professor Adams when was the Battle of Saratoga?
5. What is your opinion of the candidates Laura?
6. Please Dad may I use your pen?
7. Where my dear do you think you are going?
8. Senator Smith I have a proposal for improving our state.
9. Lisa if you apologize, I'm sure that Arlene will forget the incident.
10. You know that you shouldn't be on the couch Snoopy.

(3) Parenthetical expressions are set off by commas.

Words and phrases such as *however, for example, of course, in fact* often occur in sentences. They are called *parenthetical expressions* and are usually set off by commas.

Common Parenthetical Expressions

of course	on the other hand	in my opinion
however	I suppose	to tell the truth
for example	in fact	nevertheless
on the contrary	by the way	I believe

EXAMPLES   The weather, in fact, was perfect.

Carl, on the contrary, prefers football to baseball.

To tell the truth, Jan is one of my best friends.

▶ **NOTE** Such expressions may not be parenthetical.

Of course it is true.
I suppose we ought to go home now.

(4) Words such as *well, yes, no, why* **are followed by a comma when they are used at the beginning of a sentence or remark.**

EXAMPLES   Yes, you may borrow my bicycle.
Why, it's Lena!
Well, I think you are wrong.

EXERCISE 9. The following sentences contain parenthetical expressions and introductory words that require commas. Copy the parenthetical expressions and introductory words, inserting commas as needed.

1. Yes there are many constellations visible in the summer.
2. For instance on a summer night you can view the Scorpion, the Serpent, and the Serpent-Bearer.
3. To be sure we should not overlook the Milky Way.
4. The Milky Way in fact is more impressive in the summer than at any other time of year.
5. Of course Hercules is an interesting constellation.
6. Studying the constellations is in my opinion a most interesting hobby.
7. It does take some imagination however to pick out some of the constellations.
8. The Archer for example is hard to perceive.
9. The Scorpion on the other hand is quite clearly outlined.
10. Astronomy I think is a fascinating science.

11j. **Use a comma in certain conventional situations.**

(1) Use commas to separate items in dates and addresses.

EXAMPLES   She was born on January 26, 1981, in Cheshire, Connecticut.

A letter dated November 23, 1888, was found in the old house at 980 West Street, Davenport, Iowa.

Saturday, November 25, is the day of the party.

► **NOTE** The Post Office expects you to give the zip code number in every letter you address. The zip code number follows the state without any punctuation between it and the state.

EXAMPLE   Fargo, North Dakota 58101

EXERCISE 10. Most of the following sentences need commas; a few do not. If a sentence is correctly punctuated, write *C* after its number. Copy the other sentences, inserting commas wherever they are needed.

1. Marian Anderson was born on February 27 1902 in Philadelphia Pennsylvania.
2. My new address is 3365 Clinch Avenue Lubbock Texas 79408.
3. Gwendolyn Brooks was born in Topeka Kansas on June 7 1917.
4. Napoleon was defeated at Waterloo Belgium on June 18 1815.
5. In 1955 we moved from Ohio to Indiana.
6. On May 25 1935 Jesse Owens tied or surpassed six world track records.
7. Between 1484 and 1782 approximately three hundred thousand women in Europe were executed for witchcraft.
8. In the United States the most famous witchcraft trials were held in Salem Massachusetts.
9. The scene of the robbery was a grocery store at 650 State Street.

10. My sister's college address is P.O. Box 76 Iowa State University Ames Iowa 50010.

(2) Use a comma after the salutation of a friendly letter and after the closing of any letter.

EXAMPLES   Dear Dad,   Dear Sharon,
             With love,   Yours truly,

REVIEW EXERCISE A. From the following sentences, copy the words that should be followed by a comma on your paper. Write the comma.

1. What did you tell the interviewer Keith?
2. Kate said to forward her mail to 5525 Dogwood Road Knoxville Tennessee 37901.
3. Elizabeth Bishop a well-known American poet died in 1979.
4. They sent us a card from Dallas Texas.
5. Quick violent flashes of lightning cause approximately 27,500 forest fires a year in the United States alone.
6. Of course you shouldn't stand near electrical wires if you are caught in a lightning storm.
7. Lightning does a great deal of damage but it also does humanity a great service.
8. A flash of lightning strange as it seems could supply a home with electric power for thirty-five years.
9. Lightning strikes such tall objects as trees steeples and skyscrapers.
10. Electrical storms expected during the summer sometimes occur in the winter, too.

REVIEW EXERCISE B. From the following sentences, copy on your paper the words that should be followed by a comma. Write the comma.

1. Greece a nation with a glorious past is one of the most beautiful countries in the world.
2. Greece is chiefly an agricultural nation but its industry is increasing rapidly.
3. Greece exports olives wine figs and tobacco.
4. Much of Greece is covered by mountains lakes and rivers.
5. In fact only one fourth of the land is suitable for farming.
6. The capital of Greece is Athens a city famous for its great philosophers.
7. Athens has many museums institutes and schools.
8. Everyone to be sure is familiar with the architecture and sculpture of ancient Greece.
9. The ruins of the Parthenon the temple of Athena testify to the artistry of the Greeks.
10. The Parthenon was completed in 432 B.C. and much of it still stands in Athens.

REVIEW EXERCISE C. Copy on your paper the words that should be followed by a comma. Insert the comma.

1. Anna Mary Robertson Moses began painting when she was seventy-eight years old and she became known as Grandma Moses.
2. She continued painting almost until her death on December 13 1961 when she was 101 years old.
3. She painted many pictures in fact when she was 100 years old.
4. Grandma Moses grew up in northern New York moved to Virginia and then returned to New York.
5. She painted colorful lively scenes of rural life in New York and Virginia.
6. Critics quickly acclaimed the simplicity sincerity and charm of her paintings.
7. Her work was recognized locally nationally and abroad.
8. Grandma Moses however never had any formal art training.

9. She taught herself to paint and her memories of farm life became the subject of her paintings.
10. Many of her paintings excellent examples of American folk art are in museums and galleries.

SEMICOLONS

The semicolon is an effective mark of punctuation if it is used sparingly. Part period and part comma, it says to the reader, "Pause here a little longer than you would for a comma, but do not come to a full stop as you would for a period." You should learn two uses for semicolons.

11k. Use a semicolon between the parts of a compound sentence if they are not joined by *and, but, or, nor, for, yet.*

EXAMPLES   Take Mother's suitcase upstairs; leave Dad's in the car.

After school I went to the play rehearsal; then I studied in the library for an hour.

11l. A semicolon (rather than a comma) may be needed to separate the parts of a compound sentence if there are commas within the parts.

CONFUSING   I wrote to Ann, Beth, and Meg, and Jean notified Terry and Sue.

CLEAR   I wrote to Ann, Beth, and Meg; and Jean notified Terry and Sue.

Sometimes, instead of using a semicolon, it is better to separate a compound sentence or a heavily punctuated sentence into two sentences.

ACCEPTABLE   In the tropical jungles of South America it rains every day; the vegetation is lush and fast-growing.

BETTER	In the tropical jungles of South America it rains every day. The vegetation is lush and fast-growing.
ACCEPTABLE	Although the rest of the state has had heavy rain, Orange County is very dry; the danger of forest fires is acute.
BETTER	Although the rest of the state has had heavy rain, Orange County is very dry. The danger of forest fires is acute.

REVIEW EXERCISE D. Copy the following paragraph, inserting end marks, commas, and semicolons wherever needed. Be sure to capitalize the first word in each sentence.

Tracy went to the sideshow at the circus in Jacksonville Florida she watched a man swallow a sword another man eat fire and a woman tell fortunes these acts amazed her but the magicians pleased her more than anything else the magicians were a distinguished-looking couple who were dressed entirely in black their quick nimble hands performed strange acts they pulled rabbits out of hats made cards disappear and suspended a woman in midair the audience was awed by the magicians' skill who would not be the magicians' final act was of course their best they placed a woman in a box and proceeded to saw the box in half how the audience gasped the woman on the other hand seemed unconcerned in fact she was smiling the magicians finally put the two parts of the box back together opened the top of the box and lifted the woman out yes she was just as whole as she had been at the beginning of the act Tracy's father a former magician himself explained the trick but Tracy could not believe that people could be as quick with their hands as the magicians were after the show she went backstage to interview the magicians she wanted to submit the interview to her school paper.

REVIEW EXERCISE E. If a sentence below is correct, write *C* after its number on your paper. Copy the sentences that are not correct, inserting punctuation or omitting it as needed.

1. My grandmother showed me a letter written by her father my great grandfather in Aurora Illinois on January 1 1900 the letter was written to her.
2. What a hard test. Did anyone pass it.
3. Genni saw the danger and shouted a warning.
4. The new rules apply to everyone but a few students don't seem to understand this.
5. Audiences want to see characters they can love and hate and cheer and hiss.
6. The long steady cold rain forced us indoors we played charades checkers and card games.
7. Helen please sing soprano and Jean will sing alto.
8. Yes the statistics do in fact indicate that our team should win.
9. Mr. Mann slipped on the stairs fell to the bottom of the staircase and woke the entire household.
10. We did of course learn something from that uncomfortable boring trip.

Chapter **12**

Punctuation

Colons, Italics, Quotation Marks, Apostrophes, Hyphens

This chapter will help you to use correctly five more marks of punctuation. Together with end marks, the comma, and the semicolon, these five are the chief marks of punctuation that you will need in your writing.

COLONS

A colon is a punctuation mark that usually signals that something is to follow.

12a. Use a colon before a list of items, especially after expressions like *as follows* and *the following*.

EXAMPLES   A search showed that Jack's pocket contained the following: a knife, half an apple, a piece of gum, a dime and a nickel, and two rusty nails.

The question is as follows: if the plane leaves San Francisco at 2 P.M., at what time will it reach Chicago if it averages 500 miles per hour?

You will need these things for map work: a ruler, a box of colored pencils, and some tracing paper.

The colon is never used directly after a verb or a preposition. Omit the colon or reword the sentence.

INCORRECT My favorite sports are: basketball, tennis, swimming, and bowling.

CORRECT My favorite sports are the following: basketball, tennis, swimming, and bowling.

CORRECT My favorite sports are basketball, tennis, swimming, and bowling.

INCORRECT These cookies are made of: flour, brown sugar, butter, eggs, and nuts.

CORRECT These cookies contain the following ingredients: flour, brown sugar, butter, eggs, and nuts.

CORRECT These cookies are made of flour, brown sugar, butter, eggs, and nuts.

12b. Use a colon between the hour and the minute when you write the time.

EXAMPLES 8:30 A.M., 10:00 P.M., 9:04 this morning

12c. Use a colon after the salutation of a business letter.

EXAMPLES Dear Sir: Dear Mrs. Foster:
         Gentlemen: Dear Dr. Christiano:

EXERCISE 1. Copy the following expressions and make each into a complete sentence by supplying an appropriate list. Insert colons and commas where they are needed.

1. The following students will assemble on stage
2. The eight parts of speech are as follows
3. I am taking the following subjects this year
4. At the five-and-ten I bought

5. The mechanic listed the following damages to the car
6. You need these supplies for a picnic
7. We have studied the following kinds of punctuation marks
8. The performances will begin at
9. To succeed in sports, one should be
10. I have lived in three places

ITALICS OR UNDERLINING

In printed material, italics are letters that lean to the right—*like this*. When you write, you show that a word should be *italicized* by underlining it.

12d. Use italics (underlining) for titles of books, periodicals, works of art, ships, and so on.[1]

EXAMPLES   *Giants in the Earth* is one of my favorite novels.

One of the most famous movies ever made is *Gone with the Wind.*

On board the *Queen Elizabeth 2,* we found an old copy of the *Baltimore Sun.*

Have you heard the opera *Madame Butterfly?*

EXERCISE 2. From the following sentences, copy the words that should be printed in italics and underline them.

1. In Under the Sea-Wind Rachel Carson writes about the life of a young mackerel.
2. One of the books Louisa May Alcott has written is called Eight Cousins.

---

[1] For titles that are not italicized but enclosed in quotation marks, see rule 12n on page 224.

3. In a recent edition of Time, there is an article on our progress in space.
4. Our school newspaper, the Jackson Chronicle, received an award at the state convention.
5. Mara lent me a mystery called The Secret of the Haunted Cave.
6. The Queen Elizabeth 2 is one of the world's largest passenger ships.
7. The Emigrants had some of the most beautiful photography I have ever seen in a movie.
8. Sprayberry High School is presenting Our Town, a play by Thornton Wilder.
9. In 1927 Charles Lindbergh flew his Spirit of St. Louis nonstop from New York to Paris.
10. The first novel that I read was Treasure Island.

QUOTATION MARKS

When a person's exact words are used in writing, it is customary to use quotation marks to show where the quotation begins and ends. It is easy enough to put quotation marks before and after a quotation, but problems sometimes arise when other marks of punctuation are used in combination with them. The rules in this section will help you to solve most of your problems in punctuating quotations.

12e. Use quotation marks to enclose a direct quotation — a person's exact words.

EXAMPLES   It was Emma Lazarus who wrote, "Give me your tired, your poor."

"When the bell rings," said the teacher, "leave the room quietly."

If a person's words are not quoted exactly, no quotation marks are needed. Such a use is an *indirect* quotation.

INDIRECT QUOTATION	The reporter predicted that it would be a close game. [not the reporter's exact words]
DIRECT QUOTATION	The reporter predicted, "It will be a close game." [the reporter's exact words]

In order to write words spoken by other people, you must know more than how to use quotation marks correctly. You must learn where to use capital letters, whether to put commas and end marks inside or outside quotation marks, and when to begin a new paragraph. Study the following rules and examples until you are sure you can write conversation accurately.

12f. A direct quotation begins with a capital letter.

EXAMPLES	Maria said, "The frame isn't strong enough." Richard Lovelace wrote, "Stone walls do not a prison make."

12g. When a quoted sentence is divided into two parts by an interrupting expression, the second part begins with a small letter.

Interrupting expressions serve to break up a quotation and create variety in the passage. The expressions *he said, Mother asked,* and *replied the principal* are examples of interrupters commonly used in this way.

EXAMPLES	"Lightning has always awed people," explained Mrs. Belmont, "and many of us are still frightened by it." "The time has come," insisted the speaker, "to improve our educational program."

A quoted sentence which is divided in this way is called a broken quotation. Notice that in broken quotations, quotation marks appear before the interrupting expression and after it also.

12h. A direct quotation is set off from the rest of the sentence by commas.

To set off means to separate from the rest of the sentence. If a quotation comes at the beginning of a sentence, a comma follows it. If a quotation comes at the end of a sentence, a comma precedes it. If a quoted sentence is interrupted, a comma follows the first part and precedes the second part.

EXAMPLES   "Science is more interesting than history," said Bernie. [quotation at beginning of sentence, followed by comma]

I asked, "Who is your science teacher?" [quotation at end, preceded by comma]

"It was Mrs. Murphy," answered Gloria, "but now we have Mrs. Parkhurst." [quotation interrupted, with comma after the first part and before the second part]

▶ NOTE   No comma is needed if an end mark is used instead.

EXAMPLES   "Does she let you do experiments?" Jane wanted to know.

"I'll say she does!" Debbie exclaimed.

EXERCISE 3. Copy the following sentences, inserting commas, quotation marks, and capitals where needed. Write *C* after the number of sentences that are correct as they stand.

1. The librarian politely told me to be quiet.
2. At the same time Mike whispered hush up!

3. He asked can't you see that people are studying?
4. I replied in a whisper I'm sorry that I disturbed you.
5. I should have known better, I said to myself, than to raise my voice.
6. Next time I quietly asked the girl across from me for her science book.
7. She whispered I'll give it to you in a minute.
8. But I need it now I explained.
9. She muttered something about people who forget their own books.
10. About that time the bell rang, and the librarian said it's time to go.

12i. A period or a comma following a quotation should be placed inside the closing quotation marks.

EXAMPLES   "It's time to go," said the guide.
The man replied, "I'm ready."

12j. A question mark or an exclamation point should be placed inside the closing quotation marks if the quotation is a question or an exclamation. Otherwise it should be placed outside.

EXAMPLES   "How far have we come?" asked the exhausted man. [The question mark is inside the closing quotation marks because the quotation itself is a question.]

Who said, "Give me liberty or give me death"? [The question mark is outside the closing quotation marks because the quotation is not a question, but the entire sentence *is* a question.]

"Jump!" ordered the woman. [The exclamation point is inside the closing quotation marks because the quotation itself is an exclamation.]

I couldn't believe it when he said, "No, thank you"! [The exclamation point is outside the closing quotation marks because the quotation itself is not an exclamation, but the entire sentence *is* an exclamation.]

EXERCISE 4. Copy these sentences. Insert the proper punctuation and capitalization.

1. What do you know about the life of Lewis Carroll Mrs. Luce asked Lydia
2. His real name was Charles Dodgson Lydia said
3. He was a professor of mathematics at Oxford for many years added Lance
4. I'm sure that you've all read *Alice's Adventures in Wonderland* and *Through the Looking Glass* said Mrs. Luce
5. Yes the class chorused
6. Do you remember asked our teacher the Hatter and the March Hare
7. What a wild time Alice spent with those two characters Lydia burst out
8. Yes Lance interrupted the March Hare offered Alice wine, and then told her that there was none
9. And they both asked her foolish riddles added Lydia
10. Are you surprised asked Mrs. Luce that a professor of mathematics could write children's literature

EXERCISE 5. Rewrite each of the following sentences, changing the indirect quotation to a direct quotation. Be sure to use capital letters and punctuation wherever necessary.

EXAMPLE   1. We asked our parents if we could go on the sightseeing tour.
         1. *We asked our parents, "May we go on the sightseeing tour?"*

1. The principal announced that the annual talent parade would be held next week.
2. Our teacher asked us if we were going to enter the talent contest.
3. Jaylene said that she was going to do a modern ballet.
4. Ken suggested that he might do some rope tricks.
5. The teacher asked me what I was going to do.
6. I replied that I did not have any talent.
7. The teacher exclaimed that she was sure I was wrong.
8. Finally, I said that I would do a dramatic reading.
9. Then the teacher said that she was proud of us all.
10. We told her that we would do our best.

12k. When you write dialogue (two or more persons having a conversation), begin a new paragraph every time the speaker changes.

EXAMPLE   "Let's get going," Claire said.
        "What's your hurry, Claire?" Betty didn't seem at all worried.
        "Well, I promised we'd be there by seven thirty. It's a half-hour ride, and it's nearly seven now," Claire explained.

12l. When a quotation consists of several sentences, put quotation marks only at the beginning and end of the whole quotation, not around each sentence in the quotation.

INCORRECT   "I'll wait for you at Burke's Drug Store." "Get there as soon as you can." "We don't want to be late," he said and rushed off down the hall.

CORRECT   "I'll wait for you at Burke's Drug Store. Get there as soon as you can. We don't want to be late," he said and rushed off down the hall.

12m. Use single quotation marks to enclose a quotation within a quotation.

EXAMPLES   "Let's sing 'Home on the Range,'" suggested Jim.

"Did Ms. Numan really say, 'It's all right to use your books during the test'?" asked Sally.

12n. Use quotation marks to enclose the titles of chapters, articles, short stories, poems, songs, and other parts of books or periodicals.

EXAMPLES   Edgar Allan Poe wrote "The Raven."

Have you read Poe's short story "The Pit and the Pendulum"?

My article, "Sportsmanship at Forest Park Junior High School," was printed in the school newspaper.

Julia Ward Howe wrote "Battle Hymn of the Republic."

The fifth chapter of S. I. Hayakawa's famous book on language is called "The Double Task of Language."

EXERCISE 6. Copy the following sentences, inserting quotation marks where they are needed.

1. Nina, have you seen my catcher's mitt? asked Bob. It's been missing since Monday. I need it for practice this afternoon.
2. The Long Search was the most exciting chapter in the story of the lion cubs.
3. In what poem did Longfellow write, The thoughts of youth are long, long thoughts? asked Isabel.
4. I think it was My Lost Youth, replied her mother.
5. Lea Evans said, One of the greatest changes in architecture has been in the design of churches.

They no longer follow the traditional forms. Churches have been built that are shaped like stars, fish, and ships, among other things.

6. The latest issue of *Time* has some wonderful pictures of migrating birds.
7. Do you know the speech beginning What's in a name? from *Romeo and Juliet?* I asked her.
8. Yes, answered Emily. My mother used to say that to me when I was little. That was how I first heard of Shakespeare.
9. A human hand has more than twenty-five bones and twenty-five muscles, exclaimed Mark. No wonder a hand can do so many things!
10. There is an article called Better Health Through Nutrition in the Sunday paper.

REVIEW EXERCISE A. Copy the following paragraphs, using quotation marks and other marks of punctuation wherever necessary. Remember to begin a new paragraph each time the speaker changes. Those punctuation marks which are already included in the exercise are correct.

Halloween finally arrived. Connie and Jack asked their parents if they would go with them for tricks or treats. When their parents agreed, the children began planning their evening. We'll dress like witches and carry black cats said Connie. And we'll scare everyone in the neighborhood with our horrible masks Jack added. Oh, I can hardly wait to see the people's faces exclaimed Connie. I bet they'll be scared stiff.

Night came, and the two witches approached their first house as their parents waited by the street. It doesn't look as though anyone is home said Connie, as she eyed the almost dark house. No, there's a faint light in the window argued Jack. Anyway, we'll scare them more if they're in the dark.

The two approached the door and rang the doorbell. As the door slowly opened, a cold, moist smoke poured out. Then they heard the sounds of rattling chains and groaning voices. Suddenly, a hideous-sounding voice cackled Heh! Heh! Heh! Welcome, children.

The two witches stood frozen in their tracks. Finally, Jack cried I'm leaving. You can stay if you want to. I'm right behind you Connie gasped.

As the witches ran to where their parents were standing, a shape appeared through the smoke. A voice called after them Trick or treat.

REVIEW EXERCISE B. To show that you understand quotation marks, write a one-page narration which uses a great deal of dialogue. Put your characters — two will be enough — into an unusual situation, or have them discussing an assignment, a game, or a party. Make your conversation sound real, and be sure it is punctuated correctly.

APOSTROPHES

The apostrophe is used (1) to show ownership or relationship, (2) to show where letters have been omitted in a contraction, and (3) to form the plurals of numbers and letters.

The Possessive Case

The possessive case of a word shows ownership or relationship.

EXAMPLES   Kathleen's desk   anybody's guess
             his bat   an hour's time
             horse's mane   a nickel's worth
             student's notebook   their car

Personal pronouns in the possessive case do not require an apostrophe (hers, his, its, ours, yours, theirs).

12o. To form the possessive case of a singular noun, add an apostrophe and an *s*.

EXAMPLES   a boy's cap   Marcia's pen
            the baby's toy   Charles's opinion

EXERCISE 7.   Write a sentence for each of the following words. Use the word in the possessive case.

1. Bob	6. nobody
2. Mary	7. Geraldo
3. soldier	8. dress
4. yours	9. dime
5. minute	10. hers

12p. To form the possessive case of a plural noun not ending in *s*, add an apostrophe and an *s*.

EXAMPLES   mice's tracks
            children's choir
            children's games

12q. To form the possessive case of a plural noun ending in *s*, add only the apostrophe.

EXAMPLES   cats' basket   four days' delay
            brushes' bristles   the Carsons' bungalow

EXERCISE 8.   On your paper write the plural form for each of the following words. Then after each plural form, write a sentence using it as a possessive.

1. horse	6. student
2. carpenter	7. woman
3. dollar	8. relative
4. mouse	9. week
5. person	10. speaker

EXERCISE 9. Rewrite each of the following expressions in the possessive case. Insert an apostrophe in the right place.

1. food for the dog
2. the boots of the men
3. the hats of the ladies
4. the success of the woman
5. the grades of the students
6. the choice of the voters
7. the brooms of the witches
8. the candidate of the party
9. the licenses of the drivers
10. the duties of the examiners

Contractions

A *contraction* is a word made by combining two words and omitting some letters. An apostrophe takes the place of the letters that are left out.

EXAMPLES	there is	there's
	we are	we're
	they have	they've

12r. Use an apostrophe to show where letters have been omitted in a contraction.

Perhaps the most common contraction is that made by shortening *not* to *n't* and combining it with a verb. The spelling of the verb is usually unchanged.

is not	isn't	has not	hasn't
does not	doesn't	have not	haven't
do not	don't	had not	hadn't
was not	wasn't	should not	shouldn't
were not	weren't	would not	wouldn't

When *n't* is added to *shall, will,* or *can,* the spelling of the verb changes.

shall not	shan't [the *ll* is dropped]
will not	won't [*o* replaces *ill*]
cannot	can't [one *n* is left out]

Contractions are often formed by joining nouns or pronouns with verbs.

I am	I'm	let us	let's
you have	you've	we shall	we'll
you are	you're	she would	she'd
he had	he'd	Sam is	Sam's
she has	she's	they are	they're
Mary will	Mary'll		

Its and *It's*

The word *its,* being a personal pronoun in the possessive case, does not have an apostrophe, just as other personal pronouns (*his* and *hers*) do not have apostrophes.

The word *it's,* meaning *it is* or *it has,* is a contraction and requires an apostrophe.

EXAMPLES   Its fur is thick. [*Its* is a pronoun in the possessive case; no apostrophe is needed.]

It's time for school. [*It's* is a contraction meaning "it is." The apostrophe takes the place of the missing letter.]

It's been a great disappointment. [*It's* is a contraction of *it has.* The apostrophe takes the place of the letters *ha* in *has.*]

Write *it's* (with an apostrophe) only when it means "it is" or "it has."

Whose and *Who's*

The word *whose* is a pronoun in the possessive case. It has no apostrophe.

The word *who's* is a contraction meaning *who is* or *who has*. It requires an apostrophe.

EXAMPLES   Whose book is this? [*Whose* is a possessive pronoun meaning "To whom does it
belong?"]

Who's ready for a swim? [*Who's* is a
contraction meaning "Who is?"]

Who's been eating the pie? [*Who's* is a
contraction meaning "Who has?"]

EXERCISE 10. Write the numbers 1–20 on your paper. After each number, write *C* if the sentence is
correct. If it is not correct, copy the word requiring
an apostrophe, and insert the apostrophe.

1. The forecaster says that its going to snow tonight.
2. Wed better be sure our car has antifreeze.
3. Last year we didnt put antifreeze in our car until
December.
4. We werent prepared for snow in October, and
neither was our car.
5. Ill never forget my mothers words.
6. She said simply, "Well, the old cars had it this
time."
7. And she wasn't far wrong.
8. The old car and its radiator were frozen solid.
9. We couldnt open the doors or raise the hood.
10. We wont forget all those days of walking.
11. I wonder whos ringing the doorbell.
12. Didnt Roger bring his skates?
13. Im certain well be on time.
14. Whose turn is it to bat?
15. Dont you think theyll win the championship?
16. Lanas a good swimmer, but she cant dive.
17. Its almost ten o'clock, isnt it?
18. Our camera club didnt hold its annual picnic this
year.

19. Theyll arrive before its too late, Im sure.
20. Look at my bike; there isnt a scratch on its paint.

EXERCISE 11. Think of a suitable contraction for the blank in each of the following sentences and write it on your paper after the sentence number.

1. —— my lunch?
2. —— building sand castles on the beach.
3. We —— solve the problem.
4. —— that in your yard?
5. —— a bullfrog.
6. —— go into the water yet.
7. —— the supplies ready?
8. Why —— he here?
9. It —— time to go.
10. They —— ridden in a plane before.

REVIEW EXERCISE C. For the sentences that are correct, write *C* on your paper next to the sentence number. For the other sentences, copy the words that need apostrophes, and insert the apostrophes.

1. We cant leave until everyones finished.
2. The traffics roar and cars lights kept me awake.
3. The worlds oil supply is limited.
4. We aren't sure it's true.
5. We couldnt be sure of its size.
6. Whos the best teacher youve had?
7. Helens chances in the girls tournament are good.
8. Theres a mens clothing store on the corner.
9. Im tired of TV. Lets go to the movies.
10. Isn't this theirs?
11. She says its not hers.
12. Last years team didnt win a game.
13. My mothers office is near my fathers store.
14. Is the Smiths apartment next to yours?
15. Its not clear whos to blame.
16. The teams success is due to Julios passing.

17. Montys ice cream is the childrens favorite.
18. Clouds reflected the sun's rays.
19. The dogs leashes became entangled.
20. A trees branches fell on the Brokaws car.

Plurals

12s. Use an apostrophe and *s* to form the plural of letters, numbers, and signs, and of words referred to as words.

EXAMPLES   Your *o*'s look like *a*'s, and your *u*'s look like *n*'s.
There are three *5*'s in the telephone number.
One sign of poor writing is too many *and*'s.
There are two *o*'s, two *k*'s, and three *e*'s in *bookkeeper*.

HYPHENS

The hyphen is used (1) to indicate that a word has been broken at the end of a line and (2) to show that two or more words are being used together as one.

If there is not room for a whole word at the end of the line, you may divide it with a hyphen. Dividing words at the end of a line, however, should be avoided as much as possible.

12t. Use a hyphen to divide a word at the end of a line.

EXAMPLES

In my opinion, what this salad needs is a cu￭cumber.

Will you and Marguerite help me set the ta￭ble for supper?

That intersection at Elm and High is a bottle￭neck for eastbound traffic.

(1) Words must be divided so that each syllable can be pronounced as it is pronounced in the complete word.

UNACCEPTABLE

> Mr. Morgan looked at the board with a pu-
> zzled expression.

ACCEPTABLE

> Mr. Morgan looked at the board with a puz▪
> zled expression.

(2) Words of one syllable may not be divided.

UNACCEPTABLE

> Exercises like push-ups develop the stren-
> gth of the arm muscles.

ACCEPTABLE

> Exercises like push-ups develop the
> strength of the arm muscles.

(3) Words may not be divided so that one part is a single letter.

UNACCEPTABLE

> The seating capacity of the new gym is e-
> normous.

ACCEPTABLE

> The seating capacity of the new gym is enor▪
> mous.

12u. Use a hyphen with compound numbers from twenty-one to ninety-nine and with fractions used as adjectives.

EXAMPLES

> There are twenty▪nine days in February during a leap year.
>
> Congress may overrule a President's veto by a two▪thirds majority. [*Two-thirds* is an adjective modifying *majority*.]
>
> The pie was so good that only one sixth of it is left. [*Sixth* is a noun modified by the adjective *one*.]

EXERCISE 12. Write the numbers 1–5 on your paper. After each number, write a word or words to fit the blank in the sentence. Be sure to use hyphens where they are needed.

1. January, March, May, July, August, October, and December are the months that have —— days.
2. —— of the moon is visible from the earth, but the other half can be seen only from outer space.
3. In twenty years I will be —— years old.
4. If a quarter of the money has been spent, we must still have about —— percent of the original amount.
5. The last day of school this year will be June ——.

REVIEW EXERCISE D. Copy the following sentences and insert whatever punctuation marks are necessary: commas, colons, underlining (for italics), quotation marks, and apostrophes. The punctuation already supplied is correct.

1. Whos read Little Women?
2. There are four sisters in the novel Meg Jo Beth and Amy.
3. Beth is a frail gentle girl who is content to stay home with Marmee the girls mother.
4. Meg the oldest sister marries early.
5. Jo on the other hand vows to remain unmarried.
6. Shes interested in being a writer and she spends her spare time making up plays for the entertainment of her sisters.
7. Amy is a pretty curly-haired girl who wants to be an artist.
8. The girls have these characteristics in common kindness unselfishness and loyalty.
9. The book of course takes its title from the four sisters.
10. Its generally known that Louisa May Alcotts models for the four girls were her three sisters and herself.

REVIEW EXERCISE E. Copy the following sentences and insert whatever punctuation they need.

1. Youll need the following materials for the art course a brush an easel and some watercolors.
2. Whos taken my toothbrush? demanded Gloria.
3. Robert Burns a Scottish poet wrote the poem Flow Gently, Sweet Afton.
4. Its hard to decide whose story to read.
5. We thought that we were taking a short cruise but it turned out to be a weeks trip.
6. At 8 15 on March 1 1956 we ate the last of our provisions.
7. The next morning one of the crew shouted Land ho!
8. We werent at all sorry to be back in the harbor of Charleston South Carolina.
9. I didnt expect admitted the convict to be caught.
10. Our car license number is easy to remember because it starts with two 7s and ends with two 4s.

REVIEW EXERCISE F. Write ten sentences, following the instructions below.

1. a sentence containing an appositive
2. a sentence using a colon before a list of items
3. a sentence which states a complete date
4. a sentence containing *its*
5. a sentence containing a parenthetical expression
6. a sentence containing the title of a book
7. a sentence using the possessive case of *ladies*
8. a sentence using *whose*
9. a sentence containing a broken quotation
10. a sentence containing an indirect quotation

Sentence
Structure

PART FOUR

Chapter 13

Sentence Fragments and Run-on Sentences

Developing Sentence Sense

To punctuate a sentence correctly, you must know where it begins and ends. That sounds obvious enough, but obvious things are not always easy to do. Two very frequent errors in student writing are the *sentence fragment* and the *run-on sentence*. The first of these results from writing a period, question mark, or exclamation point before a thought is completed. The second results from omitting one of these end marks where it is needed to separate two complete sentences. To avoid these errors in your own writing, you must develop "sentence sense" — the ability to tell when you have written a complete thought.

Fortunately, you already have a strong sentence sense as far as the spoken language is concerned. Without thinking about it, you make your voice fall or rise to signal the end of a sentence. And by developing the habit of "listening" to the sentences you write, you can make use of your experience as a speaker. As you study this chapter, let your ear help you decide where the period or other end mark belongs.

THE SENTENCE FRAGMENT

A sentence expresses a complete thought. When only a part of a sentence is written with a capital letter at the beginning and a period or question mark or exclamation point at the end, the result is a sentence fragment, a part of a sentence posing as a whole sentence.

13a. A fragment is a separated part of a sentence that does not express a complete thought.

In each of the following examples, a part of a sentence has been punctuated as though it were a whole sentence. These sentence fragments are printed in *italics*. If you read only the fragments aloud, you will notice that they sound incomplete.

FRAGMENTS   Women in the civil rights movement are well known. *Including Mary McLeod Bethune and Mary Church Terrell.*

With great concentration and much discipline. Henry Aaron hit his record-breaking home run.

Antonia Brico gained fame. *When she conducted the first all-female orchestra in the 1930's.*

Detecting Fragments

If your ear leads you to suspect that you have written a sentence fragment, there are two tests that you can use to be certain. First look for a subject and a verb. If you do not find both, you have a fragment.

FRAGMENTS   Including Mary McLeod Bethune and Mary Church Terrell.

With great concentration and much discipline.

Neither of these examples has a subject or a verb. (The word *including* can be a part of a verb phrase, but it is never a verb by itself.)

Looking for the subject and verb will help you spot many fragments but not all of them. Some fragments have both.

FRAGMENT   When she conducted the first all-female orchestra in the 1930's. [*She* is the subject; *conducted* is the verb.]

If the suspected fragment has both a subject and a verb, a second test can be applied. Ask yourself whether the group of words expresses a complete thought. Separated from the rest of its sentence, the fragment above does not make sense by itself. The reader wonders what happened "when she conducted the first all-female orchestra in the 1930's."

EXERCISE 1. Number your paper 1–20. Read the following groups of words, preferably aloud. If the group of words is a sentence, put an *S* after the proper number. If the group of words is a fragment, put an *F* after the number.

1. In the center ring of the circus.
2. When the clown came on.
3. The ringmaster was smartly dressed.
4. On a wire stretched high above our heads.
5. Because no nets were used.
6. Sensing the dangerousness of the act, the crowd fell silent.
7. The dogs were dressed in evening clothes.
8. Since the elephant was well trained.
9. The graceful trapeze artists.
10. When the animal trainer put his head in the lion's mouth, the audience gasped.
11. Riding bareback was a beautiful girl.
12. Munching popcorn and drinking lemonade.

13. The man juggled cups and saucers.
14. During the tightrope walker's act.
15. With a cartwheel the acrobat landed in the ring.
16. After making a human pyramid.
17. For the grand finale the band played a march.
18. As each performer reappeared for the last time.
19. Bowing to the audience.
20. All were rewarded with loud applause.

EXERCISE 2. Some of the following items consist of two sentences. Others contain a fragment. Number your paper 1–10 and write *S* for items containing only sentences, *F* for items containing a fragment.

1. Betsy can't have the meeting at her house. Because her little brother has the measles.
2. Electricity is everywhere around us. It is in the air and in the ground.
3. We cleaned the three little fish. Hoping that nobody would ask to see our catch.
4. Thoreau spent more than two years at Walden Pond. Living in a one-room shed.
5. I promised to go to the movies with Elaine. Who would never forgive me if I went swimming instead.
6. About 245,000 students belong to Junior Achievement. Founded in 1919, it is a national organization that helps to develop leadership.
7. Pollyanna never gossips. If she can't think of something nice to say about another girl, she doesn't say anything.
8. Maria Martinez, a Pueblo Indian from San Ildefenso, New Mexico, gained fame for her outstanding pottery. Based on ancient methods.
9. If I can go, I'll call you before six. Otherwise, go without me.
10. "A stitch in time saves nine" is an old proverb. Which can be applied to many daily situations.

Correcting Fragments

The simplest way to correct a fragment is to rejoin it to the sentence from which it has been separated. Study the following examples and notice how the fragments are put back into the sentences in which they belong.

FRAGMENT   Northern California was a rather restful area. Until John Marshall discovered gold near Sacramento.

CORRECTED   Northern California was a rather restful area until John Marshall discovered gold near Sacramento.

FRAGMENT   Hansel and Gretel could not find the bread crumbs. Because the birds had eaten them.

CORRECTED   Hansel and Gretel could not find the bread crumbs because the birds had eaten them.

FRAGMENT   Ann spent the whole afternoon at the beach. Gathering shells for her collection.

CORRECTED   Ann spent the whole afternoon at the beach, gathering shells for her collection.

EXERCISE 3. Some of the following items consist of two sentences. Others contain a fragment. If an item contains only complete sentences, write *S* beside the appropriate number on your paper. If an item contains a fragment, rewrite it, joining the fragment to the sentence.

EXAMPLES   1. I will speak to the principal about you. You will be hearing from her before long.

1. *S*

2. Ramón practiced his pitching every afternoon. Hoping to become more accurate.
2. *Ramón practiced his pitching every afternoon, hoping to become more accurate.*

1. You can watch the late news. If you are willing to stay up.
2. George's excuse was ingenious. No one had ever been locked in the school bus before.
3. Ana is finally going to have her taco party. The one that she postponed three weeks ago.
4. The playoff game is at six o'clock tomorrow. Unless, of course, it rains.
5. I heard a call for help and swung the boat around. To find Jack floundering in the waves.
6. We are going to the beach tomorrow. If the day is warm.
7. Saturday was cold and rainy. With very good prospects for snow.
8. Mrs. Ikeda's car won't start because the battery is low. She says I left the headlights on all night.
9. First, I do my math homework. Which often takes me a long time.
10. We did not practice the guitar this afternoon. Because Ruth and Andrea had to write a report.

Two Common Fragments

Two kinds of fragments are especially common in the writing of junior high school students. One of these is the fragment containing a word ending in *–ing: talking with friends, hurrying to work, studying her assignment.* A word that ends in *–ing* and looks like a verb (*talking, hurrying, studying*) cannot stand as the verb in the sentence unless it has a helping verb with it (*is talking, have been hurrying, will be studying*).

When you use a group of words containing an *-ing* word, do not separate this group from the sentence.

FRAGMENT   The officer tried to hide his worries and fears. While talking with his men.

CORRECTED   The officer tried to hide his worries and fears while talking with his men.

CORRECTED   While talking with his men, the officer tried to hide his worries and fears.

FRAGMENT   Evelina forgot the time. Studying her assignment.

CORRECTED   Evelina forgot the time, studying her assignment.

CORRECTED   Studying her assignment, Evelina forgot the time.

Another common fragment is the group of words beginning with a word such as *after, although, because, if, since, unless, when, while.*

FRAGMENT   My sister will finish college this spring. If she passes all her courses.

CORRECTED   My sister will finish college this spring if she passes all her courses.

CORRECTED   If she passes all her courses, my sister will finish college this spring.

FRAGMENT   The Rothmans polished the menorah. Because Chanukah was coming.

CORRECTED   The Rothmans polished the menorah because Chanukah was coming.

CORRECTED   Because Chanukah was coming, the Rothmans polished the menorah.

EXERCISE 4.   The following groups of words are all fragments. Before or after each one, add enough words to make a sentence. Write each sentence on your paper, using correct punctuation and supplying capital letters where they are needed.

EXAMPLE 1. after the girl finished dancing
1. *The audience applauded loudly after the girl finished dancing.*

1. when she reached the top of the mountain
2. counting his money
3. although the sea was rough
4. if he had not sneezed when he did
5. moving stealthily through the jungle
6. because she was chosen the most talented girl in the contest
7. unless something is done
8. chattering among themselves
9. lying on its back
10. while the skyscraper was being constructed

EXERCISE 5. Decide which of the following expressions are sentences and which are fragments. Write *S* for each sentence after the proper number on your paper. Add enough words to each fragment to make it a sentence.

EXAMPLES 1. As the sun set behind the mountain.
1. *As the sun set behind the mountain, the natives began their ceremonial dance.*

2. Karate is fascinating to watch.
2. *S*

1. Standing near the edge of the water.
2. When the fire was finally extinguished.
3. Before leaving, the guide gave us instructions.
4. While listening to the waves hit the beach.
5. Living alone on the island, the hermit makes everything he needs himself.
6. After the door was bolted.

7. If you think it is so easy!
8. The celebrity needed no introduction, being a native of the town.
9. Before we boarded the ship.
10. Half walking and half crawling down the road.
11. The sailors felt relieved when land was sighted.
12. Our dog lay down quietly, waiting for us to notice him.
13. Because he forgot the date.
14. Unless the train is late.
15. Although she had never played backgammon.
16. Whimpering, the child went to bed.
17. Waiting impatiently for the storm to end.
18. If a person does not have a sense of humor.
19. While visiting the museum, we met some students from India.
20. Since the house was built many years before.

THE RUN-ON SENTENCE

Your sentence sense will help you to avoid another common writing fault, the *run-on sentence*. Fragments occur because the writer ends a sentence too soon. Run-on sentences, on the other hand, occur because the writer does not put a period or other end mark at the close of a sentence. Instead, the first sentence is run into the next sentence or a comma is used between sentences.

13b. A *run-on sentence* consists of two or more sentences separated by a comma or by no mark of punctuation.

RUN-ON	Finally, the supplies were delivered the settlers rejoiced.
CORRECTED	Finally, the supplies were delivered. The settlers rejoiced.

RUN-ON   The police were called, they sped to the scene of the crime.

CORRECTED   The police were called. They sped to the scene of the crime.

EXERCISE 6. The following are examples of run-on sentences. Number your paper 1–10. Decide where each sentence should end. Then write the last word of each complete sentence, the punctuation that it should have, and the first word of the next sentence. Do not forget the capital letter.

EXAMPLE   1. Mercury is the closest planet to the sun, it is also the smallest planet.
            1. *sun. It*

1. The stars, as well as the planets, are in motion, some of them move rapidly.
2. We do not see the stars move they are so far away that they seem to be motionless.
3. Pluto is far from Earth, a large telescope is needed to see it.
4. Mars is a desert of reddish rock, sand, and soil it is called the red planet.
5. People wondered if Mars had vegetation, an area of vegetation, it was once thought, had developed on the planet.
6. The largest planet is Jupiter its diameter is eleven times the diameter of Earth.
7. The atmosphere of Jupiter contains many gases, they are probably in a slushlike state because of the extremely cold surface of the planet.
8. Saturn is the second largest planet we are particularly interested in the rings of Saturn.
9. The rings are composed of billions of particles perhaps a huge explosion caused them.
10. Venus is a planet we are studying closely, it is slightly smaller than Earth.

EXERCISE 7. Some of the following items are correctly punctuated sentences. Others contain run-on sentences. Put an *S* beside the proper number on your paper for each correctly punctuated sentence. For run-ons, write the last word of the first complete sentence, the punctuation it should have, and the first word of the next sentence. Remember capital letters.

1. Arachne was famous for her skill in weaving, the story of her contest with a goddess is well known.
2. Arachne claimed her weaving was as splendid as that of Minerva, the Roman goddess of weaving.
3. Learning of Arachne's pride, Minerva disguised herself as an old woman and advised Arachne not to offend the goddess.
4. Arachne angrily replied that Minerva should engage in a weaving contest with her.
5. With that, Minerva threw off her disguise and accepted the challenge, the weavers set up looms.
6. While Minerva wove pictures of the god's famous deeds, Arachne wove scenes of their evil deeds.
7. When they were through, Minerva could find no fault with Arachne's work, she became furious with the mortal girl and decided to punish her, Minerva tore Arachne's tapestry to pieces and with her spindle struck Arachne on the head.
8. Her pride was so injured that Arachne put a noose around her neck and hanged herself.
9. Struck with pity, Minerva told Arachne she could keep her life, even though she was rude and arrogant, Minerva added, however, that Arachne and her descendants would still hang.
10. As she left, Minerva sprinkled magic juices over Arachne the girl was changed into a spider, the hanging weaver we all know today.

EXERCISE 8. Number your paper 1–25, to correspond with the line numbers in the paragraphs below.

The paragraphs contain many run-on sentences. Decide where each sentence should end, and write its last word beside the number of its line. Put a period, exclamation mark, or question mark after it; then write the first word of the next sentence, using a capital letter.

1   President Washington chose the site for the
2   White House, but he never lived in the building.
3   The cornerstone was laid in 1792, John Adams
4   moved into the building in 1800. The building was
5   then much smaller than it is now. The East Room,
6   a room used today for formal functions, was un-
7   completed, Mrs. Adams hung her wash in it.
8   In 1814 the White House was burned by the
9   British, the structure had to be rebuilt, again in
10   1950 the White House was rebuilt because it was
11   unsafe. By 1952 the reconstruction was finished,
12   President Truman returned to it from Blair House,
13   where he had lived during the rebuilding process.
14   Today the White House has 132 rooms and
15   20 baths, it has five passenger and service eleva-
16   tors. Many of the rooms are famous, the East
17   Room, the Red Room, and the Blue Room are
18   especially well known, they are used for formal
19   and informal receptions. The White House is open
20   from 10 A.M. to noon Tuesday through Saturday,
21   but, of course, only the public rooms may be
22   visited. Each day crowds line Pennsylvania Ave-
23   nue to see the Executive Mansion, one should be
24   in line early if planning to go on a tour of the
25   White House.

REVIEW EXERCISE. This exercise contains complete sentences, fragments, and run-ons. Number your paper 1–20. After each number write *S* for correct sentence, *F* for fragment, and *R* for run-on sentence.

1. People have long wondered at the noises of animals, can animals communicate with each other?
2. After several years of research.
3. Scientists are convinced that some animals have more effective communication systems than people have.
4. The porpoise can mimic a person's voice, but it speaks eight times faster than the average human.
5. Making a tape recorder essential.
6. In order to slow the porpoise's voice down enough for scientists to study it.
7. Porpoises can imitate human laughter, they can also imitate a "Bronx cheer."
8. There is some evidence that porpoises can manage to learn words and phrases.
9. Which they repeat with humanlike rhythm and enunciation.
10. After the porpoise has listened to a person who has a Southern accent.
11. It can mimic the accent.
12. A knowledge of communications among animals may help us communicate with creatures on other planets, should there be any, consequently funds are being provided for such research.
13. Animals do communicate with each other, we know that.
14. Porpoises can learn the meaning of certain words.
15. Because they do tricks after hearing words like *fish* and *jump*.
16. Can you imagine yourself communicating with a porpoise, or does this seem impossible to you?
17. Perhaps one day after getting down close to the surface of the water.
18. You will carry on a conversation with a porpoise.
19. Or maybe some other animal.
20. At one time people laughed at the idea of space travel however today we know that people can travel through space.

Chapter 14

Sentence Combining and Sentence Variety

Most of us, when we write, are so busy thinking about what we are going to say that we pay little attention to how we say it. Often the result is writing that consists of choppy, abrupt sentences that are monotonously alike, or rambling sentences that are tiresome to read. Correcting such writing is easy if you will take time to revise your compositions before making a final copy to hand in. This chapter will give you practice to help you improve and correct the sentences you write.

COMBINING SENTENCES

Reading a paragraph full of short, choppy sentences is like riding with a driver who keeps jamming on the brakes. Just when you think you are going somewhere, you are pulled up short by a period. When two or more choppy sentences are related in thought, they can usually be made smoother and clearer if they are combined into one longer sentence.

14a. Combine short, related sentences by inserting adjectives, adverbs, or prepositional phrases.

WEAK   1. The results of the test were surprising.
        2. The test was difficult.

BETTER   The results of the **difficult** test were surprising.
       (The adjective *difficult* in sentence 2 has been inserted into sentence 1.)

WEAK   1. When Phil answered, the teacher smiled.
        2. Phil answered quickly.

BETTER   When Phil answered **quickly**, the teacher smiled.
       (The adverb *quickly* in sentence 2 has been inserted into sentence 1.)

WEAK   1. Barbara Jordan spoke to the audience.
        2. She spoke with great conviction.

BETTER   Barbara Jordan spoke **with great conviction** to the audience.
                   or
       With great conviction, Barbara Jordan spoke to the audience.
       (The prepositional phrase, *with great conviction*, in sentence 2 has been inserted into sentence 1.)

EXERCISE 1. Combine the three sentences in each group into one sentence, in which you use the italicized words as adjectives. Number your sentences.

EXAMPLE 1. The doctor helped the patient.
          The doctor was *friendly*.
          The patient was *nervous*.
      1. *The friendly doctor helped the nervous patient.*

  1. Some children were frightened by a dog.
     The children were *little*.
     The dog was *big*.

2. I did my assignment in class.
   The assignment was *written*.
   The class was *English*.

3. A fence surrounds the school.
   The fence is *tall*.
   The school is *new*.

4. The crowd applauded her performance.
   The crowd was *excited*.
   The performance was *record-breaking*.

5. The city lies in a valley surrounded by mountains.
   The valley is *green*.
   The mountains are *snow-covered*.

6. All that remains of the lighthouse is its tower.
   The lighthouse is *abandoned*.
   Its tower is *white*.

7. We set up camp on a point beside a stream.
   The point was *narrow*.
   The stream was *clear* and *cold*.

8. An odor drifted from the laboratory.
   The odor was *sickening*.
   The laboratory was *new*.
   The laboratory was for *chemistry*.

9. Helicopters rescued the crew from the deck of the boat.
   There were *three* helicopters.
   The deck was *plunging*.
   The boat was *sinking*.

10. In an operation, surgeons replaced a part of the backbone with a plate.
    The operation was *long*.
    The operation was *desperate*.
    The part was *diseased*.
    The plate was *metal*.

EXERCISE 2. Combine the three sentences in each group into one sentence, in which the italicized words are used as adverbs. Number your sentences.

EXAMPLE 1. Cheryl passed the basketball to the guard.
The pass was *quick*.
The pass was *straight*.

1. *Cheryl quickly passed the basketball straight to the guard.*

1. Jules walked forward and spoke to the class.
He walked *slowly*.
He spoke *softly*.

2. Helen always does her work.
Her work is *slow*.
But it is *thorough*.

3. He picked up the letter and tore it open.
He was *eager*.
He was *impatient*.

4. We sat in the truck that Phil was driving.
We were *happy*.
Phil's driving was *slow*.

5. Mrs. Vance said goodby and departed.
Her goodby was *sad*.
Her departure was *quick*.

6. Remove the old paint and apply the new.
Remove the old paint *with care*.
Apply the new *immediately*.

7. The police officer stopped us and asked a question.
She stopped us *briefly*.
She asked a question *politely*.

8. We were distracted by the lights of a car coming toward us.
We were distracted *suddenly*.
The car was coming *rapidly*.

9. The horses bowed and trotted from the arena.
They bowed *gracefully*.
They trotted *proudly*.

10. The leading car skidded and struck the guardrail.
It skidded *wildly*.
It struck *hard*.

EXERCISE 3. Combine the three sentences in each group into one sentence, in which the italicized prepositional phrases are used. Some prepositional phrases may be inserted at more than one place in the sentence. Decide for yourself where the phrase sounds best. Number your sentences.

EXAMPLE   1. The members prepare dinner together.
They are members *of my family*.
They prepare dinner *at home*.

           1. *At home the members of my family prepare dinner together.*
                 or
           The members of my family prepare dinner together at home.

1. The team will take a plane.
They will take it *after the game*.

2. My cousin sent me a gift.
My cousin lives *in Colombia*.
It was a gift *of emerald jewelry*.

3. All members must attend the meeting.
They are members *of the newspaper staff*.
The meeting will be *after school*.

4. Hundreds wandered.
They were hundreds *of sightseers*.
They wandered *through the streets*.

5. He walks two miles.
He walks *in the morning*.
He walks *on the beach*.

6. An animal may travel.
It may travel *on your plane*.
It may travel *in a cage*.

7. New sources must be developed.
They are sources *of energy*.
They must be developed *in this century*.

8. The gathering crowd hampered the work.
It was a crowd *of curious bystanders*.
It was the work *of the firefighters*.

9. Some highways are closed.
   They are the highways *in the mountains*.
   They are closed *in winter*.
10. Prevailing winds move.
    They are winds *in temperate latitudes*.
    They move *from west to east*.

14b. Combine short, related sentences by using a compound subject.

A compound subject consists of two or more simple subjects joined by a conjunction such as *and* or *or* and having the same verb. In the following examples, the compound subjects are printed in heavy type.

EXAMPLES   Your **books** and your **lunch** are on the table.
            Roses, carnations, and **violets** were growing in the garden.

You can combine short sentences by putting the ideas they contain into a single sentence with a compound subject. The words that usually connect a compound subject are *and, or, both—and, either—or, neither—nor.* The choice of the conjunction depends upon the meaning of the sentence. In the following examples the compound subjects and the connecting words are printed in heavy type.

EXAMPLES   Spain tried to establish a colony in old California.
            Russia also tried.

            Both Spain and Russia tried to establish a colony in old California.

            Chemical foam will smother an oil fire.
            Sand will also smother an oil fire.

            Either sand or chemical foam will smother an oil fire.

Arlene will not be at the party tomorrow.
Margery will not be there either.

Neither Arlene nor Margery will be at the party tomorrow.

EXERCISE 4. Combine each pair of sentences by writing one sentence with a compound subject. Be sure the subject and verb agree in number.

1. Blocks of snow are used by Eskimos to make shelters.
   Walrus hides are also used.
2. Tahiti is an island in the South Seas.
   Mooréa, another island, is there too.
3. Green cannot be used for the uniforms.
   Blue can't be used either.
4. Corn was a popular food of the tribes of the Southwest.
   Beans were popular too.
5. Diana and Eva were early for the meeting.
   Helene was also early.
6. New homes will be built here.
   A shopping center will also be built here.
7. Wild goats are able to adapt to high altitudes.
   Sheep can adapt too.
8. Gale force winds are expected before morning.
   There will be high tides.
9. My father was not at the bus station to meet us.
   Neither was my brother.
10. Guy went to the game early to get a good seat.
    Jan and Julie went with him.

14c. Combine short, related sentences by using a compound verb.

A compound verb consists of two or more verbs that have the same subject and are joined by a conjunction. In the following examples, the compound verbs are printed in heavy type.

EXAMPLES   The bugler **arose** at dawn and **woke** the campers.

The heavy rain **flooded** highways and **washed** out bridges.

► **NOTE**   Do not confuse a compound verb and a compound sentence; do not place a comma between the parts of a compound verb.

Short sentences that have the same subject may be combined by putting the ideas they contain into one sentence with a compound verb. The connecting words most frequently used are *and, but, or, either — or, neither — nor, both — and.* In the following examples, the compound verbs and conjunctions are printed in heavy type.

EXAMPLES   Dave rang the bell.
He entered.
Dave **rang** the bell **and entered**.
María Teresa Babín praises Puerto Rican music.
She describes many dances.
María Teresa Babín **praises** Puerto Rican music **and describes** many dances.

She wrote a composition before supper.
She did not finish her history assignment.
She **wrote** a composition before supper **but did** not **finish** her history assignment.

The lost pilot had not reported his position.
He had not radioed a call for help.
The lost pilot **had neither reported** his position **nor radioed** a call for help.

EXERCISE 5. Combine each pair of short sentences into a single sentence with a compound verb.

1. She applied for the job yesterday.
   She was hired immediately.
2. The sergeant awakened his soldiers.
   He led them to the waiting truck.
3. Tom was late this morning.
   He missed the assembly.
4. Margaret finished weaving the blanket.
   She did not put the fringes on it.
5. Chris pulled to the curb.
   She let the bus pass.

REVIEW EXERCISE A. Combine each of the following groups of sentences into one smooth, well-written sentence by inserting adjectives, adverbs, or prepositional phrases and by using compound subjects or compound verbs. Number your sentences.

1. She aimed her arrow at the target.
   Her aim was careful.
   The target was distant.
   She hit it.
2. Cleavon may pitch for the Tigers.
   He may pitch in the next game.
   The Tigers are undefeated.
   On the other hand, George may pitch.
3. The painters left two cans of paint.
   The cans were open.
   They were left on the front steps.
   The painters forgot to tell me about the cans.
   They were thoughtless.
4. The old farmer had prepared an enormous breakfast.
   The farmer was generous.
   It was prepared for both of us.
   He also had packed box lunches.
   They were for later in the day.

The farmer had done all of these things before sunrise.

5. Senator Bailey spoke to our class.
She spoke about energy conservation.
She also answered questions.
The questions were many.
The questions were about solar energy.

14d. **Combine short, related sentences by making them into a compound sentence.**

A compound sentence is made up of two or more simple sentences usually joined by *and, but,* or *or.* A compound sentence, therefore, will have two or more subjects and two or more verbs.

EXAMPLE
The sun rose, and the air became warm.

(with s v s v markings above *sun rose* and *air became*)

When you use a compound sentence, you tell your reader to think of the two ideas together. Do not combine short simple sentences into a compound sentence unless the ideas are closely related and equal in importance.

RELATED IDEAS   We had won the swimming meet, and we all felt like celebrating.

UNRELATED IDEAS   We had won the swimming meet, and my dad picked us up in his car.

EQUAL IDEAS   Mary brought her mandolin to the party, and Sandra brought her guitar.

UNEQUAL IDEAS   Mary brought her mandolin to the party, and it was Leonard's birthday.

► **NOTE**   Use a comma before *and, but,* and *or* when they join the parts of a compound sentence.

EXAMPLE   The airline will sell you a discount ticket, but you must make your reservation early.

EXERCISE 6. Most of the following items consist of two or more closely related ideas. Combine these ideas into a single compound sentence, using *and,* *but,* or *or* as the connecting words. A few items contain unrelated or unequal ideas. In such cases, write *U* after the appropriate number on your paper to show that the ideas are better expressed in separate sentences. Be prepared to explain why the sentences should not be combined.

1. The British troops marched toward Lexington. The minutemen quickly gathered there to oppose them.
2. Martha got useful clothes for Christmas. Tom got a box of toys.
3. Mother invited the new neighbors to dinner. They used to live in Detroit.
4. You think fishing is fun. I think it's a very boring sport.
5. Ms. Jones planted apple and plum trees around her house. Now she has fruit as well as shade.
6. Jimmy left school early. Tom and Eddie stayed late.
7. A century ago, farmers depended on horses for power. Today they use tractors.
8. Hearing about a sale at the craft store, Nina and Rita rode downtown. Molly stayed home.
9. Nora brought Mary a birthday present. Brenda also brought one. Lucy forgot hers.
10. Horseback riding is my favorite sport. Each horse must be treated differently. I work in the stables after school.

14e. Combine short, choppy sentences into one sentence by using such words as *after, although, as, because, before, if, since, so that, when, whether,* and *while* to show the relationship between the ideas.

Sometimes the ideas expressed between two simple sentences have a special relationship with each other. For example, one sentence may explain *why, where, how,* or *when* the action in the other sentence took place. Therefore, some simple sentences can best be combined by beginning one of them with a word that expresses exactly how the two ideas are related. Study the following examples. Notice how the relationship between the ideas is expressed by the joining words.

EXAMPLES   Tom had lost his library card.
He couldn't complete the assignment.
Tom couldn't complete the assignment **because** he had lost his library card.

The judge listened to the lawyers' arguments.
She called a recess to consider her ruling.
After the judge had listened to the lawyers' arguments, she called a recess to consider her ruling.
The judge called a recess to consider her ruling **after** she had listened to the lawyers' arguments.

The children were playing in the yard.
Their mother hid the Christmas presents in a closet.
While the children were playing in the yard, their mother hid the Christmas presents in a closet.
The mother hid the Christmas presents in a closet **while** the children were playing in the yard.

Three-year-old Rosita swung hard at the piñata.
She couldn't break it.
Although three-year-old Rosita swung hard at the piñata, she couldn't break it.
Three-year-old Rosita couldn't break the piñata **even though** she swung hard at it.

Notice that your choice of a connecting word depends on the meaning you wish to give. Become familiar with the following list of words, and learn to use them effectively in your writing.

after	before	until
although	if	when
as	since	whether
because	so that	while

EXERCISE 7. Combine the sentences in each of the following groups into a single sentence by using one of the words listed below. Choose the connecting word that will best show how the two ideas are related.

as   because   although   after

1. Susan gave me only three tickets for tonight's game.
   I had asked her for at least five.
2. My study habits have improved.
   My grades are better this year.
3. Ethel sent us photographs of the Grand Canyon.
   She returned from a vacation there with her parents.
4. Richard tried to slide into second base.
   Janet tagged him with the ball.
5. We saw the Air and Space Museum.
   We all wanted to be airplane pilots.

EXERCISE 8. Combine the sentences in each of the following groups into a single sentence by using one of the words listed below. Choose the connecting word that will best show how the two ideas are related.

before   if   since   so that

1. We do not know how whales produce sounds.
   They have no vocal chords.
2. Wendy revised her composition carefully.
   Her introduction will arouse interest.
3. We could control the weather.
   Life would be much more comfortable.
4. James has been practicing his guitar every day after school.
   He decided to become a musician.
5. New cars must be tested for safety.
   They are allowed to go on sale.

EXERCISE 9. Combine the sentences in each of the following groups into a single sentence by using one of the words listed below. Choose the connecting word that will best show how the two ideas are related.

when   while   until   whether

1. Physicians do not prescribe cures.
   They have found the cause of an illness.
2. They find the cause.
   They must know what cure to prescribe.
3. A doctor cannot always know for sure.
   The patient's health will improve or will become worse.
4. Doctors wait to see the results of their work.
   They worry about the patient.
5. Some people delay going to the doctor.
   They have become seriously ill.

14f. When combining short sentences into a single sentence, be careful to choose a connecting word that expresses the exact relationship between the main ideas.

Notice that the connecting word may be placed at the beginning of the new sentence or in the middle of it. Remember also that, in combining short sentences into one sentence, your purpose is not only to make your writing smoother but also to make your meaning clearer. The word you choose to join two ideas must express the exact relationship you wish to show between the ideas.

For example, we can use a number of connecting words for these two sentences: *President Lincoln watched a play in Ford's Theater. John Wilkes Booth shot him.* But not all the connecting words would express a meaning that makes sense.

INACCURATE   Because President Lincoln watched a play at Ford's Theater, John Wilkes Booth shot him.

INACCURATE   After President Lincoln watched a play at Ford's Theater, John Wilkes Booth shot him.

These combined sentences may read smoothly, but *because* and *after* do not convey the correct relationship between the two ideas. Booth did not shoot Lincoln *because* he watched the play; nor did he shoot him *after* he watched the play.

ACCURATE   **As** President Lincoln watched a play at Ford's Theater, John Wilkes Booth shot him.

or

While President Lincoln watched a play at Ford's Theater, John Wilkes Booth shot him.

EXERCISE 10. Combine each of the following pairs of sentences by using the appropriate connecting word in parentheses. The connecting word need not come at the beginning of the new sentence.

1. The gale increased in force.
   The bridge swayed dangerously. (*as, although*)
2. The rainbow glistened brilliantly.
   The rain had fallen in torrents. (*until, after*)
3. Shirley Chisholm did not think America would elect a woman President.
   She entered the race with enthusiasm. (*although, because*)
4. They burned the useless brush.
   New forage grass would grow. (*as, so that*)
5. Mr. Bogard took Ellen's picture.
   She did not look her best. (*when, because*)
6. The doctor gave her polio vaccine.
   She will not contract polio. (*although, so that*)
7. The plow turned the rich, black soil.
   Birds darted into the furrow to snap up worms. (*as, until*)
8. Mother gave Nora a present.
   Today was her birthday. (*because, while*)
9. Fire burned the protective covering of grass.
   Heavy rains caused severe soil erosion. (*although, after*)
10. Gayle wants to go with us.
    She will have to get up early. (*so that, if*)

EXERCISE 11. Combine each of the following groups of two sentences into a single sentence, using such connecting words as *after, although, as, because, before, if, since, so that, when, whether, while.* Choose the connecting word that expresses exactly the relationship you see between the ideas.

1. He overhauled the motor.
   It ran much better.
2. Lincoln's parents were poor people.
   He became President of his country.
3. The shadow of the earth crept over the moon.
   Astronomers took photographs of the eclipse.
4. She had sanded the table top.
   She varnished it.
5. Pepe should be the guide.
   He is the only one among us who knows the way to camp.
6. Alan worked very hard.
   He did not finish the job that day.
7. A storm had grounded all planes.
   Mrs. Goldberg came home by train.
8. The huge redwood quivered, swayed, and fell with a great crash.
   The children watched breathlessly.
9. His friends were playing ball in the street.
   Jack was mowing the lawn and feeling upset.
10. I bought some new safety equipment for the boat.
    I wanted to be ready for any emergency.

REVIEW EXERCISE B. Combine the sentences in each group into one sentence by using connecting words from the following lists.

after	before	until	and
although	if	when	but
as	since	whether	or
because	so that	while	

1. A quarterback is going to pass the ball.
   He notices the speed of the running receiver.
   He can pass the ball exactly the right distance ahead of the receiver.
2. You want to hit the ball beyond your tennis opponent's reach.

You must always know where your opponent is.
You must guess the direction of your opponent's movement.

3. We entered the classroom.
We realized the teacher was going to spring a test on us.
We thought the teacher was being unfair.

4. Getting a paying job at ten years of age is difficult.
It can be done.
You are willing to work for practically nothing.

5. Mr. Johnson hired me to wash his car.
He did not hire me a second time.
The car looked worse than it had before.

6. We had filled the car trunk with luggage.
Father noticed the flat tire.
We had to unpack the trunk.

7. I unpacked the luggage.
Everyone else waited.
I finally removed the jack and spare tire from the bottom of the trunk.

8. I like to go shopping for new clothes.
I would rather go without my parents.
They always object to everything I want.

9. My grandmother gave me a book for my birthday.
She thought I should read more and watch less television.
I didn't read the book.

10. You go to the movies.
You should find out about the starting times.
You may arrive in the middle of the picture.

REVIEW EXERCISE C. The following paragraph is written in short sentences that make the style choppy. The writing can be improved by combining some of the short sentences into longer sentences. Rewrite the paragraph by inserting adjectives, adverbs, and prepositional phrases and by using compound subjects and verbs.

Trees speak a language. The language is secret. It is spoken for the lost traveler. If you are lost in the woods, examine several trees. Do this carefully. Examine trees in an exposed area. Pay attention to the size of the branches. The branches on the south side of trees are larger. The foliage is larger, also. These are trees in the Northern Hemisphere. The southern side of a tree gets more sunlight. The sunlight is direct. This is usually what happens. The southern side produces more foliage.

REVIEW EXERCISE D. Rewrite the following paragraph, combining sentences by inserting adjectives, adverbs, and prepositional phrases, using compound subjects and verbs, and using connecting words.

The Yearling is a famous story about a young boy and his pet fawn. It is by Marjorie Kinnan Rawlings. The story is set in Northern Florida. This is where Jody Baxter and his parents live. They live on a farm. One day Jody finds a fawn. The fawn is an orphan. He adopts it as his pet. He loves the fawn. His love is deep. He cares for the fawn also. His care is tender. The fawn, however, begins to eat the family's crops. This is when Jody's father becomes angry. He tells Jody to kill the fawn. For Jody, the decision is painful. It is a decision between obeying his father and saving the fawn. You will learn what Jody decides. You will learn by reading this fascinating story.

CORRECTING A RAMBLING STYLE

Sometimes, instead of writing short, choppy sentences, writers will go to the opposite extreme and run many sentences together, punctuating them as a single sentence. Using *and, so, but,* and *and then* as connectives, they will loosely tie a long succession of thoughts into a sentence that rambles on and on. One should avoid such a rambling style.

14g. Correct a rambling style by combining ideas and avoiding the overuse of *and, but,* and *so*.

The first step in correcting a rambling passage is to break it into separate, complete sentences. The second step is to combine some of the short sentences that result into better sentences.

Read the following example of a rambling sentence. Then read Step 1 in which the sentence has been broken up into six sentences. Next read Step 2, which shows how these sentences are combined and improved through the sentence combining methods included on pages 253–266.

> The afternoon was hot and sultry and so we asked my big brother Bill to drive us to the lake and he was willing and so he backed his old junk heap out of the garage and we got into our bathing suits and piled into the "heap" and we started out on our great adventure.

Step 1. Break up the passage into shorter sentences.

> The afternoon was hot and sultry. We asked my big brother Bill to drive us to the lake. He was willing. He backed his old junk heap out of the garage. We got into our bathing suits and piled into the "heap." We started out on our great adventure.

Step 2. Combine some of the short sentences into longer ones by using compound subjects and verbs, and by using the words listed on page 264.

> Because the afternoon was hot and sultry, we asked my big brother Bill to drive us to the lake. He was willing and backed his old junk heap out of the garage. After we got into our bathing suits, we piled into the "heap" and started out on our great adventure.

In revising your writing, of course, you will not need to copy it twice. You will do Step 1 in your mind and write your revised version, Step 2, only once.

EXERCISE 12. Correct the rambling style of the following passages. First, in your mind, break the passage into shorter sentences. Then combine these sentences into varied, better-written ones by using compound subjects and compound verbs, compound sentences, or the words listed on page 264. Be careful not to change the meaning of the original passage.

1. The boys had seen Cathy Bock start the outboard motor by yanking on the starting cord, and they decided to try it themselves, so they got into the boat and Andy pulled the cord, but the engine unfortunately was in gear and the throttle was wide open, so the motor caught with a roar and the boat leaped ahead and it shot up onto the beach.

2. Janey and Nora said that their first skiing lesson was a very upsetting experience, for the first time that Janey stood up, her skis slid out from under her, and she made a deep *sitzmark* in the snow, and the first time that Nora stood up on her skis they slid right out from under her, too, and she also made a deep *sitzmark* in the snow. Janey played safe, then, by sitting on her skis as she started down a slope, but she started going too fast, and she wondered where the ski patrol was. She was headed straight for a tree, and she tried to veer to one side, and she got her skis tangled, and she pitched headfirst into the snow.

CORRECTING A MONOTONOUS STYLE

If all the sentences in a passage begin the same way, the writing will be dull. Such monotony can be avoided by occasionally varying the beginnings of sentences.

14h. Correct a monotonous style by varying the beginnings of sentences.

(1) To vary sentences, begin with an adverb.

EXAMPLES   The door suddenly flew open.
            Suddenly, the door flew open.
            The game usually begins on time.
            Usually, the game begins on time.

EXERCISE 13.   Change the following sentences to begin with an adverb.

1. He handed over the letter reluctantly.
2. George grudgingly admitted that we were right.
3. He banged his fist repeatedly on the table.
4. We shall first take up old business.
5. The baby set up a howl instantly.
6. The mountains appeared in the distance gradually.
7. The injured man slowly climbed the steps.
8. We went swimming yesterday.
9. The clerk eagerly took the money.
10. The horses watched the stranger nervously.

(2) To vary sentences, begin with a prepositional phrase.

EXAMPLES   The coach had a few words to say after the game.
            After the game, the coach had a few words to say.

            A quart jar of pennies stood on the table.
            On the table stood a quart jar of pennies.

EXERCISE 14.   Change the following sentences to begin with a prepositional phrase.

1. We had traveled a hundred miles before lunch.

2. The game was tied in the last inning.
3. She was afraid to try that strategy after her last experience.
4. She wore a heart-shaped locket around her neck.
5. He had just one dime in his pocket.
6. Mr. Olivani has taught the same grade for twenty years.
7. She waited for fifteen minutes despite the rain.
8. I suddenly remembered the answer after the test.
9. Everyone is expected to remain quiet throughout the program.
10. I thought hers the most original of all the skits.

REVIEW EXERCISE E. Revise the following passages. Remember that your goal is to produce clear, well-written, varied sentences. You may not need to change every sentence. Read each passage carefully.

1. You can find the biggest money in the world on the island of Yap. It is in the Pacific Ocean. We rely on paper dollars and metal coins. The people of Yap used to trade heavy stone weights. A Yap islander may have owned a stone weighing over a ton. This would mean extreme wealth. Some of these "coins" stood over twelve feet high. Owners had to push or drag them around the island. They used heavy ropes and axles to do this. Some rich islanders had to keep their money in front of their house. It was too big to fit inside the door.

2. Joan and Elsie had colds when they visited their aunt in Hollywood but they remember the stay as a very exciting time, for they took a bus tour past the big homes of the movie stars, they shopped on Hollywood Boulevard—they couldn't come home without gifts for the family—and then Joan went alone to see a live television show, and Elsie spent a day in bed to shake off her cold, but the next day Joan stayed in bed for the same reason, and Elsie went to

a crowded movie premiere at Grauman's Chinese Theater, and on the last day of their visit their aunt took them to Disneyland.

SUMMARY

1. Combine short, related sentences by inserting adjectives, adverbs, or prepositional phrases.

2. Combine short, related sentences by using compound subjects or verbs.

3. Combine short, related sentences by making them into a compound sentence.

4. Combine short, choppy sentences into one sentence by using such connecting words as <u>after,</u> <u>although,</u> <u>as,</u> <u>because,</u> <u>before,</u> <u>if,</u> <u>since,</u> <u>so that,</u> <u>when,</u> <u>whether,</u> <u>while.</u>

5. Correct a rambling style by avoiding the overuse of <u>and,</u> <u>but,</u> and <u>so.</u>

6. Correct a rambling style by using connecting words such as <u>when,</u> <u>because,</u> <u>before,</u> etc., to show the proper relationship between ideas.

7. Correct a monotonous style by using adverbs, adjectives, and prepositional phrases to vary the beginnings of sentences.

Composition

PART FIVE

Chapter **15**

Manuscript Form

Standards for Written Work

A manuscript is any typewritten or handwritten composition, as distinguished from a printed document. In your schoolwork this year and the years ahead, you will be writing more and more manuscripts. You should learn the preferred form for your written work now, and follow it in all your papers.

15a. Follow accepted standards in preparing manuscripts.

Your teacher will find it easier to read and evaluate your papers if they are properly prepared. There is no single correct way to prepare a paper, but the rules below are widely used and accepted. Follow them unless your teacher requests you to do otherwise.

1. Use white paper $8\frac{1}{2} \times 11$ inches in size for typewritten papers and ruled composition paper for handwritten ones.

2. Write on only one side of the sheet.

3. Write in blue or black ink or typewrite. If you type, double-space the lines.

4. Leave a margin of about two inches at the top of the page and margins of about one inch at the sides and bottom. The left-hand margin must be straight;

the right-hand margin should be as straight as you can make it.

5. Indent the first line of each paragraph about one-half inch from the left.

6. Write your name, the class, and the date on the first page. Follow your teacher's instructions in the placement of these items.

7. If your paper has a title, write it in the center of the first line. Do not enclose the title in quotation marks. Skip a line between the title and the first line of your composition.

8. If the paper is more than one page in length, number the pages after the first, placing the number in the center, about one-half inch down from the top.

9. Write legibly and neatly. Form your letters carefully, so that *n*'s do not look like *u*'s, *a*'s like *o*'s, and so on. Dot the *i*'s and cross the *t*'s. If you have to erase, do it neatly.

15b. Learn the rules for using abbreviations.

In your writing, you should spell out most words rather than abbreviate them. A few abbreviations, however, are commonly used.

The following abbreviations are acceptable when they are used with a name: *Mr., Mrs., Ms., Dr., Jr.,* and *Sr.* If they do not accompany a name, spell out the words instead of using the abbreviations.

EXAMPLES **Mr.** Hastings **Dr.** Eustace
     Mrs. Galzone Frank B. Nolan, **Jr.**

     Have you called the **doctor?**
     Sylvia is a **junior** partner of the firm.

The abbreviations *A.M.* (*ante meridiem* — before noon), *P.M.* (*post meridiem* — after noon), *A.D.* (*anno Domini* — in the year of the Lord), and *B.C.*

(*before Christ*) are acceptable when they are used with numbers.

EXAMPLES   The meeting is called for 3:30 **P.M.**

Augustus Caesar lived from 63 **B.C.** to **A.D.** 14. [Notice that the abbreviation *A.D.* precedes the number, while *B.C.* follows it.]

Abbreviations for organizations are acceptable if they are generally known.

EXAMPLE   That woman works for the **FBI.** [Abbreviations for government agencies are usually written without periods.]

15c. Learn the rules for writing numbers.

Numbers of more than two words should be written in numerals, not words. If, however, you are writing several numbers, some of them one word and some more than one, write them all the same way. Always spell out a number that begins a sentence.

EXAMPLES   Dick and I set out **twenty-three** strawberry plants this morning.

From Malvern take Route **202.**

Carla started with **120** baby chicks, but now she has only **90.**

Two hundred and fifty-seven seniors graduated from our high school today.

Write out numbers like *seventh, fifty-third,* and so on. If they represent the day of the month, however, it is customary to use numerals only.

EXAMPLES   I was the **first** [not 1st] customer at the bank this morning.

Flag Day is June **14** [or **the fourteenth of June**].

15d. Learn the rules for dividing words at the end of a line.

In general you should avoid dividing a word at the end of a line to maintain an even margin, but sometimes you will find it necessary to do this by using a hyphen. Review the rules for dividing words on pages 232–33.

15e. Learn the standard correction symbols.

In marking your papers, your teacher may use some or all of the symbols given below. If you memorize these symbols, you will understand at once what is wrong in your paper. If you are not sure how to correct your error, use the index of your book to find the section that you need to review.

ms	error in manuscript form or neatness
cap	error in use of capital letters
p	error in punctuation
sp	error in spelling
frag	sentence fragment
ss	error in sentence structure
k	awkward sentence
nc	not clear
rs	run-on sentence
gr	error in grammar
w	error in word choice
¶	You should have begun a new paragraph here.
t	error in tense
∧	You have omitted something.

PARAGRAPH MARKED BY THE TEACHER

cap
p

The arrival of our new puppy, a labrador retriever brought a big change to our house. Because she was only seven weeks old,

p   she wasnt housebroken. Her teeth were
sharp as needles, and she chewed up
frag   everything she could. Including shoes,
rugs, books, and even some of the
sp   furnicher. One of her favorite stunts
gr, rs   were to hide under a bed, it was hard
to find her there because she was all
black.

PARAGRAPH CORRECTED BY THE STUDENT

cap   The arrival of our new ~~puppy~~, a ^L Labrador
p   retriever, brought a big change to our house.
Because she was only seven weeks old,
p   she wasn't housebroken. Her teeth were
sharp as needles, and she chewed up
frag   everything she could, "Including shoes
rugs, books, and even some of the
sp   furnich~~er~~^ture. One of her favorite stunts
gr, rs   ~~were~~ ^was to hide under a bed. "It was hard
to find her there because she was all
black.

Instead of working exercises for this chapter, apply
what you have learned here to every paper that you
write.

Chapter 16

Narration
and Description

Telling what happened and telling what something is like are two of the most common uses of language. Hardly a day passes in which you do not do one or the other in your conversation. Telling what happened is *narration;* creating a word picture of something is *description.*

If you have tried writing narration or description, you have probably found that it is more difficult to tell about events and people and things on paper than it is by the spoken word. When you are speaking, you use gestures, facial expressions, and tone of voice to carry part of your meaning and hold the listener's attention. When you write, your words have to do the whole job.

Learning to do the job with words alone requires careful thought and a good deal of practice. However, you do not have to learn to write narratives and descriptions by trial and error. People have been telling stories and describing things for thousands of years, and in that time they have naturally given some thought to the best way of going about these kinds of writing. The principles you will study in this chapter will help you solve some of the general problems that arise in writing narrative or description.

WRITING NARRATIVES

"And then what happened?" is not just a child's question. Adults often ask it, too. Everyone likes a story. The story may be about far-off places and strange events or about very familiar things. In either case, people are curious about things that happen to others.

Your readers will be interested in what has happened to you. Making mistakes, having fun, finding new friends, being frightened, making difficult decisions—these and many other things that you have experienced are your best sources for stories. And you are the only one who can write them.

Planning a Narrative

16a. Plan a narrative before you write it.

Planning your narrative is important. Unless you plan, you may omit essential parts of your story or get the details so mixed up that your reader is confused and the story spoiled.

A story plan should tell:

1. *Time:* when the incident occurred
2. *Place:* where the incident occurred
3. *People:* who were involved
4. *What happened:* a summary (in a sentence or two) of what happened
5. *How you felt:* a summary (in a sentence or two) of how you felt at the time

Suppose that you have been asked to write a story about a personal experience. You think awhile and decide, for example, to tell a story about an accident you had on a fishing trip. When you have jotted down notes for each heading, your finished story plan might read:

1. *Time:* last summer, while I was fishing
2. *Place:* on the dock at Lake Wyandot
3. *People:* me, crowd of scouts, my mother, a doctor
4. *What happened:* I grabbed at my fishing line and hooked my own thumb
5. *How I felt:* angry with myself for having a silly accident in front of all those people

This plan serves as a general outline and as a guide to what you should put into your story. The items of this plan should be clear and definite. As you write, *stick to your outline.*

A common error in story writing is to begin in the wrong place. If, for example, in developing this outline into a story, you begin by telling how you left home in a rainstorm, where you stopped for breakfast, the names of friends who waved to you as you passed, you would be confusing your reader with unnecessary details. Your story is about an accident you had while fishing, so begin the story on the dock at the lake, with the fishing. Read the following model narrative:

THE SHORTCUT

Jenny Jong and I had a good lesson in obeying signs last summer. When we were camping with our folks in Mount Cato State Park, Jenny and I went on a hike. We started climbing the trail up Mount Cato at daybreak, and reached the top by midday. We were tired and hungry.

"Let's shortcut, going down," I said to Jenny after we had eaten our sandwiches.

She pointed to a sign.

"It says hikers should stay on the trail."

"We'll be careful. Come on!" I said.

We were very careful. The trail zigzagged down the mountain in gentle switchbacks, but we cut straight down between zigs and zags. When we came to a slope of loose rock that our weight might have moved into a bad rock slide, we went around it on the trail. Farther down, we returned to the trail again to avoid a slope so steep that we might have broken our necks trying to climb down it. But all the rest of the way we took shortcuts, clinging to shrubs and trees as we made our way down and arriving at camp with just scratches.

We had been careful, but not careful enough. We had caught poison oak. We had such a bad case that our eyes swelled shut, and we spent one miserable week in bed.

EXERCISE 1. Draw up a story plan for the preceding narrative. Remember the five items of the plan: *Time; Place; People; What happened; How the writer felt.*

EXERCISE 2. Prepare a story plan about something that happened to you. The following suggestions may help you find the right incident. Save your plan. You will use it later as an outline for a narrative.

1. An automobile breakdown in a deserted place
2. An attempt to imitate someone older than you
3. An embarrassing moment
4. A quarrel with a friend
5. Overcoming a fear
6. A scheme for making some money
7. Your first baby-sitting assignment
8. An unexpected visitor
9. Training a pet
10. A difficult decision

16b. Make sure that your story has a beginning, a middle, and an end.

Generally, your story should be at least three paragraphs long. Usually it will be longer. The first paragraph is the beginning or introduction to your story. The last paragraph is the ending. The middle of your story may consist of several paragraphs.

The beginning. The beginning of a narrative should arouse the readers' interest and get them quickly into the story. It usually gives the *time* and the *place* and introduces the *people.* Unless the readers are supposed to be surprised, the beginning should give them a hint of what is going to happen.

The middle. This part of the narrative is mainly devoted to *what happened.* It deals with the important events in the order they occurred. Only those details that the readers have to know should be included.

The end. The end of a narrative should satisfy the readers' curiosity about *what happened* and tell them *how you felt* about it. Sometimes the way in which you tell about the final event will show your readers your attitude toward it. At other times, a brief comment will help them to see the point.

EXERCISE 3. Turn back to the narrative on pages 286–287. Be able to identify the beginning, middle, and end. Would the point be clearer if the writer had added a concluding sentence such as "Jenny and I certainly learned the hard way"? Be able to give reasons for your answer.

EXERCISE 4. Write a narrative of about two hundred words on the plan you worked out for Exercise 2.

Introduce *time, place,* and *people* in the beginning.

Narrative Details

16c. Make your details specific.

A vague and general story is likely to bore readers. A good narrative gives readers the feeling that they are actually witnessing the events. To achieve this, the details must make a strong and definite impression.

Look once more at the model narrative on pages 286–287. The long paragraph, telling how the girls climbed down the mountain, begins with the sentence, "We were very careful." But the writer does not stop with this general statement. Vivid details show how careful the girls were.

Vivid details do more than tell what happened. They *show* what happened. Suppose you were writing a narrative based on the story plan on page 286. The last two items of the plan are

4. I grabbed at my fishing line and hooked my own thumb.
5. I was angry with myself for having a silly accident in front of all those people.

These two bare statements give an idea of *what happened* and *how you felt,* but they do not hold the reader's interest or make the story vivid. Specific, vivid details will show what happened:

When I started to swing the fish onto the dock, it flopped off the hook and fell back into the water. The boys groaned, but I was too busy just then to care. I grabbed for my swinging line, realizing that I might hit somebody with my sinker or snag someone with my hook. I was right. I caught my line — by the hook. It stuck into my thumb.

I exclaimed, "Ouch!" That hook felt like a sudden jab of fire into my hand. Then I forgot the hurt in a worse kind of pain. My face got red as I realized everybody was staring at me. What a dumb thing to do! Snag yourself with your own fishing hook like a six-year-old!

EXERCISE 5. The following situations are ones that might be important parts of a longer narrative. Choose two of these situations and write, for each, three or more sentences containing specific details that will make readers feel they are *there*.

EXAMPLE   1. Putting out a brush fire
           1. *The sudden breeze swept the fire out of the small ravine in which we had been camping and onto the broad, dry meadow. We desperately beat at the flames with the one shovel we had and our raincoats. The intense heat of the flames made our faces burn as though we were feverish.*

1. Riding in a roller coaster
2. Taking an important test
3. Being caught in a thunderstorm
4. Riding on a crowded bus (or train or subway)
5. Waiting in line to buy tickets
6. Trying out for a part in a play (or a position on a team)
7. Looking for landmarks in a strange part of town
8. Meeting someone unexpectedly with whom you have quarreled
9. Trying something new for the first time
10. Entering a new school for the first time

16d. Omit unnecessary details.

A common error in writing narratives is to stray from the main idea of your story. If you are telling about how you hooked your thumb while fishing, avoid giving details about the weather or how large a fish someone else caught. These things have nothing to do with your story. One way of deciding whether a detail is necessary is to consult your story plan. If a detail will help to build an item in the plan (*time, place, people, action, feelings*), that detail is likely to be useful and appropriate. If the detail does not apply to any item in the plan, omit it.

EXERCISE 6. The following narrative contains a number of unnecessary details. Decide which details should be omitted, and copy them in a list on your paper.

I woke up in a fright and lay tense in my sleeping bag, listening. Outside the tent I could hear the wind in the pine trees. I heard an owl hoot and a burning stick crackle in the dying campfire. Then I gasped as again I heard the sound that had scared me out of sleep. Just on the opposite side of the tent wall something shuffled and snuffled.

A bear! Sniffing at our camp icebox!

I shouted, "A bear! A bear!" I shouted loud enough to shake pine cones off the trees. My father and sister woke up. People in tents around us woke up and looked out.

Dad rushed out of the tent in his pajamas. My mother, waking up, said, "Herb, calm down so we can find out what's going on."

My sister said angrily, "Quit shouting! Can't a person even get some peace and quiet out in a forest?"

Outside, Dad was moving his flashlight beam around camp. Flashlights from tents around us shone on our camp. Far in the distance, a train whistled for a crossing.

Suddenly I felt as silly as a dog with its head caught in a bucket. Dad's flashlight showed our icebox resting where it belonged, safe and sound. No bear was in sight. But slowly waddling away, making a shuffling sound in the pine needles, was a fat, harmless little raccoon. I don't think that it was able to figure out how to work the latch on the icebox door. I felt so foolish for shouting the way I did. Now I was the one who wanted some peace and quiet.

Using Dialogue

In a written story, the conversations that people have are called *dialogue*. Using dialogue is one way to make your narratives more lively and to make your characters come to life.

Even though the narratives that you are writing right now are very short, you will still find some opportunities to use dialogue. Before you do, review quickly the rules for using quotation marks on pages 218–24. Remember to start a new paragraph with each change of speaker.

EXAMPLE   "What was that noise?" I asked.
            Jerry rubbed his eyes. "I didn't hear a thing."
            "Then you were asleep."
            Jerry looked at me angrily. "Asleep? Are you accusing *me* — "

EXERCISE 7. Choose one of the following situations and write a short dialogue to fit it.

1. A girl attempts to convince her mother that her allowance should be raised.
2. Two girls try to persuade a third to come to the beach with them.
3. A student explains to his teacher why an assignment has not been completed.

4. Two boys or two girls disagree about the way to do something.
5. A baby sitter tries to reason with a small child.

EXERCISE 8. Write a narrative of about three hundred words on one of the following topics or on one of your own choice. Plan your story carefully, and make sure that it has a beginning, a middle, and an end. Use dialogue if it is appropriate.

1. What I learned from a great disappointment
2. The first trip I took alone
3. A holiday I can never forget
4. The greatest favor anyone has ever done for me
5. Lost!
6. How we won a special award
7. The last day of school
8. A false alarm
9. How I helped win (or lose) a game
10. A practical joke that backfired

WRITING DESCRIPTIONS

The purpose of a description is to make the reader see, hear, or otherwise experience something. The writer must use words to create the impression, and these words must be carefully chosen.

Descriptive Detail

16e. Use details that appeal to the senses.

Good details are as important in a description as in a narrative. Effective description appeals to the senses. You know what something is like by *seeing* or *hearing* it, or by *smelling, tasting,* or *touching* it. The best way to make a reader feel that what you are describing is real is to appeal to the senses. If you are describing a walk on a sweltering summer day, you want your reader to feel the waves of heat, see the people trying in different ways to find relief, smell the hot asphalt in the streets, and perhaps hear the refreshing sound of water splashing in a fountain or pool. A vague or general description is dull stuff. Only vivid details and sharp sense impressions will hold a reader's interest.

Like a good narrative, a good description omits unnecessary details. The main purpose of the description of the summer walk is to give an impression of the effect of the heat. A description of jewelry that you saw in a store window is not related to this main idea and should be omitted.

Read the following description:

1 Standing in the wet grass, still yawning and sleepy,
2 we did the morning exercises. Night chill was in
3 the air, but behind our backs the sun was rising,
4 and its warmth crept onto our shoulders. After
5 the exercises we raced along a wagon road to the
6 swimming pool, and as we ran up, shouting and
7 excited, two or three startled frogs made tremen-
8 dous leaps and plumped beneath the glassy sur-
9 face of the water. After the swim we dried our
10 skinny sunburned bodies and ran to the mess
11 hall. . . .
12   At mealtime we ate ravenously. . . . There were
13 steaming platters of pork and beans and cabbage
14 and stew. As we walked to the long clapboard
15 building with our hair freshly combed and water
16 glistening on our faces, which we washed at the
17 flowing pipe of a big artesian well, we existed in a
18 transport of hunger. In the steamy fragrance of
19 the mess hall we set up a clatter of knives and
20 forks and china, and afterward we went to our
21 cabins and flopped on the bunks in a state of
22 drowsy satisfaction. . . .

23   During those summers in camp a love grew up
24   in me for the rhythms of nature, for tropical rains
25   that came sweeping through the pines and oaks,
26   for the fiery midday sun, for long evenings, and
27   the deep black nights. Great campfires were lit
28   beside the bayou and a rushing column of lumi-
29   nous smoke and sparks ascended to the cypress
30   trees. Fire gleamed in the water where bass were
31   sleeping in stumps. Campers wandered toward the
32   meeting place, their flashlights swinging in the
33   woods. We sat about the fire, singing, beating
34   deep rumbling tom-toms made of hollowed oak
35   logs. . . .[1]

EXERCISE 9. On your paper, copy the words or phrases in the preceding passage that appeal to the senses, give the line in which the word or phrase appears, and indicate which of the senses the word or phrase appeals to. It may appeal to more than one sense.

EXAMPLE *Wet, line 1, touch*

EXERCISE 10. Choose five of the following objects or situations and write one sentence describing each. Include words and details that appeal to the senses.

1. Eating cold strawberry ice cream
2. A large old tree
3. A fish swimming near a dock
4. A baseball hitting a catcher's mitt
5. A car stuck in a snowbank
6. Night sounds at a lake or at the seashore
7. Musicians in a parade
8. Holding a piece of ice for a long time

---

[1] From "The Silver Horn" by Thomas Sancton from *Harper's* Magazine, copyright, 1944 by Harper's Magazine, Inc. Reprinted by permission of Russell & Volkening, Inc. as agents for the author.

9. Faces on a bus or train
10. An excited crowd at a football game

16f. Use adjectives and adverbs effectively.

An adjective, you will remember, describes a noun or pronoun and tells *what kind, which one, how many.* An adverb describes a verb, an adjective, or another adverb, and tells *when, where,* or *how.*

Many of us have times when we are lazy and fall into bad habits of thinking. Often we tend to use the same few adjectives to describe anything we happen to be talking or writing about. Such overused descriptive words become tired and weak and dull. They not only fail to do the job they are intended to do, but they bore the reader.

Among such overused adjectives and adverbs are

nice	neat	awful
swell	funny	good
terrible	terrific	bad
cute	wonderful	really

A good example of how an adjective is overused until it becomes so trite that it carries little meaning is the word *awful.* Look it up in the dictionary. It means *terrible, appalling; worthy of profound respect and fear; sublimely impressive; majestic; inspiring awe,* etc. We use the word to mean *exceedingly great, bad.* For example:

She had an awful headache.
The restaurant has awful food.
The auto horns made an awful noise.
They had an awful time at the party.

The word *awful* has been so weakened, abused, and blunted by overuse that it no longer adds much to a description.

An adjective should be fresh and exact. Replacing a dull, trite adjective with a more exact and fresher word will not only help the reader understand what you mean but will give more force and interest to your writing.

If you replace the word *awful* in the sentences on page 296 with adjectives that tell precisely what is intended, much more meaning results.

> She had an awful headache. [piercing? throbbing? agonizing?]
>
> The restaurant has awful food. [tasteless? stale? overcooked?]
>
> The auto horns made an awful noise. [loud? piercing? frightening?]
>
> They had an awful time at the party. [unhappy? painful? boring?]

EXERCISE 11. Replace the trite adjective (in italics) in each of the following sentences with an adjective that you think is fresher and more exact. Use your dictionary if you need to. List your new adjectives on a sheet of paper, numbering each one for the sentence in which it belongs.

EXAMPLE   1. We had a *grand* time sailing in the high wind.
            1. *thrilling*

1. He was in an *awful* rage.
2. Dan is a *terrific* dancer.
3. They bought a *swell* new car.
4. My aunt lives in a *cute* house.
5. The police officer found Timmy huddled in a corner, crying in a *funny* way.
6. Nora stayed home because she had a *terrible* cold.
7. Dorothy had a really *awful* case of hives.

8. When Luther stepped to the front of the class, the students gave him a *wonderful* round of applause.
9. After she finally found her broken bike, she was *good and mad.*
10. Rosa was suffering from a *bad* case of stage fright.

Like adjectives, adverbs should be fresh and exact. We tend to overuse some adverbs to such an extent that they lack precise meaning and are trite. For example:

> He was terribly good to me. [frighteningly? surprisingly? extremely?]
>
> She's so terribly shy. [severely? painfully? violently?]
>
> Diamonds are terribly expensive. [excitingly? excessively? savagely?]
>
> Nan is terribly careful about details. [savagely? frighteningly? overly?]

EXERCISE 12. Replace the trite adverb in italics in each of the following sentences with an adverb that you think is fresher and more exact. Use your dictionary. List your new adverbs on a sheet of paper, numbering each one for the proper sentence.

1. They danced together *nicely.*
2. Her sister was *terribly* good to her.
3. I didn't mind when she borrowed my book, but when she didn't return it I got *really* angry.
4. At Christmas they were *awfully* happy.
5. She thanked her parents so *cutely* that they forgot to be angry.
6. He whirled around and around until he got *wonderfully* dizzy.
7. The district attorney *neatly* trapped the witness who had lied in his testimony.
8. He is *really* tall.

9. Nora's new dress was *nice,* but Ellen's was *terribly cute.* (Substitute better adjectives and adverb.)
10. Andrea bought a *really neat* album to play on her *terrific* stereo. (Substitute better adjectives and adverb.)

16g. Use adjectives and adverbs sparingly.

Using adjectives and adverbs is such an obvious way of writing a description that we may fall into the trap of using too many, thus cluttering the impression we want to create. You should choose adjectives and adverbs as carefully as you do the details of a description. A few strong adjectives and adverbs create a more vivid and interesting word picture than many weak ones. Be especially careful not to overuse *very.*

EXERCISE 13. Number your paper 1–10. For each phrase in italics, write one adjective or adverb that will do the work of two words.

1. The *very large* police officer helped them across the street.
2. A *very smart* girl won the Science Fair award.
3. That was a *very good* dinner we just ate.
4. In a *very loud* voice he demanded to be seated.
5. She told us a *very funny* joke.
6. The football team played *very well.*
7. He described her costume *very clearly.*
8. She has a *very sad* way of speaking.
9. *Very slowly* he took out his wallet and paid the bill.
10. She has a *very musical* voice.

EXERCISE 14. Write a short description of about seventy-five words. Be sure to include details that appeal to the senses and to make effective use of adjectives and adverbs. Some suggestions are

1. A street at night
2. A department store on a bargain day
3. Riding home on the school bus
4. The last inning of a baseball game
5. A Saturday matinee at the movies

16h. Use verbs that help with the work of describing.

The careful selection of verbs also helps to make a description vivid and interesting. Verbs are especially useful in describing action. For example, the following paragraph owes its vivid quality to the use of good verbs. Adjectives like *torrid* help, but the strength of the paragraph depends mainly upon the italicized verbs.

> As the winner *flung* herself across the finish line, she *paled* and *crumpled* in a heap. The torrid sun *had beaten* down her strong body, and the final seconds of the race *had exhausted* the last of her reserves. The crowd *roared* and *swarmed* about her.

EXERCISE 15. Use verbs from the following list to improve the sentences given below. If you aren't sure of a meaning, use the dictionary.

staggered	throbbed
dawdled	careened
grimaced	squinted
sprawled	screeched
flailed	chuckled

1. The old man looked into the blinding light.
2. After a hard day, Mom lay in the hammock for a rest.
3. He made a face after taking the medicine.

4. She took her time while eating breakfast.
5. The wounded man walked into the hospital.
6. He laughed quietly when we asked for a day off.
7. Kay waved her arms in excitement.
8. She swayed to one side to avoid colliding with the man suddenly turning the corner.
9. The painful wound hurt.
10. Above us the owl gave a shrill cry.

Using Description in Narratives

16i. Use description in narratives to make your characters and setting vivid.

Because a good description makes what it describes seem real, it will also help to make narrative compositions more interesting to the reader. Notice how Erma Bombeck uses descriptive detail in her essay, "The Pampered Dog":

> The first day Arlo came home, his feet never touched the floor. In a single day he was fed eight times, burped five, danced on the TV set, slid down the banister, was given a bath, blown dry with my hair dryer, visited twelve homes, rode on a bicycle, and barked long distance on the phone to Grandma. He slept his first night under my dual-control thermal blanket.[1]

Erma Bombeck, of course, is exaggerating the details to make the narrative humorous. Her description succeeds by arousing the reader's interest and by giving a vivid picture of the pampered family pet.

A description of a setting may also play an important part in a story. Here, for example, is a paragraph from a brief story, "The Hammon and the Beans."

[1] From *The Grass Is Always Greener Over the Septic Tank* by Erma Bombeck. Copyright © 1976 by Erma Bombeck. Used with the permission of McGraw-Hill Book Company.

Notice how the setting gives a clear picture of what it was like to live in a small town near an army post.

> At this time Jonesville-on-the-Grande [in Texas] was not the thriving little city that it is today. We counted off our days by the routine on the post. At six sharp the flag was raised on the parade grounds to the cackling of the bugles, and a field piece thundered out a salute. The sound of the shot bounced away through the morning mist until its echoes worked their way into every corner of town. Jonesville-on-the-Grande woke to the cannon's roar, as if to battle, and the day began.[1]

EXERCISE 16. Write a description of a setting (no longer than one hundred words) which might be used in a narrative.

REVIEW EXERCISE A. Write a description of from one to two hundred words. Here are some suggestions:

1. A crowded beach or pool
2. An amusement park
3. A parade
4. Your block
5. A state or county fair
6. An ice-skating rink
7. An impressive setting such as the Grand Canyon

REVIEW EXERCISE B. Write a narrative of about three hundred words. If you like, you may use the same setting you wrote about in Exercise 16.

[1] From "The Hammon and the Beans" by Américo Paredes from *The Texas Observer*, April 18, 1963. Reprinted by permission of the author.

Chapter **17**

The Paragraph

Structure and Development

One might define a paragraph as a group of sentences in which the first sentence begins a little to the right of the left-hand margin. That, however, would not be a good definition of a paragraph because it does not tell how a paragraph is organized, or structured.

THE STRUCTURE OF A PARAGRAPH

17a. **A paragraph is a series of sentences developing one topic.**

A good paragraph develops only one main idea, or topic. In the following paragraph, the main idea, or topic, is stated in the first sentence. The rest of the paragraph consists of sentences that develop or explain the main idea.

Through the centuries rats have managed to survive all our efforts to destroy them. We have poisoned them and trapped them. We have fumigated, flooded, and burned them. We have tried germ warfare. Some rats even survived atomic bomb tests conducted on Eniwetok atoll in the Pacific after World War II. In spite of all our efforts, these enemies of ours continue to prove that they are the most indestructible of pests.

The following paragraph, on the other hand, is poorly structured. It does not state its main idea. The sentences do not work together to develop one point. The paragraph wanders aimlessly. Compare it with the model paragraph you have just read.

>   My big brother made $200 this summer working at a farm stand on Route 1. He says that dealing with all kinds of customers is good experience. My father wanted me to clean the basement, and my mother thought I should try washing windows. Yesterday I spent all my savings on a new set of headphones. I can't even buy a stick of bubble gum.

This piece of writing may look like a paragraph, but it is not structured like a paragraph. The main idea is certainly not clearly stated. The only order the sentences follow is the order in which they happened to occur to the writer.

EXERCISE 1. Some of the following passages are well-organized paragraphs; some are not. Write the numbers 1–5 on your paper. Read each passage. If a passage is a well-organized paragraph, write P after its number on your paper. If it is a disorganized group of sentences, or not a paragraph, write NP. Prepare to explain your opinions.

1

Communication is essential to prairie dog survival. An animal spotting an enemy gives a warning cry, which instantly sends all others scurrying to their burrows. An all-clear call later announces that the danger has passed.

2

Sometimes we would go to the new house being built in our neighborhood to watch the masons and carpenters. At first, we were angry because the house was on a lot where we used to play. We played softball on that lot. I always liked to watch the bricklayers. After the house had been closed in, we went inside and looked around. Nails and pieces of wood were scattered around. We had to watch our step. There were signs saying "Keep Out."

3

On the way home, we usually stop at Glaser's Bakery. If anyone has any money, we buy some doughnuts or cookies. Looking through the window of Rose's Pizza Palace makes everybody hungry. Rose will sell us a piece of pizza if we can't afford a whole one. The dress shop usually gets a lot of laughs. Nobody ever looks in the hardware store windows. We always take a while outside the movie, looking at the pictures. But we hardly ever go to the movies. We go on a rainy afternoon if we can afford it.

4

There are several ways to reduce the amount of trash we throw away. We can buy soda in glass bottles and return these bottles to the store. We can use both sides of a piece of paper when doing our homework. We can collect cans and other metal containers and take them to recycling centers. Finally, we can use durable dishware and utensils instead of paper plates and plastic knives, forks, and spoons.

5

Melissa is crazy about baseball. As soon as the snow melts in the spring, she is out there hitting and chasing grounders with anyone she can find to play with. She has a big collection of baseball cards and drives a hard bargain when trading. She loves to argue about which professional players are best, and her head is full of baseball facts. This year she is a catcher on her Little League team. Melissa would rather play than watch baseball on TV, but she'll do almost anything to get her parents to take her to a big league game. I think she even dreams about baseball.

The Topic Sentence

17b. The topic of a paragraph is stated in one sentence. This sentence is called the *topic sentence.*

In the following paragraphs, the topic sentence is printed in heavy type. Note that the other sentences in the paragraph support the topic sentence by giving additional information.

> **The electric motor has greatly eased housekeeping.** A willing, tireless helper, the electric motor operates the dishwasher, cleaning glassware and china far better than tired hands can do the job. A motor runs the garbage disposal that cuts waste into particles that can be washed down the drain. An electric motor operates the vacuum cleaner and the wax polisher. A motor even drives the clothes washer and the dryer.

> **The origin of furniture as we know it goes back to ancient Egypt.** The Egyptians had stools, chairs, chests, tables, and beds, examples of which can be seen in museums today. They put such everyday objects in their tombs. They also painted scenes of daily life on the walls of the tombs. Some of these were indoor scenes which showed an abundance of furniture. Many centuries later, when the sealed tombs were opened, examples of both the real furniture and the furniture painted on the walls were found.

In the paragraphs you have just read, the topic sentence is the first sentence. This is its usual position, and almost always its most effective one. A topic sentence at the beginning tells the reader what the paragraph is going to be about. Knowing this, the reader is able to follow the writer's idea easily. However, the topic sentence may be in any position and is sometimes the last sentence in the paragraph.

EXERCISE 2. Read the following paragraphs carefully. Decide which sentence in each paragraph is the topic sentence. Write the topic sentence on your paper after the number of the paragraph.

1

We associate masks with Halloween and fancy-dress balls, but in the past the mask has been an important prop in drama and in religious rites. Tribal priests among African tribes and shamans of Native American tribes wore masks in their medicine dances and religious rituals. Oriental actors wear masks when performing classic plays that are centuries old. The plays of ancient Greece were performed by actors wearing masks that represented gods and forces of nature or the emotions the characters were supposed to feel. Even in England, during the Elizabethan period, masks were worn by actors in a type of brief court play called "the masque."

2

The sport of archery has long been associated with tales of romance and valor. We all know the story of Robin Hood and his band of merry archers who roamed Sherwood Forest. We know too of William Tell, whose skill with a bow saved his life. Many a tale set in early England tells of picturesque and colorful archery contests. In fact, these contests were often the main events at country fairs.

3

Carrying a load of freight or a person, a camel can go for ten to sixteen days without water and can travel long distances over hot, shadeless sands. It can store as much as fifteen gallons of water in its peculiar stomach. Until the automobile and the airplane were invented, the camel was the only means people had for crossing the deserts of Asia and Africa. It is small wonder that the camel is called the "ship of the desert."

4

A penguin is able to adjust remarkably well to extremes of temperature. It can swim in icy water and then go ashore and spend days with the sun beating down on it. When it is swimming, its feathers form a shell that shuts out the cold water. Beneath this shell are several layers of fat that insulate it from the cold. When it is ashore, a penguin cools itself by fluffing its feathers. It pants and holds its flippers out from its body to release its body heat.

The Concluding, or Clincher, Sentence

At the end of a paragraph, writers will sometimes restate in different words the topic sentence they used at the beginning. A concluding sentence of this kind is sometimes called a *clincher sentence* because it clinches the point made in the paragraph.

While such a sentence may provide a helpful summary of a long and complicated paragraph, it is likely to seem tacked on in a shorter paragraph. Do not use the concluding sentence unless you think it is necessary to summarize the paragraph.

The 1970's were the years when Americans first began to realize that the quality of their life was threatened. The threat was caused by the way Americans were using and misusing the air, land, and water that make up the environment. Each year millions of tons of waste products from city sewage systems and factories were being dumped into rivers and lakes. Cities were unable to find

— topic sentence

new places to dump the growing
mountains of solid waste. In many of
the nation's urban areas, the air was
already dense with smoke from factories, apartment houses, and the ex-
haust from millions of automobiles.
The health of the American people
was in danger. Clearly, this *environ-* ⎫ concluding
mental crisis called for action.[1]   ⎭ sentence

FINDING A TOPIC

When you wish to write a composition, the first thing
you must do is find a topic. A good topic is one that is
interesting to you and one you are familiar with. If
your composition is limited to one paragraph, the
topic must be one that can be handled in 100 to 150
words.

To find a topic, make a list of all the possible subjects on which you might want to write a good paragraph. Search your mind for experiences, ideas,
information. Work rapidly. When your list seems long
enough to offer many choices, go back over it and
cross out topics that, on second thought, do not seem
suitable. The topics that remain will probably be right
for your composition.

Suppose the first ideas that came to mind were
related to the trip you took with your family during
the summer.

Your list of ideas might be:

> the time we ran out of gas
> the trip through the Everglades

[1] Slightly adapted from *America: Its People and Values,* Second Edition
Revised by Leonard C. Wood, et al, copyright © 1979 by Harcourt Brace
Jovanovich, Inc. Reprinted by permission of the publisher.

> going fishing
> eating places—good and bad

Next, perhaps, ideas about sports came to mind, and you added these to your list.

> a sport I like to watch on TV: gymnastics
> a sport I like to participate in: baseball
> a sport that is beneficial to health: running
> a sport that is fun: bowling

Next you think about some of the problems affecting people in your community, or, possibly, people everywhere.

> cost of living: rising prices, taxes, wages
> public services: roads and transportation, garbage and refuse disposal, recycling
> conservation of energy: oil and gas, coal, solar power, home consumption

If you are interested in current affairs, you could write a paragraph on the conservation of energy. Your list of ideas might look like the following:

SAVING ENERGY

> important for our nation
> shutting off lights
> writing letters to public officials
> getting involved
> helping to organize car pools
> using public transportation

As you go over your list, you may find more ideas than you can cover in a paragraph. Cross out ideas you think are too broad for your paragraph or not related to what you want to say. In the list above, "getting involved" is too broad a topic, and "important for our nation" is also too general. "Helping to organize car pools" might be a good idea for your paragraph, but since you are not sure how car pools are organized, it is best to leave this out, too. Now you have reduced your list to three ideas.

Writing a Topic Sentence

Next you need a topic sentence that will express the main idea of the paragraph. You ask yourself, "What is common to all three ideas left on my list?" Your answer may be, "They are all things a *student* can do to save energy." Your topic sentence then might be: There are three important actions that students can take to save energy.

The rest of your paragraph will mention the three ideas on your list. Here is the developed paragraph beginning with the topic sentence.

There are three important actions that students can take to save energy. At home, we can shut off lights that are not in use. Last night at home I counted four lights that were left on needlessly. I promptly turned them off. At school, we can write letters to public officials, reminding them of how important it is to conserve energy whenever possible. For example, I noticed a newspaper story last week about opening a bus lane on Center Street. We should support this idea in our letters. Finally, when we travel to the beach, to the ice rink, or to other places with friends, we should rely on public transportation, such as buses, subways, and trains.

EXERCISE 3. Read the following lists that can be developed into paragraphs. For each list write a topic sentence that you could use to start a paragraph containing the listed ideas.

A Good Loser
    does not offer excuses

praises the winner
learns from mistakes
resolves to win next time

A TV Program I Like
characters are always the same
the story usually has the main character in
trouble
the outcome is almost always happy
humor consists of the funny jokes, characters'
mannerisms, and crazy actions

How to Care for a Bicycle
chain and gears—how to adjust and lubricate
tires—how to change and inflate
brakes—how to adjust
reflectors—how and where to attach them

REVIEW EXERCISE A. Each of the following topics can be treated in a paragraph. Choose three topics from the list that interest you, list what you would say in a paragraph on each of these subjects, and then write a topic sentence for each of your choices.

1. The advantages of traveling by train (or auto-mobile or bicycle)
2. How to survive in the wilderness
3. A mistake that turned out to be lucky
4. The best (or worst) thing about television commercials
5. A dish that anyone can make
6. An argument that no one can win
7. Why you think there should (or should not) be billboards along our new roads
8. How an accidental event changed your way of thinking
9. Your favorite after-school activity
10. The best day of the week

REVIEW EXERCISE B. Using one of the topic sentences you wrote for Exercise 3, write a paragraph of about one hundred words.

DEVELOPING A TOPIC SENTENCE

The topic sentence tells what the paragraph is going to be about. Although it may be about a specific person or thing, the topic sentence usually makes a fairly general statement. It tells the reader that something is true. The rest of the sentences in the paragraph show more fully what the writer means in the topic sentence.

The other sentences in a paragraph should develop the topic sentence, making its generalized meaning clear and definite. For example, the following topic sentence states an idea that we can understand:

> The student who joins a school club can expect many benefits.

But we will understand this sentence better when we know what the specific benefits are. The sentences that follow this topic sentence should develop the idea by telling just which benefits the writer has in mind.

There are a number of different ways to develop a topic sentence. In this book, you will study three of the most important of them.

17c. A topic sentence may be developed by giving details.

If the topic sentence of a paragraph says, "Many strange things happened in the San Francisco earthquake of April 18, 1906," the reader expects some of these things to be mentioned. The other sentences in the paragraph would probably tell what particular strange things happened, thus supporting the topic sentence.

Read the following paragraph. Notice how the sentences support the one topic sentence by adding to the idea already stated.

Practically all the clothes worn by the pioneers were homemade. — topic sentence

At first the pelts of deer and other fur-bearing animals were used in making clothing. When sheep became common, wool came increasingly into use. The wool was sheared and washed, combed, spun into yarn, and dyed with coloring made from bark, berries, and leaves. Then it was woven into cloth. The process was, of course, long and laborious. — details supporting the topic sentence

Nevertheless, most of the pioneers learned to spin and to weave in order to be able to make the clothes the family would need. — concluding sentence

17d. A topic sentence may be developed by giving examples.

Examples, which are simply a kind of detail, are often useful in illustrating the point of a topic sentence. The examples given should be as specific as possible and should have a clear relation to the main idea.

As the season advances, other mysterious comings and goings take place. — topic sentence

Fish called capelin gather north of Russia in the deep, cold water of the Barents Sea. Flocks of birds such as auks, fulmars, and kittiwakes follow and prey upon their shoals. Cod gather off the shores of Norway and Iceland. Birds which in winter fed over the whole Atlantic, or the whole Pacific, make for some small island. The entire breeding population arrives there within the space of a few days. Whales suddenly appear off the coastal banks where the shrimplike krill are spawning. But where the whales came from or by what route no one knows.[1]

paragraph developed by examples

17e. A topic sentence may be developed by telling an incident.

Sometimes, a brief story, that is, an incident or an anecdote, is used to illustrate the point of the topic sentence. The incident or anecdote should be clearly related to the topic.

Bold, reckless Sir Francis Drake was the kind of man who inspires legends. His contemporaries were ready to believe almost any story about Drake. And why not? Many

topic sentence

Spaniards feared him more than any other English sea captain. He had seized Spanish treasure ships in the Caribbean and raided Spanish seaports under the very muzzles of Spanish cannon. . . . According to one of the legends, Drake was bowling on a lawn in Plymouth when news arrived that the Spanish Armada had been sighted approaching the English coast. The Royal navy, with Drake second in command, was anchored in Plymouth Harbor. It was ready to fight the battle that might decide the fate of England. Drake paused in his game, holding the bowling ball in his hand as he listened to the breathless messenger. "We have time enough to finish the game and beat the Spaniards, too," he said. Then he turned his back and sent the ball rolling down the green.

incident developing topic sentence

EXERCISE 4. Read each of the following paragraphs carefully. Find the topic sentence, and write it on your paper after the proper number. After each of the topic sentences, indicate whether the paragraph develops it by details, by examples, or by an incident.

1

A community of ants is a highly organized place. One ant in each community is the queen. Some members are hunters who go out and search for food which they bring back to the group. Other ants are herders who take care of "ant cows" (aphids) which produce milk on which the ants feed. Many of the ants are farmers: they harvest grass seed and store it in the nest; some grow "mushroom gardens" by preparing special beds of chewed leaves on which grows a fungus that is a chief item of diet for the group. There are ant warriors who own slaves: they sally out in raids on other ant groups, steal the young, and raise them to be workers. In every ant community, some ants take responsibility for the young, feeding them, cleaning them, keeping their quarters sanitary and healthful.

2

In 1675, the normal way to get from New York City to Philadelphia was on foot, and the trip took from three to five days. By 1775, horse-drawn coaches had lessened the time to two days. About sixty years later, a railroad connected the two cities; and by the twentieth century, fast planes and automobiles had been developed. Now we can cover the distance in a few minutes by jet airliner. In less than three hundred years, the ever-increasing speed of travel has completely changed our ideas of distance.

3

When we upset nature's balance in the relationship of wildlife to its surroundings, the results can be very unfortunate. Some years ago, in order to increase the number of deer in the Kaibab Forest, all the wolves and coyotes and mountain lions were killed by state hunters. As a result, the deer increased rapidly, multiplying in a fifteen-year period from four thousand to over a hundred thousand. The sick and weak deer, which the wolves and lions would have killed, survived. However, the enlarged herd was more than the range could feed. In two severe winters, sixty thousand deer starved to death. The herd kept dwindling, down to ten thousand animals. Damage did not stop there; the range had been so severely overgrazed that disastrous soil erosion occurred.

4

One of the many secrets of success can be expressed as "Try just a little harder." This lesson was driven home unforgettably to an oil driller in Texas named Conley. After a long effort to reach oil, he quit drilling on one site and moved away. Soon after, the driller of another well, close to Conley's, sank his well just one foot deeper than Conley's had gone. He struck oil and brought in a rich well. Conley never forgot the lesson. If he had drilled *just one foot deeper,* he, too, would have struck oil. Ever after, when drilling a well, he always sank the hole to the depth his experts recommended and then went one foot deeper.

EXERCISE 5. Some of the topic sentences below can be developed into paragraphs by giving details. Others can be developed by examples or incidents. Choose three suitable topics and develop one by using details, one by examples, and one by incident. You may substitute one or more topic sentences of your own.

1. Professional football is very different from college football.
2. Earning money is good experience for anyone.
3. Raising a puppy requires skill and patience.
4. Learning to fish takes practice.
5. Habits can be hard to break.
6. Training rules for athletes are very strict.
7. You cannot count on first impressions.
8. Anyone who goes to the beach on a hot summer day should take precautions against sunburn.
9. Giving a good party takes careful planning.
10. The old-time movies we see on television certainly give us a good idea of how movies have changed.

UNITY IN THE PARAGRAPH

17f. Every sentence in a paragraph should support the main idea expressed in the topic sentence.

The topic sentence of a paragraph states the topic or part of a topic that the paragraph will deal with. Every sentence in the paragraph should serve to make the meaning of the topic sentence clearer and more definite. Any sentence that strays from the idea expressed in the topic sentence, however interesting it may be in itself, breaks the train of thought and confuses the reader.

A paragraph in which all of the other sentences stick to the idea expressed in the topic sentence is said to have *unity*.

The following paragraph contains one sentence, printed in heavy type, that does not support the topic sentence. Notice that this sentence adds nothing to the subject of old and new sources of energy.

> As we use up the old sources of energy, we must develop new sources to replace them. Today the two most important sources of energy are oil and coal. Oil, however, is becoming scarce and more expensive. Coal is difficult to mine and dirty when burned. **Wood is not a practical source of energy.** To add to the problem, the demand for energy is rising as the earth's population is increasing. With the demand for energy increasing and the supply of oil and coal decreasing, the need for new sources of energy is obvious.

EXERCISE 6. All of the following paragraphs include a sentence that does not bear on the main idea and thus destroys the unity of the paragraph. Find the unnecessary sentence and copy it beside the proper number on your paper. If there is no unrelated sentence in a paragraph, write *C* beside the number.

1

Everyone uses tin cans, but few people know much about them. A tin can, first of all, has very little tin in it. The can is made of tin plate which is over 98 percent steel with only a coating of tin. A firecracker exploded under a tin can makes a satisfying roar. Coating a metal with tin is a process which has been known a long time. As long ago as 55 B.C., the early Romans coated copper vessels with tin in order to make them suitable as food containers. Today, over twenty-one billion tin cans are used to contain packed food.

2

Coal is a vital ingredient in the manufacture of steel. Over 60 percent of the 100 million tons of coal used in making steel is converted into coke. The loss of iron and steel through rusting is a great waste each year. For every ton of iron ore dumped into a blast furnace, a ton of coke must be added. The coke, burning with intense heat, melts the iron. In addition, the coke supplies the carbon which, next to the iron, is the most important element in steel.

3

Diamonds, which are a form of carbon, were formed from coal, which is basically carbon. Thousands of years ago, deep in the ground, the coal was subjected to great heat and pressure. The heat turned the carbon into a liquid, and the pressure caused it to crystallize. The carbon lost its unattractive appearance and became the most precious of stones. Industrial diamonds are made artificially.

4

America's efforts to save endangered wildlife have been successful in some cases. For example, there were only 551 bison in our country in 1889. Today there are between 25,000 and 30,000 head. Bison live by grazing on grassy plains. Recently the whooping crane has also been saved from extinction. In 1940 there were fewer than 15 whooping cranes left alive. By 1980, through painstaking conservation efforts, nearly 120 of these majestic birds were nesting on Texas' Gulf Coast.

COHERENCE IN PARAGRAPHS

In addition to sticking to the point, the sentences in a paragraph should flow smoothly and naturally from one to the next. When they do, the paragraph is said to have *coherence*. The ideas in a coherent paragraph have a clear and logical relation to each other.

In many paragraphs, coherence can be achieved by simply putting the details or examples or incidents in the paragraph in a logical order. A paragraph about baking a cake will tell how to mix the batter before it says anything about putting the cake pan in the oven. Sometimes, however, you will need to give the reader a clue to the way in which one sentence is related to another or to the topic sentence.

Within paragraphs in this part of the chapter, you will study first the ordering of details and then some of the ways of helping the reader follow your train of thought.

Organizing Details

The natural way of telling a story is to give the events in the order they happened. This way of organizing information is called *chronological* — the order of time. Chronological order is useful in other kinds of writing as well as narratives. For example, the paragraph below explains how to make a simple electromagnet by taking each step in chronological order.

A simple electromagnet can be made by wrapping insulated wire around a spool, then sticking a long spike or bolt up through the hole. When the ends of the wire are attached to the poles of a battery and a current is sent through the coils around the spool, the spike inside the spool is made magnetic. It loses its magnetism, however, as soon as the current is stopped.

Just as it is natural to take up events in the order they happen, it is natural to describe objects by their position in relation to one another. In the following example the position of the things the writer sees is shown by the words or phrases in heavy type.

A man stood **upon** a railroad bridge in northern Alabama, looking **down** into the swift water twenty feet **below.** The man's hands were **behind** his back, the wrists bound with cord. A rope closely encircled his neck. It was attached to a stout cross timber **above** his head and the slack fell **to the level** of his knees. Some loose boards . . . supplied a footing for him and his executioners —two private soldiers of the Federal army, directed by a sergeant who in civil life may have been a deputy sheriff. **Upon** the same temporary platform was an officer in the uniform of his rank, armed. He was a captain. A sentinel **at each end** of the bridge stood with his rifle in the position known as "support" . . . .[1]

A paragraph that deals with ideas that do not involve time or position requires a different kind of order. In such a paragraph, the details or examples may be organized in order of their importance. The order may be from least to most important or the other way

---

[1] From "An Occurrence at Owl Creek Bridge" by Ambrose Bierce.

around. Either method, if followed consistently, should result in an understandable arrangement.

Student self-government has many benefits for young people. Students are more likely to follow rules they have made themselves than rules handed down to them by adults. Penalties devised by students are likely to fit the crime, and students generally accept such punishments as fair and deserved. Students are likely to obey regulations that the students themselves have made. But most important of all, the experience that students gain in making and enforcing their own rules will help them to understand and appreciate the need for laws in any society.

EXERCISE 7. Each of the following topics can be treated in a single paragraph. Number your paper 1–10 and indicate which kind of order—chronological order, spatial order, or order of importance—you would use in developing each topic.

1. The life cycle of an insect
2. The advantages of learning to dance
3. The arrangement of a room in your house
4. How a basketball court is laid out
5. The best method of artificial respiration
6. Your reasons for belonging to the Boy Scouts, the Girl Scouts, or some other organization
7. The duties of a cheerleader
8. The preparation of a favorite dish
9. The view from a tall building
10. Reasons for fighting pollution

EXERCISE 8. Choose one of the topics from Exercise 7 that you think should be developed chronologically, and write a paragraph using this kind of order.

EXERCISE 9. Choose one of the topics in Exercise 7 that you think should be developed by order of importance, and write the paragraph.

Connecting Sentences Within Paragraphs

In a good paragraph the thought flows easily from one sentence to the next. Putting your ideas in an understandable order will help the readers follow your thinking, but you can help them still more by giving some thought to the relation between your sentences. If you are developing your paragraph in chronological order, try to use such expressions as *first, meanwhile, later, afterward, finally,* etc. Paragraphs organized spatially are likely to need expressions like *next to, in front of, beside, between,* and *behind.* Words like these, which help to make the organization of the paragraph clear to the readers are called *transitional expressions.*

Still other transitional expressions show the relationship between ideas. Some of these, like *and, but,* and *or,* are used mainly within sentences; others are used to link the idea of one sentence with the one that precedes or follows. Some examples are *however, furthermore, as a result, in fact, yet,* and *therefore.*

The transitional expressions in the following paragraph are printed with underscores. Notice how they help readers grasp the relation of the supporting sentences to each other and to the topic sentence.

The National Park Service does a big and important job. It is the government agency that operates our National Parks. Our first National Park was Yellowstone National Park, |— topic sentence which was established in Wyoming, Idaho, and Montana in 1872. However, the National Park Service was not created until 1916. It was established to bring together under one bureau work that had been done by a number of different government agencies. According to Congress, the Service's job is to "conserve natural and historic objects in such manner as will leave them unimpaired for future generations." The National Park Service administers parks, monuments, historic sites, and recreational spots in 300 areas in all parts of the United States. Many of the parks include spectacular scenery, such as the Grand Canyon in Arizona, or Lassen Peak, an active volcano. In addition to protecting and preserving the natural and historic objects, the Service must provide for the comfort and safety of the millions of visitors who come to the parks every year. As a result, it operates hotels, cabins, campgrounds, parkways, and trails. It also collects and sends out information about our hundreds of parks. Anyone who has visited any of our National Parks understands the importance of the National Park Service.

transitional expressions

concluding sentence

EXERCISE 10. Transitional expressions have been omitted in the following paragraph. For each blank, choose an appropriate transitional expression from the list below, and write it beside the proper number on your paper. You may use some of the transitional expressions more than once if you need to. You will not need all of them.

actually	then
after a short while	nevertheless
after that	therefore
first	meanwhile

The old-time beekeeper had a clever way of locating a cluster of wild bees. Equipped with a small wooden box that had a sliding cover, he would go to a meadow. __1__, he would find a bee in a flower and capture it in his box. __2__, he would pull back the cover and release the bee. __3__, since he knew that the pollen-laden insect would make a "beeline" to the tree where the wild bees were clustered, he would carefully note the direction of the flight. He would __4__ move to the other side of the meadow, capture another bee, release it, and note the direction in which it flew. He knew that both bees had headed home by the most direct route. __5__, he knew that the cluster of bees must be located at the point where his imaginary lines crossed. __6__, it was easy to capture the swarm in a large net and move it to his own orchard. __7__, the beekeeper was simply using mathematics.

REVIEW EXERCISE C. Choose one of the topics below, decide what you would like to write about it, make a list of ideas, make up a topic sentence, and then develop it in an interesting paragraph. Underline the topic sentence and any transitional expressions you use.

1. A favorite program (radio, TV, disc jockey, singer, band, etc.)

2. Someone I admire
3. A great performance (athletic, stage, movie, etc.)
4. How school is different this year from last year
5. A needed reform
6. An experience with bad weather
7. Why it's important to keep a secret
8. An unusual relative
9. How to stay healthy
10. The one store I like to visit often
11. The job I dislike the most
12. What I would tell the President
13. A shop project (crafts, art, etc.)
14. A disaster
15. Rules in my home
16. The hiding place no one knows
17. Why safety comes first
18. Foods I can't eat (don't like)
19. Another school I attended
20. Why I believe (or do not believe) in luck

TYPES OF PARAGRAPHS

The Narrative Paragraph

A narrative is a story. A narrative paragraph is a paragraph that tells a story.

Usually a narrative paragraph is structured like any other kind of paragraph. It begins with an introductory sentence—like a topic sentence—and then clarifies this opening sentence by telling a story.

The following paragraph is a narrative paragraph. As you read it, notice how the story supports, or clarifies, the opening sentence.

Monk and Glennie were playing catch on the side lawn of the firehouse when Scho caught sight of them. They were good at it, for seventh-graders, as anyone could see right away. Monk, wearing a catcher's mitt, would lean easily sidewise and back, with one leg lifted and his throwing hand almost down to the grass, and then lob the white ball straight up into the sunlight. Glennie would shield his eyes with his left hand and, just as the ball fell past him, snag it with a little dart of his glove. Then he would burn the ball straight toward Monk, and it would spank into the round mitt and sit, like a still-life apple on a plate, until Monk flipped it over into his right hand and, with a negligent flick of his hanging arm, gave Glennie a fast grounder.[1]

When you write a narrative paragraph, you tell what happened in the order in which it happened. This is chronological, or time, order. It is not the only way a story may be told, but it is the usual way, especially in the narrative paragraph.

EXERCISE 11.   Each of the following sentences could be the introductory sentence of a narrative paragraph. Select one and use it as the introductory sentence. Then write the rest of a narrative paragraph. Or make up an introductory sentence of your own and use it as the opening sentence of a narrative paragraph.

1. I had a hard time training my dog, Major.
2. My father (or mother) once had to admit to being wrong.
3. Sometimes it is better to take a chance than to do nothing.
4. When I was ten, I learned some ways to save money.
5. One afternoon I found out which was the safer of the two routes I could follow on my way home from school.
6. The surest way to make friends is to be friendly.

[1] From "A Game of Catch" by Richard Wilbur. © 1953 The New Yorker Magazine, Inc. Reprinted by permission of the publisher.

7. We have more fun at the farm than anywhere else.
8. I learned the importance of the motto, "Be Prepared."
9. You learn more from failure than from success.
10. Being late to school isn't always your own fault.

The Descriptive Paragraph

When you describe something, you draw a picture of it in words. A descriptive paragraph is a paragraph that describes something. Like most paragraphs, a descriptive paragraph usually begins with an introductory sentence. This sentence announces what the paragraph is going to describe.

In the following one-paragraph description of a place, the introductory sentence tells us that the author is remembering a favorite childhood scene, a store. Notice how the many details in this description contribute to a vivid picture of the scene being remembered.

Until I was thirteen and left Arkansas for good, the Store was my favorite place to be. Alone and empty in the mornings, it looked like an unopened present from a stranger. Opening the front doors was pulling the ribbon off the unexpected gift. The light would come in softly (we faced north), easing itself over the shelves of mackerel, salmon, tobacco, thread. It fell flat on the big vat of lard and by noontime during the summer the grease had softened to a thick soup. Whenever I walked into the Store in the afternoon, I sensed that it was tired. I alone could hear the slow pulse of its job half done. But just before bedtime, after numerous people had walked in and out, had argued over their bills, or joked about their neighbors, or just dropped in "to give Sister Henderson a 'Hi y'all,'" the promise of magic mornings returned to the Store and spread itself over the family in washed life waves.[1]

The following paragraph describes a person. The details support the introductory sentence, which tells us the man was English-looking.

He was just about the most English-looking man I had ever seen. Long, humorous, strong-jawed face. Small, clipped moustache, untidy, sandy hair. He was wearing an old tweed jacket and shapeless flannel trousers. The collar of his check shirt was frayed and the tie carelessly knotted. He looked as though he didn't spend much time in front of a mirror.[2]

EXERCISE 12. Search your memory for an event, a place, or a person you could describe vividly in a descriptive paragraph. A review of "Writing Descriptions" on pages 293–302 will help you. Write a descriptive paragraph of approximately one hundred words.

The Expository Paragraph

An expository paragraph gives information about something or explains something, or it may do both. The following expository paragraph gives information about two kinds of falcon, the peregrine and the kestrel. Like most informational paragraphs, it is developed by facts.

---

[1] From *I Know Why the Caged Bird Sings* by Maya Angelou. Copyright © 1969 by Maya Angelou. Reprinted by permission of Random House, Inc.
[2] From *All Creatures Great and Small* by James Herriot, copyright © 1972 by James Herriot. Reprinted by permission of St. Martin's Press, Inc. and Harold Ober Associates, Inc.

No bird in the world is better equipped for pursuit than the peregrine falcon, bulletheaded, broad in the shoulder and tapering to the tail, a powerful, perfectly streamlined machine whose pointed wings are capable of putting it into a power dive estimated to reach 175 miles per hour. But the peregrine is effective only in open terrain; for this reason falconry as a sport has never caught on in wooded eastern North America as it has on the moorlands of north England and Scotland. Most falcons are strong fliers of the open country, although some of the smaller ones, the kestrels, are more like helicopters, hovering for mice, grasshoppers, and other petty prey.[1]

The following expository paragraph *explains* why you cannot breathe when you are swallowing.

You are not able to breathe when you swallow because your breathing system is closely linked to your nourishing system. In fact, both the air you breathe and the food you eat travel down the pharynx, a wide muscular tube situated behind the nose and mouth. The air must reach the larynx or "voice box" on its way to the lungs, while the food has to go by way of the gullet and stomach. Obviously, some kind of device must be used to prevent the two from becoming mixed up. Swallowing temporarily interrupts breathing by closing the air passages while food is propelled from the mouth to the gullet and stomach. If a particle of food goes the wrong way, the lungs respond immediately by trying to expel the food with a cough.[2]

[1] From *The Birds* by Roger Tory Peterson and the Editors of Time Life Books. © 1963, 1968 Time Inc. Reprinted by permission of Life Nature Library.

[2] From *1000 Questions and Answers* by Elizabeth Hardy, published by Octopus Books Limited. Reprinted by permission of the publisher.

EXERCISE 13. The following list is intended to suggest subjects about which you can write an expository paragraph. Your purpose will be to give information or to explain, or to do both. Select a subject or make up one of your own and write an expository paragraph about it.

1. How something works (a pump, refrigerator, sewing machine, camera)
2. How a game is played (soccer, parcheesi, checkers)
3. How to build something (skateboard, kite, puppet, stamp collection)
4. How to care for a pet
5. How to make friends
6. How not to make friends
7. Characteristics of a particular animal, bird, fish
8. Ways to improve your marks in school
9. Ways to earn spending money
10. Why we have different seasons

Chapter 18

The Whole Composition

**Planning and Organizing
a Longer Piece of Writing**

Much of what you learned about paragraphs in Chapter 17 applies to the composition as a whole. The paragraph consists of sentences closely related in meaning; the composition is made up of related paragraphs. Like the paragraph, the composition focuses on a single idea, which is often stated near the beginning.

Because compositions consist of a number of paragraphs, it stands to reason that the topic must be bigger or more fully treated than that of a paragraph. Usually the composition deals with an idea that has several parts, each of which can be discussed in a separate paragraph. For example, a composition comparing winter sports with summer sports may have two paragraphs, one dealing with each kind. Similarly, a composition on carelessness as a cause of accidents may have one paragraph on accidents in the home, another on accidents on the highway, another on boating accidents, and so on. Often the composition has a short introductory paragraph stating the topic. It may also have a short concluding paragraph that sums up what has been said in the same way as the concluding sentence does for the content of a paragraph.

CHOOSING A TOPIC

Although the topic of a composition will usually be broader than that of a paragraph, it should not be too broad. A composition of the kind you will be writing this year is still a short piece of writing. Avoid choosing a topic so large that you would have to write a book to do it justice.

18a. Choose a subject that you know something about.

Knowing your subject is the first principle of good writing. It is easy to make general statements like, "Life as we know it cannot exist on the planet Mars." You have to know something about the subject to provide the supporting details. General statements are useful to introduce or sum up a number of specific statements, but the specific statements, the details, have to be there. It is the details that really inform your reader, and knowing details means knowing your subject.

(1) You may choose a topic from your own experience.

The subjects you know best are to be found in your everyday life—in your interests and hobbies, your experience with friends and family, your memories of places you have seen and things you have done. Perhaps you can build and fly model airplanes or design a dress or make hand puppets. Perhaps you know how to shoot a basketball, ride a surfboard, or paint a lifelike picture. Whatever your interests happen to be, they are bound to provide you with material you can handle successfully in compositions.

(2) You may choose a topic from other sources.

Naturally there are many things that you come to know about at second hand. Possibly, through reading a magazine article, you have become interested in space travel, the War Between the States, or a famous person from history. If so, you may have followed up your original interest by reading other articles and books or watching television programs on your subject. Information that you collect in this way becomes part of your experience, too.

EXERCISE 1. The following topics are intended to suggest things that you might write about. Some of them you may know about from personal experience; others you may have read about. Choose one topic of each kind and write only the title that you would use for a composition on this subject. Indicate after each title whether you know about the topic mainly from personal experience or from other sources. You may substitute similar topics of your own if none of these suggestions fit your interests. Consider your choices carefully, for you will later be asked to write a composition on one of them.

1. How an animal trains its young
2. Breaking a bad habit
3. Careers in medicine (or science or teaching or journalism)
4. A promising new source of energy
5. Your reasons for admiring a famous person
6. How to preserve fruits and vegetables
7. Houses (or apartments) I have lived in
8. Making friends in a new school (or in a new neighborhood)
9. Shopping at a general store (or a supermarket)
10. An invention that changed history

18b. Limit the topic.

Once you have found a subject to write about, you must decide whether it is too big to handle in the time and space you have to work with. Big subjects are *not* easier to write about than smaller ones. The bigger the subject, the more detailed knowledge you will have to include in your composition. A composition on "The War Between the States" would have to be book length to cover the subject; on the other hand, one on the importance of the Battle of Gettysburg could be managed in a reasonable amount of space.

EXERCISE 2. Each of the following topics is too broad to be covered in a short composition. Choose five, and find for each a more limited topic. Write the narrower topic beside the proper number on your paper.

EXAMPLE   1. Careers in medicine
                1. *The duties of a doctor*

1. Pets
2. Earning money during vacation
3. Clothes
4. Sports
5. Automobiles
6. Music
7. Courtesy
8. Conservation
9. Science
10. Television programs

18c. Determine the purpose of your composition.

In limiting your topic, you must consider the purpose of your composition. Taking a particular attitude toward your subject will help you define that purpose. The topic "Television" is too big. However, the narrower topic "My favorite television program" does indicate a purpose — to explain why a particular program is your favorite. If your purpose is to show how much can be learned from certain programs, your topic might be "The educational benefits of television." Another topic, "The dangers of watching too much television," indicates a third purpose and still another way of limiting your topic.

EXERCISE 3. Choose three of the topics you wrote for Exercise 2. State what your purpose would be if you were to write a composition on each of these topics. You may revise your topics if you wish.

EXAMPLE	*Original topic*	*Sports*
	Narrowed topic	*How to be a guard in basketball*
	Purpose	*To explain what skills a guard needs and how to develop these skills.*

EXERCISE 4. Write a composition of about two hundred words on one of the two topics you chose for Exercise 1. At the top of your paper, state the purpose of your composition. Be sure that all the details support this purpose.

PLANNING THE COMPOSITION

18d. Plan your composition before writing.

A clear, well-organized composition always has a plan behind it. The best kind of plan is an outline, like the one on page 342, which gives the main and supporting ideas in the order you will write about them. Before you reach the stage of making an outline, however, you must think of ideas and details to put in your composition.

(1) List your ideas.

After you have chosen a topic, make a list of the ideas that seem to fit within the topic. Do not worry at this point about organizing your ideas. Jot them down as they come to you.

Title of Composition: Training a Dog
Purpose: To show how a dog may be trained to respond to simple commands

what obedience training is	repetition of command
need for firmness	some obedience com-
need of praise	mands — sit, lie down,
a dog's desire to please	heel
using the words of com-	a dog's intelligence
mand	give one command at a
	time

(2) Group your ideas under headings.

Now you are ready to decide what the larger divisions of your composition will be. Find the ideas that belong together and group them under a common heading. Sometimes this heading will be one of the ideas you have already jotted down. At other times you will have to supply the heading. For example, in the list for "Training a Dog," two ideas, *a dog's desire to please* and *a dog's intelligence,* seem to belong together. What larger idea do they share in common? Since both intelligence and the desire to please are qualities that make a dog easy to train, these ideas can be grouped under *qualities needed for training.* Similarly *what obedience training is* and *some obedience commands — sit, lie down, heel —* can be grouped under a larger idea, *obedience training.*

The complete list of notes can be grouped as follows:

Qualities needed for training   heading
    desire to please ⎱ related
    intelligence ⎰ ideas

Obedience training   heading
    what obedience training is
    obedience commands — sit,   related
      lie down, heel   ideas

Some rules for training   heading
    praise as an incentive
    firmness
    repetition of command   related
    one command at a time   ideas
    using words of command

EXERCISE 5. The ideas for each of the following topics should be grouped under two major headings. First write the topic as a title. Then write the two headings and the ideas that belong under each of them. In topics 1, 2, and 3 the major headings are included in the list of ideas. You supply the headings for topics 4 and 5.

EXAMPLE   1. How to build a signal fire: choose location; pick dry wood for start; look for high ground; find clear space; choose green wood to make smoke; build fire to make visible signal.

1. *How to Build a Signal Fire*
   I. *Choose location*
      look for high ground
      find clear space
   II. *Build fire to make visible signal*
      pick dry wood for start
      choose green wood to make smoke

1. Autumn activities: Halloween party; sports; school dance; football; social activities; hiking
2. How to fry an egg: procedure; pan; pancake turner; grease; equipment and materials; egg; heat grease in pan; add egg and cook
3. How to find a book: card catalogue; sources of information; asking librarian; biography shelved by subject's name; system of placing books on shelves; fiction by author's name
4. Our drama club: getting members; casting a play; electing officers; rehearsing; performing the play; writing the club constitution; choosing a play
5. Description of my cat: lying by fire; pouncing; playing; sleeping; running smoothly

(3) Arrange your ideas.

The final step in planning a composition is to arrange your ideas in the order they will appear in your composition.

Outlining

18e. Make an outline for a composition.

An outline is a guide to your subject which not only shows your ideas in their correct order but also indicates their relative importance. Here is the form of a typical outline:

I. First main idea
   A. Supporting idea
   B. Supporting idea

II. Second main idea
   A. Supporting idea
   B. Supporting idea
   C. Supporting idea
      1. Supporting detail
      2. Detail
      3. Detail

III. Third main idea
   A. Supporting idea
   B. Supporting idea

Notice that Roman numerals precede the main headings, followed by capital letters and Arabic numerals for subtopics. Notice that each level of the outline is indented.

Notice too that there are at least two subtopics for each major heading. Subtopics are divisions of a more important topic. It is impossible to divide a piece of land, a cake, or a topic into less than two parts. A correct outline will not show

I. Main idea
   A. Supporting idea [There should be at least two supporting ideas here.]
II. Main idea

The order in which you arrange the ideas in your outline will depend on your subject. Sometimes you will arrange them in chronological order or in order of importance. Often the ideas themselves will suggest the proper order. For example, these ideas obviously should follow the order of time: *the beginning of our trip, incidents during our trip, the end of our trip.*

How can the main ideas for the composition "Training a Dog" be arranged? One idea, *Obedience training,* is clearly more specific than the others, since it involves specific commands. Furthermore, *Qualities needed for training* is the most general idea and should probably be discussed first. Thus the main ideas would be arranged in the order of general to specific:

I. Qualities needed for training
II. Some rules for training
III. Obedience training

Now the supporting ideas should be arranged with some indication of their relative importance. Notice, for example, that the specific commands, *heel, sit, lie down,* are really developments of the idea *Obedience commands,* and should be treated as details under this idea.

Notice in the sample outline which follows that a fourth main idea has been added to provide a conclusion to the composition. The role of a conclusion will be discussed later in this chapter.

TRAINING A DOG

I. Qualities needed for training
  A. Intelligence
  B. Desire to please

II. Some rules for training
  A. Importance of firmness
  B. Teaching one command at a time
    1. Repetition of command
    2. Using words of command
  C. Praise as an incentive

III. Obedience training
  A. Definition
  B. Obedience commands
    1. Heel
    2. Sit
    3. Lie down

IV. The qualities of a good trainer

EXERCISE 6. Copy the incomplete outline at the left. Fill the blanks with the items at the right.

POLISHING SHOES

I. Materials	Small brush
A.	Wax polish
B.	Procedure
C.	Polishing cloth
D. Brushes	Applying polish evenly
1.	Rag
2.	Polishing with cloth
	Polishing brush

II.
   A. Removing loose dirt
   B.
   C. Using polishing brush
   D.

EXERCISE 7. Arrange the following ideas and details into an outline. Your outline, like the one on page 342, should have three levels.

GIVING A PARTY

Main Ideas:
      Cleaning up after the party
      Preparing for the party
      Entertaining at the party

Supporting ideas and details:
      Making a guest list
      Washing dishes
      Suggesting party games
      Cleaning the room
      Inviting guests
      Preparing refreshments
      Serving refreshments
      Making decorations

Sandwiches
Greeting guests
Ice cream
Cake
Making everyone feel at home
Soft drinks

EXERCISE 8. Prepare an outline on a subject of your own choice. If you wish, use one of the topics suggested in Exercise 1, page 335. Later you will use this outline to write a composition. Be sure your outline has the following:

a. a title
b. at least two main headings
c. supporting ideas for each main heading

The Parts of a Composition

18f. Be sure that your composition has an introduction, a body, and a conclusion.

In Chapter 16 you learned the importance of a beginning, a middle, and an ending in narratives. Similarly, other kinds of compositions need an introduction (beginning), a main discussion, or body (middle), and a conclusion (ending).

The *introduction* should state the purpose of the composition. A good way to indicate purpose is with a statement of fact. Notice that the sample composition on pages 345–47 begins, "A dog has two qualities that make it one of the easiest animals to train." This statement of fact not only leads to a discussion of these qualities but also indicates the purpose of the composition—to tell how to train a dog.

The *body* is the longest part of a composition. It contains most of the information and must fulfill the purpose you have set out to accomplish. In the sample composition that follows, the body consists of the second, third, and fourth paragraphs, corresponding to parts II and III of the sample outline.

The *conclusion* should sum up the main points of the composition. It need not be long or complicated. Notice that the conclusion of the sample composition, while discussing the qualities of a good trainer, also restates two of the basic rules for training a dog.

The composition that follows was developed from the outline on page 342. The outline topics appear in the right margin in shortened form to show the relationship of outline and finished composition.

TRAINING A DOG

A dog has two qualities that make it one of the easiest animals to train. Its intelligence helps it to learn quickly and to understand what you want. Its desire to please makes it eager to learn and obey.

introduction

qualities for train-
ing—I, A-B

Before learning about specific commands, you should know some general rules about training a dog. First, always be firm. Being firm does not mean being harsh or cruel to your dog. It means making sure your dog understands very clearly that it must obey you even if it is playful or not paying attention. Next, teach only one command at a time. Always use the same words of command, and repeat the lesson every day until your dog has learned

body

importance of
firmness—II, A

one command at
a time—II, B

it. Finally, praise your dog when it has done well. Praise is one of the greatest rewards you can give a dog, and it will help a dog to learn.

praise as incentive—II, C

The basic kind of training to give a dog is obedience training, which teaches certain simple commands. A dog that has learned obedience commands, like "heel," "sit," or "lie down" has formed the habit of obedience, and other commands will come easily to it. One of the basic commands is "heel," because it controls a dog when it is moving. To teach your dog this command, jerk its leash and give the word of command whenever it moves ahead or steps behind you. Praise your dog when it moves to the correct position. In time it will obey even when it is not on a leash. Another command, "sit," is taught by jerking the leash and pushing the dog's haunches as you give the word of command.

obedience training defined—III, A

obedience commands—III, B

1. "heel"

2. "sit"

To teach a third important command, "lie down," put your dog in a sitting position, and pull the leash almost tight. Then bring your free hand down on the leash, gently forcing the dog into the desired position as you say the command.

3. "lie down"

In training a dog, the trainer's qualities are as important as the dog's. A dog learns best from a patient, kind trainer, who is firm in giving commands and ready to reward the dog with praise.

conclusion

qualities of a good trainer — IV

18g. Revise your composition.

There are at least three things you should do before you hand your composition in. Try to follow the same procedure for each composition. Good habits of revising will be useful whenever you have writing to do.

1. Strike out words or phrases — even whole sentences — that now seem unnecessary or that you think may confuse the reader.

2. Check all the punctuation by reading the composition aloud. Remember that full pauses are likely to require periods.

3. Check the spelling of all words.

At first, planning and writing a good composition may take more time than you have previously spent on writing. But as following the steps given in this chapter grows into a habit, you will find you have become a much better writer and writing a composition has become easier.

EXERCISE 9. Write a composition based on the outline you made for Exercise 8. Perhaps you have had second thoughts about the ideas for the composition. If so, revise your outline. Your teacher may want you to hand it in with your composition. Be sure to revise your composition carefully before you hand it in.

SUMMARY

1. Choose a subject you know, either from personal experience or reading.

2. Limit your topic, and decide the purpose of your composition.

3. Jot down ideas.

4. Organize these ideas in an outline.

5. Write the first draft.

6. Revise carefully.

Chapter 19

Writing Explanations and Reports

Steps in Organizing Information

Writing explanations, reports, and book reports involves some of the same problems as writing other compositions. You must carefully choose words that will exactly convey your meaning. You must select and organize details. You must be sure that every sentence and paragraph is perfectly clear. In addition, there are some special problems. In writing an explanation, you must often divide a process into a series of steps. To write a report, you must gather information and then put the information in your own words. In a book report, you must give an accurate idea of the book's content and present solid reasons for your opinion of the book.

EXPLANATIONS

Usually, to answer the question *Who? What? When?* or *Where?* you need little time and only a few words. But to answer the question *How?* you need to explain a relationship or process. This kind of explanation requires time and thought.

19a. Write explanations which are complete, clear, and accurate.

Before you can explain something, you must be sure that you understand it yourself.

If you are going to explain how to make or do something, think of the important steps and present them in the order they must be performed. Make the order clear by using transitional words like *first, next, then,* and *finally.* Give each step simply, clearly, and briefly without leaving any gaps or omitting essential information. If you use technical terms or unfamiliar words, make their meaning clear to the reader. Be sure to mention all necessary equipment and materials.

EXAMPLE   HOW TO BUILD A CAMPFIRE

First, collect three kinds of fuel: tinder to start the fire, kindling (small pieces of wood), and larger wood. Various items will serve as tinder — shredded bark, wood shavings, clumps of dry grass, newspapers, or anything else that catches fire easily. In addition to fuel, get three wet or green logs.

Next, put two of the logs at an angle to each other with the open side facing the wind. Between the angle of the logs place the tinder, the kindling, and finally the larger wood. Set fire to the tinder. When the larger wood has caught fire, place the cooking pan on the logs where they meet. After the fire has burned a while, cover the open side of the fire with the third log.

19b. Give examples and comparisons to help convey what you mean.

When you are explaining something that is unfamiliar, complicated, or technical, help your reader to understand the explanation by giving a simple example or a comparison with something familiar. Notice in the following paragraph how a comparison makes a basic principle of health easy to understand.

> Your body is like a bank in which you deposit good food, good exercise, recreation, rest and sleep, good thinking, and good work. If these deposits are regular, you will be able to withdraw more than enough energy for work and play.[1]

In the following paragraphs, a simple example is used to explain the economic term *inflation*.

> With prices up, consumers find that their dollars buy less than they did in the past. We call this situation *inflation*.
>
> For example: Suppose last year the items the Johnsons bought on their weekly trip to the supermarket usually cost $22. This year, the same list of items costs $24. If this situation is part of a rise in price levels everywhere, we have inflation. It means that the Johnsons have to choose. If they still want to spend only $22, they will have to remove some items from their shopping list. Or, if they decide that they need all the things on their shopping list, they will have to cut some other part of their budget by $2.[2]

EXERCISE 1. Match the subjects in the first column with the examples or comparisons in the second column which would help explain the subjects.

1. The nervous system   a. A magnet

[1] From *You and Your Resources* by Paul F. Brandwein, et al. Reprinted by permission of Harcourt Brace Jovanovich, Inc.

[2] Slightly adapted from *Free Enterprise in America* by Andrew Hacker, copyright © 1977 by Harcourt Brace Jovanovich, Inc. Reprinted by permission of the publisher.

2. Your city council

3. The force of gravity

4. Fractions

5. The development of a living thing

b. Telephone lines and central switchboard

c. A tadpole becoming a frog

d. Your club passing or defeating a motion

e. Slices of a pie

A picture, the Chinese say, is worth a thousand words. Using an illustration, a map, a chart, or a diagram will often help your reader to understand your explanation.

19c. Use illustrations, maps, charts, or diagrams that might help the reader better understand what is being explained.

Review the sample explanation on page 350. Although a person following these directions can easily build a campfire, the explanation can be made still clearer by including the following illustration:

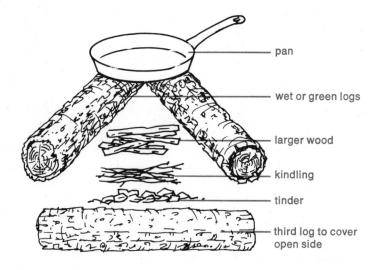

pan

wet or green logs

larger wood

kindling

tinder

third log to cover open side

EXERCISE 2. From the following list of subjects for explanations, choose five for which you could use illustrative material—illustrations, maps, charts, diagrams, and graphs. List these five subjects on your paper, along with a sentence or two indicating what illustrative material might be used.

EXAMPLE   1. *How to set a table. I would use a diagram showing the position of the plate, cup, glass, and silverware for one place setting.*

1. How to paddle a canoe
2. How to paint with water colors
3. How to find the nearest police station
4. How to repair a flat bicycle tire
5. How to set up a tent
6. How to make a batik
7. How to apply make-up
8. How to run a fast break in basketball
9. How the earth rotates on its axis
10. How to find your way by the stars

EXERCISE 3. Write an explanation of something you can do well. Present the steps in the order in which they must be performed. Be sure that your explanation is clear, complete, and accurate. Here are some suggestions:

1. How to polish a car
2. How to bake your favorite cake
3. How to make decorations for a party
4. How to ride a horse
5. How to make a box kite
6. How to tune a guitar
7. How to plant tomatoes
8. How to prepare an exhibit for a science fair
9. How to collect stamps or coins
10. How to take flash pictures with a camera

REPORTS

As you go on in school, you will be asked to write more and more reports in English, social studies, and science. Writing a report is not difficult if you go about it in a logical way and follow a few simple rules.

19d. Be sure you understand the assignment.

Obviously you cannot write a good report unless you fully understand the assignment. Listen carefully to your teacher and ask questions if you need to. Be sure you know how long your report is supposed to be and what kind of material it is to cover.

For example, if you have been asked to write a report on the kinds of trees and plants that grow in your area, you would not describe the wild animals that live there. If you did, you would be wandering from your topic.

Always try to keep in mind the purpose of your assignment. Notice that trees or plants would be discussed for all three topics listed below. However, what you would write about trees or plants would be very different for each topic:

1. Trees that grow in a wilderness area or park near your school.
2. Forest conservation programs in your state.
3. Plants grown for food in your state.

19e. Gather all the necessary information for the report.

Usually the best place to begin gathering information is the reference section of the library. An encyclopedia or other general reference work will give a good introduction to the subject and furnish many facts.

Often you will find further information in a specialized reference work. (See pages 395–401 for instructions on using reference works.)

Suppose you want to write a report on Juliette Low, who did so much to start the Girl Scouts of America. You will find a biographical sketch of her in the *World Book Encyclopedia,* in the volume marked *L.* Or, you are asked to write something about the material cork. In the same encyclopedia, in volume *C,* you will find an article on cork. If you want to write on a scientific topic such as helicopters or refrigeration, you will probably find articles on these topics by looking in a large encyclopedia or in the table of contents or index of a one-volume encyclopedia, such as the *Lincoln Library of Essential Information.*

More specialized reference works are also available. Suppose you want to get information—for a report, or for your own use—on how to play chess or anagrams or charades. You would find it in such a book as *The Complete Book of Games* by Clement Wood and Gloria Goddard.

Your teacher or school librarian will help you find the special reference book you need.

▶ **NOTE** You may also wish to use books other than reference books. Such books may be found by consulting the card catalogue in the library. See pages 391–94 for instructions in using the card catalogue.

EXERCISE 4. Choose a topic for a report which you will later write. Review the material in the previous chapter on limiting your topic. (See pages 336–37.) Be sure your topic is not too large to cover in one report.

Find information on your topic in at least three different reference works or other books. On a sheet of paper write the name of your topic. Number 1-3. After each number give the title and author (if given) of your reference work or book, the volume number (if necessary), and the number of the page on which you found your information.

If you have difficulty in thinking of a topic, here are ten suggestions. Some of these topics are too broad to cover in a short report and have to be limited to a more specific topic.

1. The Navajo Indians
2. The U.S. Virgin Islands
3. Musical instruments
4. An outstanding athlete
5. The Equal Rights Amendment
6. Contributions of minority groups
7. Solar energy
8. Nuclear submarines
9. The history of Braille
10. The Olympic Games

Taking Notes

After locating sources of information about your topic, your next step is to select facts for your report, that is, to take notes. Carefully write down each item of information that you think should be in your paper. Be careful to get your facts straight and to note the source.

When taking notes, do not copy the exact words of an encyclopedia or any other book without using quotation marks. In general, do not use quotations unless they are particularly apt or striking. A good report is written in the writer's own words, not in the words of others. Taking notes in your own words will help you avoid the bad habit of copying. A teacher can easily tell the difference between your writing and a passage from a book. Be ready to hand in a list

of your sources with your report, if your teacher requests it.

   Suppose you have chosen to write a report on gold
as a precious metal. On pages 239–43 of volume 8 of
World Book Encyclopedia, you would find information telling the reasons for gold's value, how it is
used in jewelry making and as a currency, and where
it is found in nature. You would want to take separate
notes about each of these facts. Your first note might
be:

1. Gold has great value because it is scarce. It is
   also valuable because it is beautiful, it is soft,
   and it is tarnish-resistant.

Then you would take notes about some of the other
facts you might use in your report. In volume 6 of
Compton's Pictured Encyclopedia, you would find
other useful facts about the history of gold searches
and the types of gold mining. Your final notes for the
report might look like this:

From *World Book Encyclopedia*, volume 8, pages
239–43:

1. Gold has great value because it is scarce. It is
   also valuable because it is beautiful, it is soft,
   and it is tarnish-resistant.
2. It can be beaten into thin sheets, pulled into fine
   wire, or hammered into different shapes.
3. To be hard, gold must be mixed with another,
   harder metal to form an alloy. The proportion of
   gold in an alloy is measured in karats. Pure gold
   is twenty-four karats. Eighteen-karat gold means
   that the alloy is eighteen twenty-fourths gold, or
   seventy-five percent gold.
4. Gold is found in vein deposits below the surface
   of the earth. It is also found in nuggets, called
   placer deposits, in streambeds. Gold is also present in small amounts in seawater.

5. Gold is used to make gold coins and jewelry. When it is beaten into gold leaf (thin strips), it is used for gold lettering, gilding, and dental fillings.
6. Gold was used for jewelry as early as 3500 B.C. in Mesopotamia and Egypt.
7. Spanish explorers came to Mexico and Peru in the 1500's looking for gold.
8. In 1849, people from all over the world came to California to search for gold.

From volume 6 of *Compton's Pictured Encyclopedia,* pages 149–52:

1. Despite people's search for gold, only 50,000 tons (45,000 metric tons) were produced from 1492 to 1942. This amount could make a cube 44 feet (approximately 13.5 meters) on a side.
2. Today, platinum is an even more valuable metal.
3. California was the site of the gold rush of 1849.
4. Australia's frontier attracted thousands of people after gold was found there in 1851.
5. Other places where gold was discovered include Alaska and South Africa.
6. Most of today's gold is mined in South Africa, the U.S.S.R., Canada, and the United States.

EXERCISE 5. Refer back to the three sources that you used in Exercise 4. From each source, write at least three notes about your topic. Make sure that your notes are accurate, that they are in your own words, and that they are related to your topic. They are the second stage of your report.

Organizing Your Notes

19f. Organize your information.

Now that you have gathered the information for your report in the form of notes, prepare the notes for use.

Read your notes. You will discover that some information is duplicated. You may also find that some statements do not fit into the topic as you have limited it. Your job now is to organize the information that you will use.

Ask yourself: What are the most important ideas in these notes that I have gathered? Choose only ideas related to your topic. If your topic is gold as a precious metal, it makes sense to include the reasons gold is so valuable. It does not make sense to include technical details on the mining of gold. Write a list of these main ideas. Here is a list of ideas based on the notes on gold.

1. Gold has certain properties and commercial uses that make it valuable.
2. Gold has been sought for thousands of years.
3. Gold is found below the earth's surface, in streambeds, and in seawater.

Are these ideas listed in the order that you will use them? Which idea should come first in your report? Which last? Where do the other ideas belong?

When you have arranged these ideas in a sensible, logical order, you will have a rough outline for your report. (Review pages 340–42.) Here is a rough outline for the report on gold.

GOLD

I. Sought after throughout history
II. Valued highly for its properties and its commercial uses
III. Found in nature in three different forms

EXERCISE 6. Choose the main ideas from the notes that you have taken for Exercise 5. Organize them into a rough outline like the one above. This rough outline is the third stage of your report.

After you have made your rough outline, organize the other details under your main ideas. Here is a complete outline for the report on gold.

GOLD

I. Sought after throughout history
   A. Used for jewelry and ornaments in Egypt and Mesopotamia as long ago as 3500 B.C.
   B. In the 1500's, looked for by Spanish explorers in Mexico and Peru
   C. Discovered in California in 1849 — started the gold rush and opened up the American West
   D. Found in Australia in 1851 — accelerated the settlement of the frontier
   E. Discovered in such diverse places as Alaska and South Africa

II. Valued highly for many reasons
   A. Valued for scarcity — only 50,000 tons (45,000 metric tons) produced in 1492–1942, enough to make a cube 44 feet (13.5 meters) on each side
   B. Valued for beautiful color
   C. Prized because it doesn't tarnish
   D. Valued for softness — can be worked into shapes or beaten into gold leaf
      1. Can be minted as coins
      2. As gold leaf, is used for lettering, gilding, and dental fillings
   E. Can be hardened for jewelry by being combined with other metals
      1. Pure gold called twenty-four-karat
      2. Eighteen parts gold plus six parts other metal called eighteen-karat gold

III. Found in nature in three different forms
   A. Found as vein deposits in the earth
   B. Found as nuggets, called placer deposits, that lie at the bottom of streambeds
   C. Found in minute quantities in seawater

EXERCISE 7. Using the main ideas you have written for Exercise 6 and the notes which you have written for Exercise 5, prepare an outline for your own report. (To review outlining, see pages 340–42.)

Writing the Report

By now you have chosen or been assigned a topic for your report, gathered information and made notes on your topic, and organized your notes in the form of an outline. What remains is to write the report and then to revise it.

19g. Use your own words in writing the report.

A report copied word for word from books shows you can find information but nothing more. A report in your words shows you can use the information.

It is tempting to copy a passage from a book. You may feel that the passage does a better job of organizing and conveying the information than you can do. But copying is not writing. Putting the information in your own words means that you have learned it and organized it, and perhaps even added to it, yourself. You can increase your skill in writing reports only by seeking to understand the information and striving to find the best words possible to communicate it.

EXERCISE 8. Using your outline and your notes, write a first draft of your report. Be sure the report is in your own words.

19h. Check and revise your report.

All writing assignments may contain errors, some minor and some serious. Since a report may contain errors of fact as well as writing errors, you should be especially careful in checking and revising it. A useful way of writing your report is to write a first draft, and then to check it for accuracy and improve the writing. Your last step is to write the final copy of the report.

After you have written the first draft, you are ready to improve it.

First, read it over for *content:*
   (a) Does the report cover the subject adequately?
   (b) Are all the facts accurate?
   (c) Have you included a list of sources in your report?

Next, read it over for *construction* and *style:*
   (a) Do the title and opening paragraph arouse the reader's interest?
   (b) Is there a concluding paragraph?
   (c) Is each paragraph well constructed, with a topic sentence and supporting details or examples?
   (d) Are the facts in your report well organized?
   (e) Are the sentences varied, and have you avoided fragments and run-on sentences?

Finally, check for matters of *form:*
   (a) Does the paper have a heading—name, class, and date?
   (b) Is there a title, and is it capitalized properly?
   (c) Is there a one-inch margin at the left, a slightly narrower one at the right?
   (d) Are the pages numbered? Is your name on each page?

Here is the final copy for the report on gold.

THE LURE OF GOLD

No other substance on earth has been sought after for so long and with such passion as gold. Ornaments and jewelry made from gold have been found in Egyptian tombs and Mesopotamian ruins dating back to 3500 B.C. Spanish explorers sailed across the stormy Atlantic Ocean in the 1500's, hoping to find gold treasure in Mexico and Peru. The gold rush of 1849 opened California and the American West. Australia's frontier attracted thousands of settlers after gold was found there in 1851. Such widely separated places as South Africa and Alaska have also had gold rushes.

Although people have been looking for gold for centuries, not that much has been found. If all the gold produced from 1492 to 1942 were melted into a cube, it would measure only 44 feet (13.5 meters) on a side. It is gold's scarcity, in fact, that makes it so valuable.

Other properties of gold that make it valuable are its beautiful color, its resistance to tarnishing, and its softness. Pure gold is soft enough to be worked into various shapes or can be minted as coins. It can be beaten flat into gold leaf, which is used for lettering, gilding, and dental fillings.

When gold is used in jewelry, it is usually combined with another metal to make it harder and more durable. Jewelers use the term *karat* to measure the purity of gold in a ring or other piece of jewelry. Twenty-four-karat gold is equal to one hundred percent gold. Eighteen-karat gold, the kind of gold more often used in jewelry, is equal to eighteen parts of gold and six parts of another metal.

However, finding gold at a jewelry store is easier than finding it in its natural state. In nature, gold is found in veins of ore far below the earth's surface. It is also found occasionally in nuggets, called placer deposits, that lie in streambeds. But no matter how inaccessible these gold deposits are or how difficult it is to extract the gold, people with gold fever continue to follow the lure of gold. Even today, scientists are trying to find an economical way of extracting minute particles of gold from seawater!

Sources: *Compton's Pictured Encyclopedia,* volume 6, pages 149–52.
World Book Encyclopedia, volume 8, pages 239–43.

EXERCISE 9. Prepare the final copy of your report. If your teacher wishes, hand in your outline and first draft with it.

WRITING BOOK REPORTS

A book report gives two kinds of information: what the book is about and what you thought of the book.

19i. In giving an idea of the book's content, avoid getting bogged down in details.

Many students who write a summary of a book's content begin with the first incident of the book, go on to the next incident and then the next. They soon find that they have a long, tedious account which includes every single incident in the book. A report on a book should tell only the book's highlights. It should be carefully planned.

The kind of information you give in your summary will depend on the type of book. A report on a novel should indicate the background of the story — the time, the place, and the main characters. It should also give a general idea of what happens and mention some of the chief incidents. A report on a nonfiction book should indicate the importance of the subject, according to the author, and briefly describe several parts of the book. A report on a biography should indicate why the person written about is important enough to be the subject of a biography and mention several of the chief incidents in that person's life.

19j. Give specific reasons for liking or disliking a book.

Here are two statements of opinion about a book.

> POOR   I liked this book because I am interested in the War Between the States.

BETTER   This book deals with the progress of the War Between the States—from the moment Fort Sumter was fired on, to Lee's surrender at Appomattox. Besides making the readers feel that they are present at the events, the author explains the causes of the War Between the States, shows why particular battles were won and lost, and points out why the South eventually lost the war. This book is both exciting and informative.

In your book reports, give the specific reasons behind your opinion of the book. Try also to show why others might share your opinion—why, in other words, the book may be called good or poor. These are reasons which should go beyond, "I am interested in the subject of this book"; or, "This book bored me."

Some guides for book reports are these:

1. Be sure to give the title of the book and the name of the author.

2. When you refer to the title of the book, be sure to underline it.

3. Be careful in your use of tense. In writing the summary of the book, decide on present tense or past tense and stick to it. Do not shift from present to past or past to present.

4. Refer directly to the characters by name. Do not say "this man" or "this woman."

EXERCISE 10. Write a book report. Tell briefly what the book is about. Give solid reasons for your opinion of the book.

Chapter 20

Letter Writing

Friendly Letters, Social Notes, Business Letters

Everyone likes to get letters. One of the first things that people do when they return home after a short absence is to look for mail. Telegrams and telephones are handy in emergencies and on special occasions, but for really keeping in touch with far-off friends and relatives there is nothing like a newsy letter.

How often you find a letter in your mailbox depends to a great extent on you. If you write frequent, interesting letters, you are likely to be satisfied with the mail you get in return. If, on the other hand, you are in the habit of waiting until you have more time or until something really exciting comes along to write about, the letters that come for you are likely to be few and far between. Exchanging letters is like carrying on a conversation: one person can't do it alone.

THE FRIENDLY LETTER

Have you ever felt, when you sat down to write a letter, that you didn't have much to say? Most of us feel this way at times; but it is rarely, if ever, true.

20a. In a friendly letter, write about things that interest you and the person to whom you are writing.

There are several helpful ways of deciding what to put in a letter. Think of the person to whom you are writing. *What would he or she like to hear about?* Suppose you're writing to your grandparents. Everyday happenings in the family will interest them. Has someone had a birthday? Taken a trip? Had the measles? Have you taken up a new hobby?

Another kind of material is supplied by the letter you are answering. If you were talking with a friend who told you about an interesting experience or an unusual piece of luck, you would certainly have something to say about it. If your friend writes you some interesting news, you will want to comment on it in your reply. People often ask questions in their letters about what you are doing and plan to do. The answers to such questions are still another thing to go in your letters.

EXERCISE 1. Read the letter on the following page and note the items of news that you would want to comment on if you were replying to this letter.

20b. Write friendly letters neatly on appropriate stationery.

You may use tinted paper, if you wish, but white paper of good quality is always suitable. Use a pen and write in blue or black ink. If you can use a typewriter well, it is all right to type a friendly letter.

Write neatly. A letter that is blotched with inky fingerprints, crossed-out words, spatterings, or erasures will make a bad impression on the reader.

Center a short note on the page. Keep equal margins on the sides and on the top and bottom of a long letter. If you are using folding stationery and the letter is so long that more than two pages are required, use the page order of a book; write the second page on the

59 Hobart Avenue
Summit, New Jersey 07901
January 25, 1982

Dear Tony,

Thanks for the letter and the picture of San Antonio. I envy you for having the Alamo practically in your backyard. That's a place I would really like to see.

The big news from the old neighborhood is that we finally got Dad, Mr. Blake, and some of the other fathers to play football with us yesterday morning. There were eleven of us altogether - practically six-man football. Charlie Adams was the extra player. Every time one team got behind they put him on it. You should have seen him grab those passes! You know how small he is. He would sneak right past the safety man and be in the clear before they even noticed him.

Toward the end of the game, the little kids came around and we let them play. Jimmy Nelson was one of them. I guess he's about eight. When we were all in the huddle he asked me which side I wanted to have win. "Why, our side," I told him. "Which side is that?" he asked me. With a team like that, how can you lose?

We finally won 36 to 30. The other side gave up when Charlie had to go home for dinner.

Write soon and let me know what you're doing.

Your friend,
Jack

back of the first, and so on. If you foresee that your letter will be only two pages long, leave the back of your first page blank and start a fresh sheet, or, if your stationery is folded, continue on page three.

20c. Follow generally accepted rules for the form of a friendly letter.

You have seen many letters, and you probably have a fairly clear idea of letter form. Actually, the form is not hard to master. Study the following instructions and example.

1. *Heading*

Write your address in two lines in the upper right-hand corner. Put a comma between the city and the state. Skip a few spaces after the state and write your zip code number. Do not use a comma between state and zip code number. Write the date on the third line, with a comma between the day of the month and the year. Do not use any punctuation at the ends of the lines in the heading.

2. *Salutation*

Write the salutation a short space below the heading, flush with the left-hand margin. In a friendly letter, the salutation usually begins with *Dear* ——. Put a comma after the salutation.

3. *Body*

Indent the first line of the body of the letter, and use the same indention for the first line of each paragraph that follows. Other lines should begin at the left-hand margin.

4. *Closing*

Begin the closing a little to the right of center. Capitalize the first word of the closing, and put a comma at the end. The closing of a friendly letter is usually *Sincerely, Your friend, With love,* or something similar.

5. *Signature*

Sign your first name beneath the closing, either centered (if your name is shorter than the closing) or lined up at the left with the closing. Do not put any punctuation after your name.

The letter shown on page 368 is in *block style.* That is, the second and third lines of the heading begin directly below the beginning of the first line. Another style that is often used for handwritten friendly letters is *indented style,* in which the heading looks like this:

> 1183 West Street
> Green Bay, Wisconsin 54301
> June 11, 1982

A heading in either block or indented style is appropriate for a friendly letter.

> *1183 West Street*
> *Green Bay, Wisconsin 54301*
> *June 11, 1982*
>
> *Dear Andy,*
>
>
>
>
>
>
>
>
>
>   *Sincerely yours,*
>   *Walt*

Model Form of a Friendly Letter

EXERCISE 2. Think of a friend or relative who would like to get a letter from you. With that person's interests in mind, choose several incidents from your recent experience and write a short letter about them.

THE ENVELOPE

You should address the envelope for your letter with care. Quite often letters cannot be delivered because of faulty addressing. Lack of a return address may result in your letter's being lost if your correspondent has moved. Study the following instructions and example.

Place the address of the person to whom the letter is going just below the middle and to the left of the center of the envelope. Place your own name and address in the upper left-hand corner. No title is used before your name in the return address.

John Davis
1649 Muir Drive
Port Huron, Michigan 48060

      Mr. Stephen Kinnery
      325 South Ames Street
      Marion
      Indiana 46952

A Model Envelope

Notice that the zip code number is included in the address, and is written after the state. The state may be written on a separate line, as in the example, or on the same line as the city. Every word begins with a capital. In the return address, a comma is used between city and state.

EXERCISE 3. Address an envelope for the letter you wrote in Exercise 2.

EXERCISE 4. For practice in following the correct form for friendly letters, choose one of the following situations and write the letter it suggests. If you prefer to make up a different situation to write about, you may do so.

1. Write to someone you know who is living in another country, asking for information about living conditions in whatever country the person is living. Explain that you need the information for a composition. Ask specific questions.

2. As a surprise for your parents, you planned a party for their wedding anniversary. Describe to a friend everything that happened.

3. You have just attended a movie that you know your friend will want to see. Describe it enthusiastically so that your friend will be sure not to miss it.

4. You have just completed your first baby-sitting assignment. The friend you are writing to has done some baby-sitting, too, but does not know these particular children. Describe how it went.

5. You have just moved to a different neighborhood and are writing about it to a friend who still lives in your old neighborhood. Describe what you like or don't like about your new surroundings.

6. You have just been to see an important baseball (or football or hockey) game. Both you and the friend you are writing to are fans of the same team. Describe what happened.

7. You have just taken an after-school job. Write to a friend urging your friend to get a similar job or not to, depending upon your experiences.

8. You have just transferred to a new school and are writing about it to a friend who still attends your old school. Tell what you like or don't like about your new surroundings.

9. You are giving your dog a course in obedience training. Write to a friend or relative reporting on your progress. (Use information from the explanation on pages 345–47, if you wish.)

10. You want to set up a darkroom to develop your own photographs. The friend to whom you are writing already has one. Ask your friend what you will have to buy, how much you will have to spend, and generally how to go about it.

THE SOCIAL NOTE

20d. Social notes are short letters, such as invitations and thank-you notes, written to meet certain social demands.

Everyone has occasion to write social notes now and then, and you should learn to do it properly. The social note has the same form as a friendly letter.

The Thank-You Note

The form of a letter of thanks is the same as that of a friendly letter. Such a letter should be written on personal stationery. The purpose of a letter of thanks is, of course, to show the person who will receive it that you really appreciate the kindness shown to you. However, it will seem less like a duty letter if you say a word about something else as well. Write a thank-you letter as soon as possible after you have received a gift or a favor.

5455 South Blackstone Street
Chicago, Illinois 60615
March 20, 1982

Dear Aunt Jane,

Thank you ever so much for the beautiful blouse you sent on my birthday. It is exactly the right size and the color goes perfectly with the blue skirt Mother made for me.

Maybe I'm getting too old for birthday parties, but when Mother asked me if I'd like to have some of my friends over, I was all for it. I had four for a pajama party Saturday night. I slept all Sunday afternoon!

For my birthday, Daddy gave me plane fare for a trip to Cleveland to visit Ginnie Taylor during Spring vacation. I can hardly wait!

Love,
Linda

A Thank-You Note

EXERCISE 5. Write a letter of thanks for an actual gift or favor you have received. Or, if you prefer, select one of the following situations as the occasion for a letter, and write the letter.

1. You have been ill for two weeks and will not be able to return to school for another two weeks. Your class has sent you a get-well card and a gift. You want to thank them.

2. A friend who lives in another city has sent you a special stamp for your collection.
3. A relative visiting Arizona has sent you pictures of the Grand Canyon.
4. A relative whom you have not seen for some time remembers your birthday and sends you a present.

The Bread-and-Butter Note

If you have spent a weekend at the home of a friend, or if you have paid a longer visit to friends or relatives, you should write a letter of thanks to your hosts as soon as you return. If you were visiting someone of your own age, the letter should be addressed to your friend's parents. Such a letter is called a "bread-and-butter" note. It is important for you to show the family that you enjoyed your stay with them and that you appreciate their kindness and generosity.

The form of the "bread-and-butter" note is the same as that for any friendly letter.

EXERCISE 6. If you have visited someone recently, write a bread-and-butter note expressing your thanks for the hospitality you received. Or, if you prefer, imagine that you were in one of the following situations, and write a bread-and-butter note.

1. You have spent a month of your summer vacation on your uncle's ranch.
2. You have stayed for the weekend with your best friend, who lives on the other side of the city. There was a party Saturday night.
3. Your grandmother has taken you on a three-day sightseeing trip to a nearby city.
4. You and your family have visited your aunt and uncle and their family at their summer camp. Their family includes two cousins, Bob and Joan, about your age.

532 Fifth Street Southeast
Minneapolis, Minnesota 55414
July 15, 1982

Dear Mr. and Mrs. Berman,

Everyone is getting tired of hearing me talk about my big weekend at your farm. Jack and I had so much fun. I can't stop talking about it - the swimming and riding, how I didn't learn to milk a cow, the trip to town on Saturday, and your wonderful meals. Mom says I have been spoiled rotten.

I appreciate all the things both of you did to give me a good time. Tell Jack I will write to him soon.

Sincerely,
Al

A "Bread-and-Butter" Note

THE BUSINESS LETTER

Many of the letters which you and members of your family write are not letters to friends or relatives but are business letters: letters ordering goods, asking for information, applying for jobs or entrance into schools, and so on. Such letters are important in our daily life, and they should be correctly written.

20e. Follow generally accepted rules for the form of a business letter.

Use suitable stationery. White paper is appropriate. Write your business letter on a typewriter if you type well. If not, write it in pen and ink. Make your letter look attractive by centering it properly on the page. You will have to figure out in advance how much room you need, and you cannot always make the lines come out exactly right; nevertheless, try to get even margins all around. Keep the letter neat by avoiding erasures, messy blotting, or splotching. Keep your letter brief. If your letter is too long for one page, do not write on the back but continue on a second page. Try to carry over at least three lines onto the second page. Begin them two inches down from the top.

Business letters should be polite and very clear. When writing an order for merchandise, for example, it is important to give full and exact information. Otherwise, exasperating mistakes and delays may result.

The form of a business letter is slightly different from that of a friendly letter. Study the model and explanation on the pages that follow.

1. *Heading*
Write a complete heading: street address on the first line; city, state, and zip code on the second line, with a comma between the city and state; date on the third line, with a comma between the day and the year.

2. *Inside Address*
Unlike a friendly letter, a business letter has an inside address placed a short space below the heading, beginning at the left margin. Give the name of the person or firm, or both, to whom you are writing. Give the address, with a comma between city and state and

1811 Kindy Avenue
1   Covington, Kentucky 41012
May 11, 1982

H. C. Laurel Hardware Company
2   160 North Main Street
Memphis, Tennessee 38103

3 Mail Order Department:

    In the Memphis Press-Scimitar for Monday,
May 10, you advertise a woodcarving set for
4   $4.98, postpaid. Please send me this item.

    I am enclosing a money order for $4.98.

5   Very truly yours,

6   *John J. Mack*

     John J. Mack

A Model Business Letter

about one-quarter inch space between state and zip code number.

The reason for the inside address on a business letter is that in a business office where carbon copies of all letters are filed, it must be clearly indicated on each letter to whom it was addressed. A letter which had only the salutation "Dear Mr. Smith" would not make this clear. You may not keep a file of the few business letters you write; nevertheless, you should follow the regular form used everywhere.

3. *Salutation*

Place the salutation two typewriter spaces (one-quarter inch) below the inside address, flush with the left-hand margin. Follow it with a colon. If you are writing to a firm rather than to an individual, you may use an impersonal salutation (*Customer Service:, Editors:*) or the traditional salutation (*Gentlemen:*). It is understood that the group you are writing to may be composed of both men and women. If you are writing to an individual whose name you do not know, the proper salutation is *Dear Sir* or *Dear Madam.* If you are writing to an individual whose name you do know, the salutation should be *Dear Mr. ——, Dear Miss ——, Dear Mrs. ——,* or *Dear Ms. ——. Ms.* may be used when writing to a woman who does not use *Mrs.* or *Miss* in her typed signature. It is also acceptable to address a person you do not know by using both first and last names: *Dear Henry Walker, Dear Susan Farrell.*

4. *Body*

The first line of the body of a business letter begins two spaces below the salutation. It may be indented five typewriter spaces (one inch in handwriting) from the left-hand margin. The first line of all succeeding paragraphs should be indented the same distance.

5. *Closing*

The standard form for the closing of a business letter is *Yours truly* or *Very truly yours.* The first word is capitalized. The closing should begin just to the right of the middle of the page and should be followed by a comma.

6. *Signature*

The signature should be placed below the closing and flush with it. Sign your first and last names. If you have typed the letter, type your name several spaces below the closing, and then write your name in ink between the closing and your typed signature. Do not put a title (Mr., Miss, etc.) before your handwritten signature.

The way you fold a business letter depends on the size of the paper and the envelope. If the sheet is the same width as the envelope, fold it up from the bottom and down from the top, as shown in the first three steps of the illustration. If the sheet is wider than the

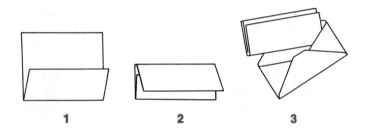

envelope, follow the steps pictured below. Fold the paper up from the bottom almost to the top of the sheet. Then fold the right side over a third of the way; fold the left side over that. Always put the folded edge of the letter into the envelope first.

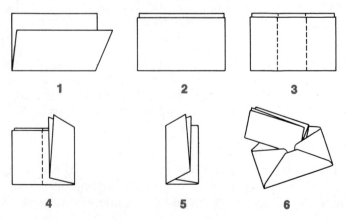

You may have occasion to write business letters requesting information or correcting a mistake, as well as letters ordering merchandise. No matter what the purpose of your business letter, make sure you meet these requirements:

1. *Be clear.* State exactly what you want or whatever information you intend to convey. Tell the reader as much as you feel necessary to convey the situation.

2. *Be brief.* Do not put any unnecessary information in your letter, and do not write it in a rambling, wordy style. Be as concise as possible. However, do not leave out any important details; if you do, the reader of your letter will not be able to fulfill your request promptly.

3. *Be courteous.* Your letter will make a better impression if its tone is polite and reasonable. If you must make a complaint in a letter, do so courteously.

The block style is preferred for a business letter; the indented style is not usually used. The envelope for a business letter is addressed the same as that for a friendly letter. The inside address in the letter should be identical with the address on the envelope.

▶ **NOTE** The United States Postal Service recommends the use of two-letter codes for states, the District of Columbia, and Puerto Rico. The Service also recommends the use of nine-digit zip codes. When you use these codes, the address should look like this:

EXAMPLE Ms. Dorothy Brooke
206 Greenside Ave.
San Francisco, CA 94116-1412

The two-letter code is never followed by a period. The following is a list of two-letter codes for states, the District of Columbia, and Puerto Rico.

Alabama   AL
Alaska   AK
Arizona   AZ
Arkansas   AR
California   CA
Colorado   CO
Connecticut   CT
Delaware   DE
District of Columbia   DC
Florida   FL
Georgia   GA
Hawaii   HI
Idaho   ID
Illinois   IL
Indiana   IN
Iowa   IA
Kansas   KS
Kentucky   KY
Louisiana   LA
Maine   ME
Maryland   MD
Massachusetts   MA
Michigan   MI
Minnesota   MN
Mississippi   MS
Missouri   MO

Montana   MT
Nebraska   NE
Nevada   NV
New Hampshire   NH
New Jersey   NJ
New Mexico   NM
New York   NY
North Carolina   NC
North Dakota   ND
Ohio   OH
Oklahoma   OK
Oregon   OR
Pennsylvania   PA
Puerto Rico   PR
Rhode Island   RI
South Carolina   SC
South Dakota   SD
Tennessee   TN
Texas   TX
Utah   UT
Vermont   VT
Virginia   VA
Washington   WA
West Virginia   WV
Wisconsin   WI
Wyoming   WY

EXERCISE 7.   Write a short business letter to Camper's Camp, 3412 Mahan St., Baton Rouge, Louisiana 70806. Ask what camping lanterns are available, how they are operated, and how much they cost. Be sure that the letter form is correct.

EXERCISE 8.   Bring to school an advertisement of an item you would like to own. Write a business letter ordering this item.

CHECKLIST

Friendly letters and social notes

1. Include your address and the date in the heading.
2. Place a comma after the salutation.
3. Include news the other person would like to know or find interesting. Answer any questions that may have been asked in your friend's last letter.
4. Write as if you were talking face to face, but be careful to organize your thoughts.
5. In a note of thanks, be specific about whatever it is you are grateful for.

Business letters

1. Use block style for the heading, not indented style.
2. After the salutation use a colon, not a comma.
3. Be careful to include all information necessary to understand or act upon your letter.

Aids to
Good English

PART SIX

Chapter 21

Using the Library

The Card Catalogue, the Dewey Decimal System, Reference Books

You are already well acquainted with one important service your library provides—that of supplying you with books for your spare-time reading. Your library should certainly continue to be a source of pleasure for you, but more and more as you get on in school you will be using it as a source of information as well.

A library is a storehouse of human knowledge. It has books of one kind or another on most of the subjects that people have found worth thinking about. No one person can learn all of these things. But it is the mark of an educated person to know how to find out a particular fact or piece of information when it is needed. In most cases, the library is the answer.

THE ARRANGEMENT OF YOUR LIBRARY

Probably there is more than one library that you can use. There is your school library, and there is the library in your community. If you live in a large city, you can use the large main library as well as the branch library in your neighborhood. Become familiar with these libraries so that you can take full advantage of their resources. If you are not already familiar with your school library, get acquainted with it by using it. Learn where the fiction and nonfiction books, the reference books, and the magazines are kept. Learn the location of the card catalogue. Your school librarian will answer your questions, but the more you use the library, the better you will be able to locate books by yourself. Your community library is likely to be larger than your school library, and there you will be able to find books not available at school. There, too, you should become familiar with the different parts of the library by asking questions and, above all, *using* the library.

Fiction

21a. **Learn to find books of fiction.**

In most libraries, books of fiction can be found in one section, arranged in alphabetical order according to the author's last name. Several books by the same author are further arranged alphabetically by the first word of the title (not counting *A, An,* or *The*).

Suppose you want to find *Phantom of the Blockade* by Stephen W. Meader. First you find the fiction section of the library and then those books by authors whose last names begin with M. Among these you will find Meader. After locating novels by the author you want, you then look at titles. Before coming to *Phantom of the Blockade,* you may find *Away to Sea, Bulldozer, The Fish Hawk's Nest* (arranged under F, not T), and *Lumberjack.*

▶ **NOTE** Books by authors (like Robert McCloskey) whose names begin with *Mc* are arranged in most libraries as though the name were spelled *Mac; St.* is arranged as though it were spelled out, *Saint.*

EXERCISE 1. Number 1–15. After these numbers, write the letters of the following books in the order in which they would be arranged on the library shelves.

A. *Bright Island* by Mabel Louise Robinson
B. *Cimarron* by Edna Ferber
C. *Homer Price* by Robert McCloskey
D. *The Incredible Journey* by Sheila Burnford
E. *Old Jules* by Mari Sandoz
F. *A Certain Measure* by Ellen Glasgow
G. *Cress Delahanty* by Jessamyn West
H. *National Velvet* by Enid Bagnold
I. *Johnny Tremaine* by Esther Forbes
J. *Call It Courage* by Armstrong Sperry
K. *The Time Machine* by H. G. Wells
L. *Jim Davis* by John Masefield
M. *Treasure Island* by Robert Louis Stevenson
N. *Charlotte's Web* by E. B. White
O. *The Return of Silver Chief* by Jack O'Brien

Nonfiction

21b. Learn to understand the Dewey decimal system of arranging nonfiction.

As you use your library, you will learn that non-fiction books are arranged primarily not by author and title but according to the numbers of the Dewey decimal system.

The Dewey decimal system gets its name from Melvil Dewey, the American librarian who developed it. According to this system, all books except fiction are classified under ten headings and arranged by numbers. These numbers and headings are as follows:

000–099   General works (encyclopedias and other reference materials)
100–199   Philosophy
200–299   Religion
300–399   Social sciences (economics, government, etc.)
400–499   Language
500–599   Science
600–699   Technology (engineering, aviation, inventions, etc.)
700–799   The Arts (architecture, music, sports, etc.)
800–899   Literature
900–999   History (including geography, travel books, and biography)

All of the following books about science would be in the 500 series of the Dewey decimal system and could be found in the same section of the library:

The Story of Atomic Energy by Laura Fermi
A Dipper Full of Stars: a Beginner's Guide to the Heavens by Lou Page Williams
The Mysterious Earth by Lester Del Ray
Plants That Changed the World by Bertha S. Dodge

Every book of nonfiction has a call number printed on its spine. This number places the book under one of the ten headings of the Dewey decimal system and then into still smaller categories. For example, *A Dipper Full of Stars* may be found on the 500 shelves under the special category 520–529, *astronomy.* Its specific call number, 523.8, narrows the category even more. All books numbered 523 belong under *descriptive astronomy,* while 523.8 indicates that the book is about *the stars.*

▶ **NOTE** While biographies dealing with the lives of several persons may be found under the number 920, individual biographies are in a special section of the library and are marked with a B on their spines. (In some libraries they are marked 92.) Under the B appears the initial of the last name of the biography's subject. *The Life of Clara Barton* by Percy H. Epler would be marked: B
B

Still another way of classifying biographies is to spell out the name of the person who is the subject of the biography, with the number above it.

The Card Catalogue

You don't have to remember the headings of the Dewey decimal system to find a book in the library. You can find out the call number of a nonfiction book and much other information besides from the card catalogue of the library.

21c. Learn to use the card catalogue.

In some prominent place in your library, you will find a cabinet with small drawers. Each drawer is filled with cards arranged in alphabetical order by the information on the top line. This cabinet and its contents is called the *card catalogue.*

The card catalogue contains at least three cards for each book of nonfiction in the library: an *author card,* a *title card,* and a *subject card.* There may be several subject cards and, in the case of joint authors, several author cards.

The Author Card

If you are looking for a book by a particular author,

you would look for the card with the author's name, last name first, printed at the top. If there is more than one author, there will be a card for each name. All books by an author are arranged in the alphabetical order of the titles under the author's name.

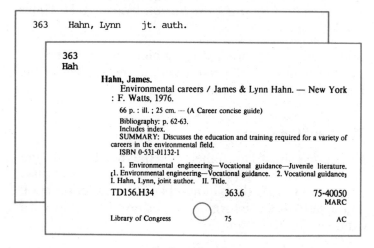

363   Hahn, Lynn   jt. auth.

363
Hah

Hahn, James.
Environmental careers / James & Lynn Hahn. — New York : F. Watts, 1976.

66 p. : ill. ; 25 cm. — (A Career concise guide)

Bibliography: p. 62-63.
Includes index.
SUMMARY: Discusses the education and training required for a variety of careers in the environmental field.
ISBN 0-531-01132-1

1. Environmental engineering—Vocational guidance—Juvenile literature. [1. Environmental engineering—Vocational guidance. 2. Vocational guidance] I. Hahn, Lynn, joint author. II. Title.

TD156.H34   363.6   75-40050
                                            MARC

Library of Congress   75   AC

Author Card

The Title Card

If you know the title of a book but do not know the name of the author, you can find the book listed on the *title card*. On this card, the title of the book is printed at the top. This card is placed alphabetically in the card catalogue according to the first word in the title, unless the first word is *a, an,* or *the,* in which case the card is filed alphabetically according to the second word in the title.

The Subject Card

If you do not have a book in mind but are looking

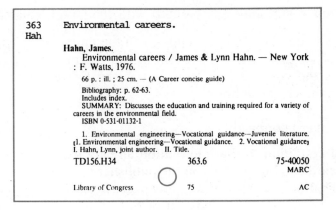

Title Card

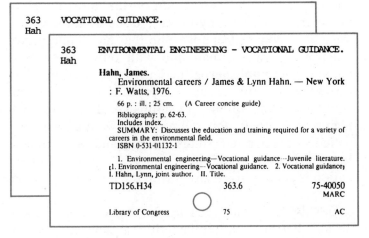

Subject Card

for any available information on a particular subject, you hunt up the *subject card*. Subject cards refer you to specific books on the subject. Like author cards and title cards, they are arranged alphabetically in the card catalogue.

The Call Number

The number 363 that appears in the upper left corner of all the sample cards shown on the previous page is the *call number*. It gives you the Dewey decimal number of the book.

Other Information

In addition to the information already discussed, the card catalogue tells you the publisher and date of publication of a book, how many pages it has, and whether or not it is illustrated. All of this information can be important. Obviously, if you want a book about airplanes, you will look for one published recently enough to include information on the latest developments in jet aircraft. If you want to see what the planes look like, you will choose one that has a number of illustrations rather than one with only a few. The name of the publisher is the least important bit of information on the cards in the card catalogue, but sometimes you will find it useful also. If you are reading up on football, you will probably want a book published in the United States. In England and Canada, football is quite a different game. The place of publication is always given along with the publisher's name.

EXERCISE 2.   Using the card catalogue in your school library, list the call number, title, author, and date of publication of one book on each of the following topics.

1. Space travel
2. Harriet Tubman
3. The sun
4. Football
5. Flowers of North America
6. Greek myths
7. Early explorations of America
8. Maria Tallchief
9. California history
10. Careers

REFERENCE BOOKS

21d. Learn to use reference books.

In addition to its many books on special subjects, a library also has reference books — books which contain information on a wide variety of subjects or which tell you where to find such information. Reference books are always kept together in a special section of the library.

Encyclopedias

When you want a good, detailed introduction to a subject, whether it is fossils, Alexander the Great, or the Battle of Bull Run, the reference book to use is an encyclopedia. An encyclopedia is a collection of articles on many different subjects. Often these articles contain special features like pictures, charts, maps, and lists of facts and figures about population, natural resources, and so on. When you are writing a report, you will probably go to an encyclopedia first for an overall view of your subject before you go on to more detailed sources of information.

Some encyclopedias you are likely to find useful are

> *Britannica Junior Encyclopedia*
> *Compton's Pictured Encyclopedia*
> *World Book Encyclopedia*
> *Collier's Encyclopedia*

All these encyclopedias consist of many volumes, and all arrange their articles alphabetically by title. To find information on a particular subject, use the guide letter or letters on the spine of each volume. An article on *mining* can probably be found near the middle of the volume marked M. To find a specific article in a volume, use the guide words at the top of the pages exactly as you use guide words in a dictionary. (See page 408.) If you cannot find a subject under a particular title, look for similar titles or for a larger subject that includes your subject. For example, information on *doctors* might be found in an article on *medicine.*

If you still cannot find the subject or wish to know if the encyclopedia contains more information on the subject, use the index. The index may be the first volume of the encyclopedia (as in *Britannica Junior*), the last volume (as in *Collier's Encyclopedia*), or at the end of each volume (as in *Compton's Encyclopedia*). Every encyclopedia has a section on how to use the index, usually at the beginning of the index itself. In addition to volume and page number of a subject, the index will also indicate the location of illustrations, charts, maps, and tables.

EXERCISE 3. Look up in an encyclopedia five of the topics listed below. Write down the name of the encyclopedia which contains information about the topic. After the name, write the volume number or letter, and the number of the page on which you found the information. Take brief notes on two of these topics, and be prepared to report on them in class.

EXAMPLE   1. The founding of the Red Cross
          1. *Compton's Encyclopedia, volume 12, page 117*
             Founded in 1864 in Geneva, Switzerland. Inspired by a pamphlet, "A Memory of Solferino," written by a young Swiss businessman, Henri Dunant.

1. The pony express
2. The first television broadcast
3. The manufacture of polio vaccine
4. The life cycle of the salmon
5. Where amber is found
6. How rice is cultivated
7. Who invented the telescope and when
8. When the last ice age was
9. The mining of diamonds
10. The origin of Halloween
11. How to keep score at bowling
12. How the Amazon River got its name
13. The paintings of Mary Cassatt
14. Why the dinosaur disappeared

Atlases

Atlases are books containing detailed maps and much information about cities and countries. In an atlas you can find such information as the climate, industries, natural resources, and population of a country. You can also learn the location of cities and towns, lakes, mountains, and so on. A few of the common atlases are

> *The Encyclopaedia Britannica Atlas*
> *Hammond Contemporary World Atlas*
> *National Geographic World Atlas*
> *Rand McNally Popular World Atlas*

An atlas is a valuable book in social studies courses such as history and geography. Become thoroughly familiar with at least one atlas.

Almanacs

An almanac is a collection of miscellaneous information. More than anything else, it consists of lists of facts—for example, a list of actors, actresses, and motion pictures that have won Academy Awards; a list of the leading magazines of the United States and Canada; a list of All-Star baseball games, including the dates the games were played, the final scores, and the names of the winning and losing managers; a list of colleges and universities of the United States, the names of their presidents, and the number of students attending them; a list of noted authors, scientists, engineers, and political and military leaders of various nations. Almanacs are published annually and bring you much up-to-date information, but they also present many facts of historical interest.

Three useful almanacs are *The World Almanac and Book of Facts,* the *Information Please Almanac,* and *The CBS News Almanac.* The best way to find information in an almanac is to use the index. In *The World Almanac* the index is at the front of the book, while in the others it is in the back.

Biographical Dictionaries

A biographical dictionary will give you information about the lives of famous persons. Some well-known biographical dictionaries are *Who's Who, Who's Who in America, Webster's Biographical Dictionary,* and *Twentieth Century Authors.*

EXERCISE 4. Number 1–10 on your paper. After the appropriate number, indicate whether you would look first in an atlas, an almanac, or a collection of biographies for information about the items listed below. Use the abbreviations *At* for atlas, *Al* for almanac, and *B* for a collection of biographies.

1. The place and date of birth of Abigail Smith Adams
2. The population of Portland, Oregon
3. The continent on which Timbuctoo is located
4. The winner of the 1980 World Series
5. The chief industries of Sweden
6. The principal novels of James Baldwin
7. The total vote cast in the presidential election of 1980
8. The approximate distance from New York to Moscow by the shortest air route
9. The newspaper career of Richard Harding Davis, the American short story writer
10. The winner of the Nobel prize for literature in 1979

The *Readers' Guide*

Information on many topics, particularly information about recent events, discoveries, and inventions, is likely to be found in magazines rather than in books. Magazine articles may also supply new information or new points of view about people and things of other times.

To help you locate a particular article or find out what has appeared in magazines on a certain subject, your library has a special reference book called the *Readers' Guide to Periodical Literature,* which indexes by author and subject the articles in each issue of more than one hundred magazines.

You will find the *Readers' Guide* in two forms: as a paperbound booklet published 22 times a year and as a large volume containing all the booklets published in a two-year period. The magazine articles themselves are listed by subject (like Farm buildings) and by author (like Cain, S.). If you look at the sample on this page, you will see that each entry presents a brief description of the article and employs special abbreviations. A "Key to Abbreviations" is provided at the front of the *Readers' Guide*. Some abbreviations are

abr	abridged	**por**	portrait
arr	arranged	**tr**	translated, translation,
bi-m	bimonthly		or translator
cond	condensed	**w**	weekly
F	February		

FARLOW, Robert L.   author entry
Romania: the politics of autonomy. bibl f Cur
Hist 74:168-71+ Ap '78
FARM accidents. See Agriculture—Accidents
FARM animals. See Livestock
FARM auctions. See Auctions
FARM building fire insurance. See Insurance,
Fire
FARM buildings   subject entry
See also
Barns and stables
Silos   cross references
Swine houses

Heating and ventilation
Little light on the solar question. L. Reichen-   title of magazine
berger. il Suc Farm 76:26-7+ O '78
FARM buildings, Remodeled   volume number
Remodeling. S. Cain. il Suc Farm 76:26-7 Ag '78
FARM Bureau Federation, American. See Ameri-
can Farm Bureau Federation
FARM cooperatives. See Agriculture, Cooperative
FARM corporations
Farm corporation's most important document;   title of article
stock purchase agreement. S. Cain. il Suc Farm
76:u04 C32 Mr '78

Taxation   division of
Incorporation: three little-known money savers.   main subject
Suc Farm 76:18 S '78
No reason to pay estate taxes on farmland;
adopting an employee stock ownership plan.   page number
L. Kruse. il Suc Farm 76:23+ S '78
Warning: double entities may be hazardous to   author's name
your farm business health. S. Cain. il Suc
Farm 76:30 Ag '78
FARM credit. See Agricultural credit
FARM equipment
Homemade ideas for the shop and field. il Suc   date of magazine
Farm 76:26 Ja '78

Suppose you are writing a composition on solar heating for farm buildings. The *Readers' Guide* would lead you to an article on the subject from the October

1978 issue of *Successful Farming.* The *Readers' Guide* entry for this article gives the following information:

> An article about solar heating in farm buildings called "Little Light on the Solar Question" by L. Reichenberger may be found in *Successful Farming.* The article, which is illustrated (il), is in volume 76; it begins on pages 26–27 and is continued on later pages (76:26–7+) of the October 1978 issue (O '78).

At first, entries in the *Readers' Guide to Periodical Literature* may seem difficult to read, but actually most of the abbreviations (like *il* for *illustrated*) are easy to recognize with a little practice. When you come to a new, unfamiliar abbreviation, refer to the key at the front.

EXERCISE 5. In the *Readers' Guide,* find an article listed under any five of the following subjects. Copy the entry for the article. Then, in a sentence or two, explain the information in the entry.

EXAMPLE   Pet care

> *Pet grooming pointers. B. Humeston. Bet Hom & Gard 57:200+ O '79*
> *An article about pet care called "Pet Grooming Pointers" by B. Humeston appears in the October 1979 issue of <u>Better Homes and Gardens</u> (volume 57). The article begins on page 200 and continues on later pages of the issue.*

1. Movies
2. United States Congress
3. Bicycles
4. Ecology
5. Mexican-Americans
6. Television
7. Basketball
8. Automobile racing
9. Photography
10. Yachts

REVIEW EXERCISE. Answer the following questions. If necessary, look up information in the chapter.

1. Under which of the ten number ranges of the Dewey decimal system would the following books be found? Refer to page 390.
   A. *Our Literary Heritage: A Pictorial History of the Writer in America*
   B. *Know Your Government*
   C. *Your Art Heritage*
   D. *All About Language*

2. What is the quickest way to find the call number of a book?

3. Name two different kinds of books in which the following information might be found:
   A. The birth and death dates of Lucy Stone
   B. A map of New Hampshire
   C. A biography of Ralph Waldo Emerson, the essay writer
   D. A list of winners of the Nobel Peace Prize

4. Name the three kinds of cards in a card catalogue. Which kind would you use most in gathering information for a report?

5. A book has $\overset{B}{W}$ on its spine. What kind of book is it? What or whom might the book be about?

6. Which of these fiction books would come first on a library shelf? Which second? Which last? Identify them by letter.
   A. *Jane Eyre* by Charlotte Brontë
   B. *The Good Earth* by Pearl Buck
   C. *Wuthering Heights* by Emily Brontë

7. You probably would not find an article on the World Series in an encyclopedia. Under what topic might you find information on this subject?

8. What part of an encyclopedia can be used to locate information quickly? Where is this part located? (Name the encyclopedia you consult.)

9. In which reference book would the following entry be found? In a sentence, explain the entry.

   TRAVEL photography

   > Your adventurous camera. K. Reading. Seventeen 37:98 Je '78

10. Give the names of two widely used almanacs. List five different kinds of information that you find in an almanac.

Chapter 22

Using the Dictionary

What a Dictionary Tells You About Words

If you are like most people, you use a dictionary mainly to find out the spelling or meaning of a word. Your dictionary is certainly the right place to look for spellings and meanings, but it contains a wealth of other information as well. It tells you what part of speech a word is, how it is pronounced, how it is used, and many other things about it.

There is probably no other single reference book that you will consult so often while you are in school and afterward. But like any tool, a dictionary is most useful to those who know how to use it well. This chapter reviews some of the important features of dictionaries. Since dictionaries differ in their practices, a chapter like this one can only be a general guide. For specific help with your own dictionary, study carefully the introductory instructions it contains. All dictionaries designed for students of your age contain a guide of this kind. You will find the reading of it well worthwhile and interesting, too.

The sample column on the opposite page illustrates some important features to be found in all dictionaries. You will find it helpful to refer to this page from time to time as you work through this chapter.

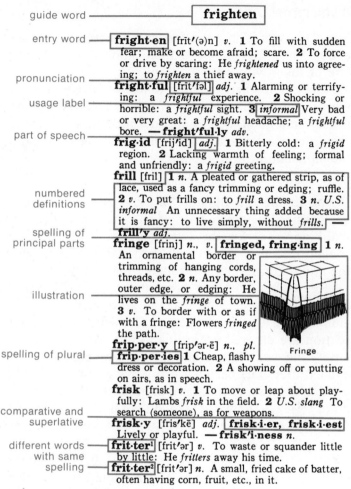

guide word ——————————— **frighten**

entry word —— **fright·en** [frīt′(ə)n] *v.* **1** To fill with sudden fear; make or become afraid; scare. **2** To force or drive by scaring: He *frightened* us into agreeing; to *frighten* a thief away.

pronunciation —— **fright·ful** [frīt′fəl] *adj.* **1** Alarming or terrifying: a *frightful* experience. **2** Shocking or horrible: a *frightful* sight. **3** *informal* Very bad or very great: a *frightful* headache; a *frightful* bore. — **fright′ful·ly** *adv.*

usage label ——

part of speech —— **frig·id** [frij′id] *adj.* **1** Bitterly cold: a *frigid* region. **2** Lacking warmth of feeling; formal and unfriendly: a *frigid* greeting.

frill [fril] **1** *n.* A pleated or gathered strip, as of lace, used as a fancy trimming or edging; ruffle. **2** *v.* To put frills on: to *frill* a dress. **3** *n.* *U.S. informal* An unnecessary thing added because it is fancy: to live simply, without *frills*. — **frill′y** *adj.*

numbered definitions ——

spelling of principal parts

fringe [frinj] *n.*, *v.* **fringed, fring·ing** **1** *n.* An ornamental border or trimming of hanging cords, threads, etc. **2** *n.* Any border, outer edge, or edging: He lives on the *fringe* of town. **3** *v.* To border with or as if with a fringe: Flowers *fringed* the path.

illustration ——

Fringe

frip·per·y [frip′ər·ē] *n.*, *pl.* **frip·per·ies** **1** Cheap, flashy dress or decoration. **2** A showing off or putting on airs, as in speech.

spelling of plural ——

frisk [frisk] *v.* **1** To move or leap about playfully: Lambs *frisk* in the field. **2** *U.S. slang* To search (someone), as for weapons.

comparative and superlative

frisk·y [fris′kē] *adj.* **frisk·i·er, frisk·i·est** Lively or playful. — **frisk′i·ness** *n.*

different words with same spelling ——

frit·ter[1] [frit′ər] *v.* To waste or squander little by little: He *fritters* away his time.

frit·ter[2] [frit′ər] *n.* A small, fried cake of batter, often having corn, fruit, etc., in it.

ARRANGEMENT OF A DICTIONARY

22a. Learn how to find a word in the dictionary.

Two devices help you to find words in a dictionary: *alphabetical arrangement* and the *guide words* on each page.

Alphabetical Order

Since the words in a dictionary are entered in alphabetical order, your speed in locating any particular one of them will depend on how well you know your alphabet. The exercises that follow require you to put words in alphabetical order. If you find this slow going, it may be a good idea to spend a little time reviewing the order of letters. The best way to do this is to divide the alphabet into three parts:

abcde   fghijklmnop   qrstuvwxyz

If you divide the alphabet in this way, you will also be learning in which part of the dictionary a given word appears, for the letters *a* through *e* take up roughly the first third of all dictionaries, *f* through *p* the middle third, and *q* through *z* the last third.

Remember that you are not through with alphabetical order when you find the section of words beginning with a particular letter. The words within each section are entered according to the order of the first letter, the next letter, and so on. For example, *pen* comes after *pat,* because *e* follows *a.* In words like *about* and *absent,* you have to go to the third letter in order to place the word. To find out if *basin* comes before or after *basic,* you have to look at the fifth letter.

EXERCISE 1. Number your paper 1–20. Arrange the words below and on page 407 in alphabetical order.

ship	explanation
export	reception
industrial	sensation
product	beneficial
shelter	forty
fertile	hindrance
indistinct	transportation
velocity	preposterous

calamity   rhythm
navigation   astonishment

EXERCISE 2. Number your paper 1–5. Working as rapidly as you can, put each of the following rows of words in dictionary order after the proper number.

1. bottom   butter   boil   bread   build
2. even   envy   evil   ever   event
3. carriage callow   cartwheel carried   careful
4. dome   dog   doll   doltish   dominion
5. ski   slight   skillful   sky   skin

Phrase Entries

Most of the entries in a dictionary are single words. Sometimes, however, two or more words are used together with a special meaning (*plum pudding, baker's dozen, Roman numeral,* etc.). Such words are entered in the dictionary as though they were spelled as one word. For example, *Roman numeral* comes after *romance* but before *romantic* because the *n* in *numeral* comes after *c* but before *t*. In this case, it is the sixth letter that decides.

Abbreviations

Some dictionaries include abbreviations in the main body of the book, while others group all of them in a special section at the back. It is likely that the dictionary you are using this year defines abbreviations right along with other words. If this is the case, you will find an abbreviation in the place it would naturally fall in alphabetical order. That is, you will find *lb.,* the abbreviation for *pound,* right after *lazy,* and *LP* (for *long-playing record*) after *lozenge,* or whatever the last word is that begins with *lo.*

EXERCISE 3. Number your paper 1–25 and arrange the following words in alphabetical order.

dryer	jackknife	no.
another	dry cell	already
quilt	jack rabbit	thresh
latitude	nuclear	quill
nosy	boisterous	threat
lately	boiler	nose dive
dry goods	threadbare	villager
anthem	position	
village	Dr.	

Guide Words

As an aid in helping you find the word you want quickly, dictionaries print at the top of each page the first and last word defined on that page. These words, usually printed in heavy type, are called *guide words*. The one at the left shows the first word defined in the left-hand column of the page. The one at the right shows the last word on the page—at the bottom of the right-hand column. If the spelling of the word you are looking for falls alphabetically between these two guide words, the word you want is on that page. Guide words can be great time-savers when you are looking up a word. Get into the habit of using them.

EXERCISE 4. Number your paper 1–10. Suppose that the guide words *café* and *calamity* appear at the top of a page in your dictionary. Make a plus (+) beside the number of each of the following words that you would expect to find on the page that has these guide words. If the word would appear on an earlier page, write *before.* If it would appear on a later page, write *after.*

EXAMPLES 1. cage
            1. +
            2. cave
            2. *after*

1. cake	6. calcium
2. cattle	7. cabbage
3. cafeteria	8. calamity
4. California	9. calf
5. coal	10. Cajun

EXERCISE 5. Using the guide words on each page, look up the following words in your dictionary. On your paper, copy the guide words and the page number from the page on which each of the words appears.

EXAMPLE 1. mature
           1. *matron* 402 *maze*

1. warlike	7. protection
2. empress	8. chief
3. unpredictable	9. superhuman
4. frontier	10. government
5. tenant	11. heartily
6. lb.	12. birthright

INFORMATION IN A DICTIONARY

22b. Learn how to find the meaning you want.

Many English words have more than one meaning. In fact, some common words like *point* and *run* may have twenty, or even more, depending upon the size and completeness of the dictionary. However many meanings are given for a word, each one is defined separately and numbered. The following example shows how one dictionary defines the different meanings of the word *drift*. Each number indicates a different meaning for the word.

> **drift** [drift] **1** *v*. To move or float along in a current of water or air: We let the boat *drift;* Leaves *drifted* down. **2** *v*. To become piled up by water or wind: The snow *drifted* as high as the door. **3** *n*. Something piled or heaped up by the wind or water: a *drift* of snow. **4** *v*. To move or live without any particular goal or purpose: He *drifted* from city to city. **5** *n*. The act of drifting, or the direction or speed of drifting: a westward *drift*. **6** *n*. The meaning of something: the *drift* of a speech. **— drift'er** *n*.

From *The HBJ School Dictionary,* copyright © 1977 by Harcourt Brace Jovanovich, Inc. Reprinted by permission of the publisher.

Always read a dictionary entry carefully. When more than one meaning is given for a word, read all of them and decide which definition fits the sentence you have in mind. Frequently, one of the definitions will actually *fit* into your sentences. Suppose, for example, you read the sentence, "I understood the *drift* of her remarks." You know that the remarks were not floating on water or piled up like snow, and therefore, none of the first three meanings is the one you want. But when you come to the last entry, you find, "The meaning of something: the *drift* of a speech." This is the definition you want, and it makes reasonably good sense to substitute *meaning* for *drift* in your original sentence.

Dictionaries often supply a sample phrase or sentence after numbered meanings to help you see the differences among them. Notice how the examples help you to keep straight the several meanings of *luck* in the following definition:

luck [luk] *n.* **1** Good fortune; success: He had *luck* in finding a good job. **2** Something that happens by chance; fortune: John always seems to have bad *luck* in sports. — **in luck** Successful; lucky. — **out of luck** Unlucky.

From *The HBJ School Dictionary,* copyright © 1977 by Harcourt Brace Jovanovich, Inc. Reprinted by permission of the publisher.

EXERCISE 6. Number your paper 1–10. Look at the italicized words in the following sentences. For each italicized word, write the meaning which best fits the sentence. Use the dictionary if you need to.

1. The damaged vessel is *listing* badly.
2. When you have finished *listing* the names, give your paper to Barbara.
3. Do you know the *fare* to Chicago?
4. At this restaurant, the *fare* is always excellent.
5. This *trail* was blazed by the forest ranger.
6. Don't *trail* behind; you'll be late.
7. Grace found three *quarters* in the sofa.
8. The soldiers were well pleased with their *quarters*.
9. The *base* of the statue was made of metal.
10. The new student's vocabulary was very *base*.

Synonyms and Antonyms

Words that are similar in meaning are *synonyms*. Words that are opposite in meaning are *antonyms*.

Many definitions employ synonyms. You are very likely to find the word *dry* used in the definition for *arid* and the word *deep* used in the definition for *profound*. Some dictionaries give lists of synonyms, and some include short paragraphs discussing the differences in meaning among these synonyms. You may find the abbreviation *Syn.* after the list of meanings given for a word; and after *Syn.* will be the word or words that are similar in meaning to the defined word.

mer·cy (mûr′sē) *n., pl.* **-cies.** **1.** Kind and compassionate treatment of an offender, enemy, prisoner, or other person under one's power; clemency. **2.** A disposition to be kind and forgiving: *I threw myself on his mercy.* **3.** Something for which to be thankful; a fortunate occurrence: *It's a mercy he survived.* **4.** Alleviation of distress; relief: *Her death was a mercy.* [Middle English *merci,* from Old French *merci,* compassion, forbearance (to someone in one's power), from Late Latin *mercēs,* reward, God's gratuitous compassion, from Latin *mercēs,* pay, reward. See **merc-** in Appendix.*]
    Synonyms: *mercy, leniency, clemency, forbearance, charity. Mercy* emphasizes compassion in a general way; it suggests reprieve from a fate of considerable severity, without further implication. *Leniency* applies to a specific act of indulgence. *Clemency* is usually applied to a specific act of a person or agency charged with administering justice; the recipient therefore is considered an offender. *Forbearance,* especially in its legal sense, is allied to *clemency* in denoting the act of foregoing the execution of a right. *Charity,* in this context, is a nonspecific term denoting benevolence.

© 1979 by Houghton Mifflin Company. Reprinted by permission from *The American Heritage Dictionary of the English Language, High-School Edition.*

If the dictionary treats antonyms, it may handle them similarly, using the abbreviation *Ant.*

EXERCISE 7. Copy from your dictionary (if it gives them) synonyms for five of the following words.

1. injurious	9. drab
2. begin	10. dislike
3. eternal	11. like
4. hideous	12. say
5. false	13. possible
6. imply	14. join
7. reckless	15. excel
8. immortal	

Part of Speech

The dictionary tells you what part of speech a word is. Many words may be used as more than one part of speech. In a dictionary, each part of speech is indicated by an abbreviation which comes either before or after the definition of the word:

n.	noun	*pron.*	pronoun
v.	verb	*prep.*	preposition
adv.	adverb	*interj.*	interjection
adj.	adjective	*conj.*	conjunction

Related Forms of a Word

For many words, there are closely related words and expressions the meaning of which can easily be seen once the meaning of the main word has been explained. For example, *fawnlike* presents no problem if you know the meaning of *fawn,* nor does *fearlessly* once you know *fearless.* Many dictionaries include such words within the entry for the word to which they are related.

Since the related forms are often different parts of speech from the entry word, the new part-of-speech label is given. Some dictionaries give pronunciations for these related words, unless they are very easy to figure out. Most dictionaries at least indicate how the related words are accented.

You will be hearing more about related word forms in Chapter 23. When you are looking up a new word, do not neglect any of these close relatives that may be listed. If you can learn two or three new words at a time, why not take the opportunity to expand your vocabulary?

22c. Learn to use your dictionary for spelling and capitalization.

The dictionary shows you how to spell a word. Simply following the principles of alphabetical order and using the guide words will lead you to most spellings that you want. Following these principles will lead you to the information that there are two *r*'s in *occurrence* and that there is an *i* after the *l* in *peculiar*. But if you try to look up *perhaps* and *omission* as though they were spelled as "prehaps" and "ommission," you naturally will not find them. If you cannot find a word in your dictionary, the chances are you have guessed wrong about the spelling. In that case, you must try to discover your error and look elsewhere. Even very bad spellers can find words in a dictionary. It just takes them longer.

Variant Spellings

You may find two spellings given for a word; thus you are likely to find in your dictionary both *raccoon/racoon, theater/theatre,* and *gray/grey*. In such situations the dictionary is likely to tell you — often by printing it first — which form is preferred.

Unusual Plurals

Although most nouns form their plurals by adding *−s* or *−es,* some do not. The words *fly* and *dowry,* for example, form the plural by changing the *y* to *i* and then adding *−es*. Thus the plural of *fly* is *flies* and that of *dowry* is *dowries*. When a plural is formed in an irregular way, the dictionary will show it, placing the abbreviation *pl.* before the plural form. (Notice the form *fripperies* on page 405.)

Past Tense Forms

Some verbs do not form the past tense in the usual way by adding *−d* or *−ed,* but in other ways. For example, if you look up the words *draw* and *deal* and *see* in your dictionary, you will find the following past forms given:

draw	**drew**
deal	**dealt**
see	**saw**

The omitting of a final silent *e* before *–ed* or the changing from *y* to *i* before *–ed* is regular but may be troublesome. Therefore, your dictionary is likely to list verb forms involving these operations. (Notice the inclusion of *fringed* on page 405.)

Present Participles

Usually you form the present participle of a verb by adding *–ing*. Thus the present participle of *draw* is *drawing*. Some verbs, however, present special problems. For example, to form the present participle of the verb *starve* you drop the *e* and add *–ing: starving*. Similarly, the present participle of *stare* is *staring;* of *hope* is *hoping*. Other words double the final consonant: *hop, hopping; prefer, preferring*.

Dictionaries usually include forms that involve spelling problems like these. (Notice the inclusion of *fringing* on page 405.)

Comparatives and Superlatives

The dictionary shows the comparative and superlative forms of adjectives when they present any spelling problems. When we add to *hot* the ending *–er* we must double the *t* to spell *hotter*. When we add *–est* to *merry* we must change the *y* to *i* to form *merriest*.

EXERCISE 8. Using a dictionary if you need to, follow directions for each of the items on the next page, and write the correctly spelled word on your paper.

EXAMPLE   1. Add *–ing* to *write*
       1. *writing*

1. Add –*s* to *spy*.
2. Add –*ing* to *dance*.
3. Add –*s* to *monkey*.
4. Add –*ing* to *duel*.
5. Add –*ly* to *neutral*.
6. Add –*ence* to *recur*.
7. Add –*ed* to *pry*.
8. Add –*est* to *happy*.
9. Add –*er* to *win*.
10. Add –*s* to *hero*.

EXERCISE 9. Write the past tense and present participle form of each of the following verbs on your paper. Use a dictionary if necessary.

1. write
2. sleep
3. begin
4. lie
5. lay
6. weep
7. fortify
8. ski
9. hurt
10. dive

Capitalization

In general, proper nouns are capitalized in English and common nouns written with lower-case, or small, letters. Most dictionaries print proper nouns with a capital letter and common nouns with a small letter. (See how your dictionary prints the entries for the nouns *Canadian* and *Sioux*.)

Sometimes a word is capitalized in one sense but printed with a lower-case letter in another. (Compare your dictionary entries for *God* as the supreme being and for *god* meaning a Latin or Greek deity.)

If you are in doubt about using a capital, the dictionary will help you. Remember that, in addition to consulting the dictionary, you should know the rules for capitalization (see Chapter 10).

EXERCISE 10. Look up the following words in a dictionary to see when they are capitalized. Be able to explain in each case why a capital letter should or should not be used.

1. arctic	6. capitol
2. congress	7. pole
3. house	8. roman
4. sister	9. catholic
5. president	10. republican

Syllable Division

The term *syllable* is not easy to define simply and clearly, but in general a syllable is a short word or part of a longer word containing a single vowel sound with or without adjacent consonants. A dictionary divides into syllables each defined word that contains more than one syllable.

Some dictionaries separate the syllables by a hyphen: sim-plic-i-ty.

Some dictionaries use a dot in the center of the space between syllables: e·ven·tu·al·ly.

Still others simply leave a space between syllables: dread ful ly.

Knowing the syllables in a word sometimes helps you to pronounce and spell the word correctly. In your writing, if you must divide a word at the end of a line, you need to know the syllables, so that you can divide it between syllables.

EXERCISE 11. Look up the following words in a dictionary. (Use the guide words.) Copy this list, separating the words into syllables. Leave spaces between the syllables.

1. jewel	6. opportunity
2. monastery	7. profuse
3. industrious	8. invention
4. merchant	9. canal
5. companion	10. knightly

22d. Learn to use your dictionary for pronunciation.

The dictionary gives a pronunciation for every entry word. The pronunciation indication is usually given immediately after the entry word, in brackets (as on page 405), but sometimes it is given between bars. Find out which procedure your dictionary uses.

Notice that the spelling given within the brackets or bars has no necessary connection with the spelling of the word. It is an indication of pronunciation alone. For example, you will probably find in your dictionary the respelling "rīd" after *ride*. This does not mean that you can ever correctly spell *ride* in this way; it means that the three sounds, those connected with *r, i,* and *d,* are the only ones used in pronouncing the word. Follow the entry word for spelling.

The Accent Mark

When a word has more than one syllable, one, at least, of its syllables is stressed or accented—that is, uttered with greater force or volume than the others. Notice the difference in pronunciation between *beacon,* with the accent on the first syllable, and *begin,* with the accent on the second.

Sometimes the position of the accent makes a great deal of difference. If we pronounce *entrance* with the accent on the first syllable, we have the noun meaning "act of entering" or "way of entering," but if we pronounce this same combination of letters with the accent on the second syllable, we have the verb meaning "to fill with delight and wonder." Notice the position of the accent in every new word that you learn.

Dictionaries commonly indicate the accented syllable by placing the mark ' after it: *fav' or a ble.* Some dictionaries use the mark ' instead, placing it in front of the syllable accented: 'fav or a ble.

EXERCISE 12. Look up the following words in your dictionary. Copy the words on your paper, dividing them into syllables and placing the accent mark as your dictionary places it. Leave spaces between the syllables.

1. reduce	11. invent
2. queenly	12. occupation
3. embark	13. machinist
4. diffuse	14. odor
5. consider	15. inflict
6. political	16. resist
7. encourage	17. possess
8. misfortune	18. possessive
9. meander	19. public
10. differential	20. publicity

Sometimes for words of three or more syllables a dictionary indicates two accents, one the primary accent, the other the secondary accent. The word *popularity* has five syllables: *pop, u, lar, i,* and *ty.* When you pronounce this word, you will have no doubt that the syllable *lar* is accented, but you will also notice that the syllable *pop* receives greater stress than *u, i,* or *ty.* Sometimes the secondary accent is indicated by the mark ˌ before and below the syllable in question.

In many dictionaries the primary accent is given in heavy print ('), the secondary in lighter print ('). The word *popularity,* for example, is marked *pop' u lar' i ty.* In other dictionaries the secondary accent is shown by two accent marks ('') or by the mark (ˌ): *pop'' u-lar' i ty* or *ˌpop u 'lar i ty.*

The introductory section of your dictionary will tell which of these systems is used in that book.

EXERCISE 13. Look up the following words in your dictionary. Copy the words on your paper, dividing them into syllables and placing the accent marks where they belong. Follow the system of your dictionary in showing syllable division and accent. Practice pronouncing the words.

1. ruination
2. tributary
3. photographic
4. opposition
5. luminary

6. fumigation
7. graduation
8. classification
9. optimistic
10. senatorial

Symbols for Sounds

We have in English many more sounds than we have letters to show these sounds. The vowels in the words *cat, mate,* and *father* have different sounds, but we spell all the words with the letter *a.* The dictionary maker cannot show the difference between these pronunciations without using more symbols.

Diacritical Marks

To solve this problem, dictionaries use diacritical marks—special symbols placed above conventional letters.

Recording of pronunciation is among the dictionary maker's most difficult tasks; few specialists on pronunciation are completely satisfied with any one system of recording pronunciation, and dictionaries vary widely in the systems of diacritical marks they use.

In order to use the pronunciations given in your dictionary, you must familiarize yourself with the diacritical marks it uses. These are explained in a key that usually appears inside the front cover and sometimes on each page as well.

In this chapter you will study only a few of the more important diacritical marks that are common to most systems.

Long Vowels

The long straight mark over a vowel is called the *macron* (pronounced *mā′kron*). When the macron appears over a vowel, the vowel is often said to have the sound of its own name. Such vowels are called long vowels.

EXAMPLES   dāt   date
               sēt   seat
               hī   high
               gōt   goat
               ūnit   unit

EXERCISE 14. Look up the following words in a dictionary. Copy each word on your paper, dividing it into syllables and using the accent mark. Put a macron over each long vowel. For now, ignore all other diacritical marks.

  1. invade   6. mistake
  2. slope   7. mining
  3. checkmate   8. useful
  4. exaggerate   9. seaweed
  5. outline   10. dome

Short Vowels

Vowels customarily called "short" include the following:

         a as in bat   *o* as in top
         e as in net   *oo* as in wood
         i as in pick   *u* as in but

Dictionaries vary in their method of showing the pronunciation of short vowels.

One method is to place a *breve* (pronounced *brēv*) over the vowel. Thus in the *American Heritage School Dictionary* the pronunciation of *establish* is shown like this: ĭ stăb′lĭsh. The curved marks over the vowels are breves. Another method is to leave short vowels unmarked: es tab′lish.

The Schwa

Today's dictionary maker is becoming increasingly aware that devices other than diacritical marks are needed to indicate the truth about English pronunciation, and probably the dictionaries of the future will make more use of special symbols. One pronunciation symbol that is now very commonly used is called the *schwa*. Look at the last symbol used on page 405 in the pronunciation of *fritter:* frit′ər. This "upside-down *e*" is a schwa. The schwa indicates the blurred, unclear sound — the sound that might be spelled as "uh." Notice the use of the schwa in the pronunciation for *frightful* on page 405.

EXERCISE 15. Look up the following words. Copy the dictionary pronunciations of the words on your paper.

1. dreadfully
2. drama
3. boa
4. complimentary
5. coverall

6. discontentment
7. fission
8. historical
9. narrative
10. obligation

REVIEW EXERCISE. Write out the answers to the following questions on your paper. Use complete sentences.

1. What is a synonym?
2. What is an antonym?
3. What does the accent mark tell?
4. What is meant by "guide words"?
5. The words *gave, general, gear,* and *gasoline* all appear on one page of a dictionary. Two of them are the guide words for that page. Which two?
6. What does the macron tell about a vowel?

7–10. List four kinds of information that the dictionary gives you about a word.

Chapter **23**

Vocabulary

Learning and Using New Words

The number of words you know and use today is much greater than the number you knew four or five years ago. This is true whether or not you have ever consciously tried to enlarge your vocabulary. You have learned many new words from your parents and friends, from the subjects you have studied in school, from books, movies, television programs, and games. There is almost nothing that you do in school or in your free time that doesn't increase your supply of words.

But though you are always learning some new words just by going about your everyday affairs, the chances are that you can learn many more if you make an effort to do so. This chapter will show you some ways in which you can add to your vocabulary many of the new words that you see and hear. It is very important that you should learn to do so. A good vocabulary is a great advantage in everything you do. It will help you to succeed in school and in your later life.

Before studying ways of developing a better vocabulary, you may be interested to see how your knowledge of words compares with the vocabularies of other students. An average student your age should score between 65 and 70 percent on the following diagnostic test. Can you do better?

EXERCISE 1. Number your paper 1–25. Each numbered word below is followed by four words. Beside the number on your paper, write the letter of the word that is closest in meaning to the numbered word.

EXAMPLE 1. vacant   a. useless   c. stupid
                               b. empty   d. clean

       1. *b*

1. brawny   a. powerful   c. intelligent
               b. ancient   d. delicate

2. catastrophe a. magazine   c. store
               b. disaster   d. outlook

3. combustion a. group   c. friend
               b. excitement d. burning

4. decoy   a. watch   c. vision
               b. copy   d. lure

5. diminish   a. make older c. make easy
               b. make less   d. finish

6. elicit   a. draw forth c. exchange
               b. give away   d. unravel

7. fatigue   a. make-believe c. weariness
               b. door   d. appearance

8. gibberish   a. high fever c. old song
               b. combination d. senseless
                                    chatter

9. hilt   a. mountain   c. towel
               b. handle   d. doorway

10. inarticulate a. compact   c. not cheap
               b. not stated d. unable to
                                    speak

11. inflation   a. suit   c. swelling
               b. revelation d. confidence

12. isolate   a. place apart c. protect
               b. collect   d. vote

13. larceny
  a. raft
  b. theft
  c. money
  d. cloud

14. methodical
  a. orderly
  b. tired
  c. religious
  d. modern

15. opaque
  a. not near
  b. liquid
  c. not transparent
  d. gentle

16. predict
  a. deny
  b. ignore
  c. request
  d. prophesy

17. punctual
  a. speedy
  b. tasty
  c. honest
  d. on time

18. ramble
  a. sing
  b. grasp
  c. cover
  d. wander

19. renown
  a. awareness
  b. desire
  c. fame
  d. cabinet

20. seclude
  a. tie up
  b. move
  c. keep apart
  d. unlock

21. sullen
  a. gloomy
  b. white
  c. heavy
  d. lonely

22. tendency
  a. weariness
  b. inclination
  c. tool
  d. balcony

23. tangible
  a. solid
  b. massive
  c. ignorant
  d. imaginary

24. unkempt
  a. snowy
  b. untidy
  c. not known
  d. unready

25. variation
  a. violin
  b. vapor
  c. change
  d. violence

23a. As you learn new words, list them with their meanings in your notebook, and use them in your speech and writing.

Keeping a vocabulary list in your notebook is one of the surest ways to enlarge your knowledge of words. After each new word, write a definition of it. Then write a sentence in which the word is used. Keep a special section of your notebook for this purpose. Add words you learn from day to day in other classes and outside school. Review your list occasionally, and use the words in speech and writing as often as you can in order to make them a permanent part of your vocabulary.

MEANING FROM CONTEXT

One obvious way of learning the meaning of a new word is to look it up in a dictionary. The chances are, however, that you have learned only a small percentage of the words you know by this method. More often you guessed the meaning from the situation in which you heard the new word used, or you recognized that it was formed from other words you already knew. You will be using all three of these methods in this chapter and from now on.

23b. Learn new words from context.

The *context* of a word means the other words and sentences that surround it. From the context, you can sometimes guess at the meaning of an unfamiliar word. For example, if you did not know the meaning of the word *accompanist,* you could probably guess it from the way it is used in the following sentence: *The accompanist played so loudly that he interfered with the singer.* From the context, you can tell that "accompanist" means one who plays (probably the piano) while someone sings. The word can hardly mean anything else. If you look up the word in the dictionary, you will find that your guess is right; that, in fact, anyone who performs with a soloist (whether a singer or an instrumentalist) is an accompanist.

Use of context clues in learning new words is so important that a longer illustration will be worthwhile here. Ernest Lawrence Thayer's poem called "Casey at the Bat" tells how mighty Casey, the star of the Mudville team, comes to bat in the last half of the ninth with two out, runners on second and third, and two runs needed for Mudville to tie the opponents. Casey does not swing at the first pitch, and the umpire calls it a strike.

> From the benches, black with people, there
>   went up a muffled roar,
> Like the beating of the storm waves on the
>   stern and distant shore.
> "Kill him! kill the umpire!" shouted someone
>   on the stand;
> And it's likely they'd have killed him had not
>   Casey raised his hand.
> With a smile of Christian charity great Casey's
>   visage shone;
> He stilled the rising tumult, he made the game
>   go on;
> He signaled to the pitcher, and once more the
>   spheroid flew;
> But Casey still ignored it, and the umpire said,
>   "Strike two."

The words *visage, tumult,* and *spheroid* may give you some trouble, but if you think about the context you may be able to see that *visage* is unlikely to mean anything other than "face," that *tumult* may be read as "noisy, threatening agitation," and that *spheroid,* at least in this passage, must mean "baseball." The words and sentences that surround these three words lead us to safe guesses about their meanings. (Incidentally, mighty Casey struck out on the next pitch, Mudville lost, and there was no joy whatever in the town that night.)

EXERCISE 2. Number your paper 1-10. For each

numbered word in the paragraph below, select the word closest in meaning from the list preceding the paragraph. Write that word next to the appropriate number. Look for clues to meaning in the context. After you have finished, check your answers with the dictionary, and correct them where necessary. You will not need all of the words in the list.

automobile	realized
beginner	roadway
false impression	scattered
patient acceptance	instruction book
picture	speeded up
pretend	stern

The (1) *novice* got into the (2) *vehicle* with his mother, asked his mom to hold his learner's permit, and started up the motor. The car began to move, and the boy (3) *accelerated* slowly and carefully. He tried to keep in mind all the directions in the driver's (4) *manual* and at the same time to control the car. He attempted to (5) *feign* confidence, but the (6) *grim* expression on his face showed the strain. Although he was going only 20 miles per hour, he had the (7) *illusion* of going at high speed. The onlookers saw the mother look back, her face a (8) *portrait* of hopeless (9) *resignation,* and then they (10) *dispersed* as the car went out of sight in a cloud of dust.

EXERCISE 3. Number your paper 1–10. Next to each number, copy from column B the word or phrase that is closest in meaning to the italicized word in column A. Refer to the dictionary if necessary.

A	B
1. an *audition* for the singer	cartoon
2. the *bravado* of the trapped wrongdoer	carry
	false boldness
3. an amusing *caricature*	go on board ship

4. tourists about to *embark* trial hearing
5. a *humane* judge make up one's mind
6. *lubricate* the motor merciful
7. a *partial* count trivial
8. *resolve* to work harder incomplete
9. an ancient *scroll* roll of parchment
10. *transport* the luggage oil

Often authors know that they may be using words unfamiliar to their readers and, accordingly, add brief definitions themselves. Notice how the words in heavy type in the following sentences have been defined by the authors.

The university owns a **seismograph,** a machine for measuring the force of earthquakes.

Leading from the heart are two major **arteries,** vessels that carry blood to other parts of the body.

This plastic is **translucent** in that it permits some light to pass through it but prevents one's seeing through it.

23c. Learn the meaning of new words by looking them up in the dictionary.

You may not always be able to guess the meanings of words from the context. Frequently you must use a dictionary. As you know, the dictionary lists words alphabetically and gives much information about them in addition to their meanings. In this chapter, however, we are concentrating on meanings. When you have found the word you are looking for, there may be several meanings given. You must read all of these meanings to find the one which applies in the sentence you have in mind.

EXERCISE 4. Copy column A on your paper, and

next to each item copy the item from column B that is closest in meaning. Refer to the dictionary when you need to. You will not use all the words in column B.

A	B
1. authentic	invitation to a game
2. challenge	put off
3. postpone	agreement
4. harmony	call to mind
5. juvenile	frequent
6. nocturnal	genuine
7. perpetual	hold back
8. restrain	issue
9. sequel	lasting forever
10. utter	of the night
	speak
	that which follows
	youthful

EXERCISE 5. Write numbers 1–5 on your paper, corresponding to the following numbered questions. Next to each number, copy from the following list the word that answers the question. You will not use all the words. You may refer to the dictionary to find the meanings of the words.

censure	eludes	pompous
confiscates	inert	profound

1. What does a good base runner do when the catcher has the ball, and the runner is trying to slide into home plate?
2. How do you describe something that seems inactive and motionless?
3. What does a police officer do when stolen goods are found?
4. What word describes a person who thinks or feels deeply?
5. What is the manner of a self-important person?

EXERCISE 6. Follow the directions for Exercise 5.

beneficiary maternal phenomenon
farce migrate rumor

1. What is a play that is supposed to make people laugh?
2. What is a piece of news that spreads without proof of its truth?
3. What is a person who receives money through a will or insurance policy?
4. What is the attitude of a mother to her children?
5. What do groups of animals sometimes do when food becomes scarce where they live?

EXERCISE 7. Number your paper 1–10. Next to each number, copy a word from the following list which conveys an idea appropriate to the sentence having that number. Look up the words in the dictionary if you do not know their meanings.

EXAMPLE 1. He was admired by all for his brave and generous nature.
  1. *noble*

controversial frivolous rigid
credible lenient sallow
desolate overt tepid
flawless weary noble

1. The steel beam did not bend, in spite of the great weight on it.
2. Robinson Crusoe was shipwrecked alone on a barren island.
3. There was nothing sneaky about the action, which was done in full view of everyone.
4. The subject aroused a great deal of debate, and much was said pro and con.
5. The teacher did not scold the boy, despite his lateness to class.

6. The story was easy to believe when we heard the evidence.
7. His unhealthy complexion was caused by lack of sunshine.
8. The waters off the coast of Florida are almost lukewarm, many swimmers report.
9. The club members giggled and refused to be serious at the rehearsal.
10. The perfect diamond glittered on top of the golden ring.

EXERCISE 8. Number your paper 1–5. Next to each number, write a word selected from the list below which correctly completes the sentence of the same number. Refer to your dictionary for word meanings.

antecedent	epitaph	pacifist
debris	manuscript	synopsis

1. A summary that gives the main points of a story is called a ——.
2. "O Rare Ben Johnson," the inscription on the poet's tomb, is a famous ——.
3. After the hurricane the streets were littered with ——.
4. Because he regarded war as wrong and useless, he was called a ——.
5. The original copy of Gertrude Stein's novel is a valuable ——.

EXERCISE 9. Follow the directions for Exercise 8.

utility	hermit
enmity	opponent
grandeur	strategy

1. As the traveler looked at the Greek temple, she was impressed by its ——.
2. For a long time Thoreau lived at Walden Pond, away from people, almost as a ——.

3. The chess master won the game by a clever ——.
4. Because of a long-standing —— between their families, Romeo and Juliet were married secretly.
5. By her speed and strength, the tennis champion overwhelmed her ——.

EXERCISE 10. Number 1–10 on your paper. For each number, choose and copy the word or phrase from column B which has the meaning of the numbered word in column A. Use the dictionary.

A	B
1. antedate	a. shut out
2. bulwark	b. ruler
3. caliber	c. light up
4. exclude	d. force one's self in
5. illumine	e. farm
6. incite	f. quality
7. intrude	g. stir up
8. moderate	h. find out
9. envelop	i. happen before
10. terminate	j. not extreme
	k. cover from all sides
	l. strong means of defense
	m. bring to an end

REVIEW EXERCISE A. The words listed below are selected from the words you have studied so far in this chapter. Number your paper 1–20. Beside each number write the letter of the word that is closest in meaning to the numbered word.

1. tepid   a. calm   c. weary
           b. lukewarm   d. enclosed
2. bravado   a. false boldness   c. exploration
           b. volume   d. shallowness
3. caliber   a. character   c. quality
           b. shade   d. dimensions

4. maternal
   - a. motherly
   - b. ancestral
   - c. ever-increasing
   - d. anxious

5. epitaph
   - a. witty saying
   - b. inscription on a tomb
   - c. puzzle
   - d. short poem

6. credible
   - a. believable
   - b. obscure
   - c. breakable
   - d. not difficult

7. elude
   - a. oil thoroughly
   - b. perceive
   - c. hit savagely
   - d. escape from

8. grandeur
   - a. sum
   - b. magnificence
   - c. old age
   - d. location

9. sequel
   - a. chapter
   - b. that which follows
   - c. shrill cry
   - d. development

10. terminate
    - a. period of weeks
    - b. infest with insects
    - c. bring to an end
    - d. railroad depot

11. partial
    - a. incomplete
    - b. slightly ill
    - c. separately
    - d. filled up

12. authentic
    - a. antique
    - b. literary
    - c. genuine
    - d. false

13. lenient
    - a. not severe
    - b. soothing
    - c. transparent
    - d. melodious

14. inert
    - a. repulsive
    - b. heavy
    - c. unmoving
    - d. waxy

15. pompous
    - a. mild
    - b. self-important
    - c. ceremonial
    - d. lengthy

16. feign
    - a. rule
    - b. pretend
    - c. hope for
    - d. cool quickly

17. debris
    - a. proclamation
    - b. state of exhaustion
    - c. severe cold
    - d. rubbish

18. incite
    - a. dislike
    - b. stir up
    - c. make calm
    - d. speak to

19. caricature
    - a. slight damage
    - b. scene in color
    - c. cartoon
    - d. circus performer

20. illusion   a. light   c. a pattern
of stars
                    b. picture   d. false impres-
sion

WORD ANALYSIS

Some English words can be divided into parts. You can see that *untrue* can be divided into *un–* and *true,* that *foretell* is composed of *fore–* and *tell,* and that *mistrust* is made up of *mis–* and *trust.* You can also see that *wildly* can be divided into *wild* and *–ly, coldness* into *cold* and *–ness,* and *golden* into *gold* and *–en.* Many other words can be divided like these examples.

23d. Learn the meaning of new words by dividing them into their parts.

Roots

Although English has many words that can be divided, it has some that cannot. *Man* cannot be divided into *m* and *an; room* is not made up of *r* and *oom, ro* and *om,* or *roo* and *m.* *Water* cannot be divided into *wat* and *er,* nor can *summer* be divided.

Words like *man, room, water,* and *summer* that cannot be broken up into separate parts are called *roots.* Scan a column of your dictionary, paying attention only to the shorter and simpler words. If you happen to start with *cr,* for instance, you will find that the following words are roots: *crab, crack, craft, crag, cram, crane, crank, crash,* and *crate.*

Now consider once more the words *untrue, foretell, mistrust, wildly, coldness,* and *golden. Untrue* divides into *un–* and *true,* but the form *true* cannot be further divided. It is a unit by itself; it is not made up of *t* and *rue, tr* and *ue,* or *tru* and *e*. And *wildly* divides into *wild* and *–ly*, but *wild* itself is a unit that cannot be divided. *True* and *wild* are roots. Similarly, *tell* in *foretell, trust* in *mistrust, cold* in *coldness,* and *gold* in *golden* are roots. *Untrue, foretell,* and *wildly* consist of roots with something more added to them.

Prefixes and Suffixes

The groups of letters *un–* (in *untrue*), *fore–* (in *foretell*), and *mis–* (in *mistrust*), are called *prefixes;* they are added to the beginning of the word.

In *wildly, coldness,* and *golden, –ly, –ness,* and *–en* are *suffixes*. They are added to the end of the root. Study this small table:

PREFIX	ROOT	SUFFIX	WORD
un–	true		untrue
en–	courage	–ment	encouragement
re–	create	–ion	recreation
	man	–hood	manhood
un–	happy	–ness	unhappiness

Being able to recognize certain words as made up of roots and prefixes or suffixes almost always helps in learning the spelling and the pronunciation of such words and often, although not always, helps in arriving at their meaning.

EXERCISE 11. Number your paper 1–10. Write *root* after the number of each root word below and on page 438. Write *root and prefix* or *root and suffix* for words made up of a root and one of these elements.

1. friendless
2. sweeten
3. miscount
4. dismount
5. father
6. recapture

7. paper	9. arc
8. aunt	10. picture

EXERCISE 12. Follow directions for Exercise 11.

1. undo	6. booklet
2. apple	7. unable
3. deem	8. discard
4. placement	9. lioness
5. intake	10. uncle

23e. Learn the meaning of some common prefixes.

PREFIX	MEANING	EXAMPLE
anti–	against	antiwar
post–	after	postdated
sub–	under	submarine

You can see how these prefixes affect the meaning of the words in which they occur. An *antiwar* point of view is one that is *against* war. A *postdated* letter is one that is dated *after* the time of writing. A *submarine* is a boat that travels *under* water.

EXERCISE 13. Each of the ten words below uses one of the prefixes you have learned. Copy the numbers on your paper and write the meaning of the word after the number. Use the dictionary.

EXAMPLE   1. subterranean
　　　　　1. *under the surface of the earth*

1. antiseptic	6. antifreeze
2. postscript	7. subtract
3. subdivide	8. antiaircraft
4. postgraduate	9. postlude
5. subsoil	10. antisocial

Here are seven additional prefixes. Learn their meanings and study the examples carefully.

PREFIX	MEANING	EXAMPLE
ante–	before	anteroom
contra–	against	contradict
in–	not	inarticulate
inter–	between	interstate
per–	through	perforate
re–	again, back	recall
trans–	across	transfer

EXERCISE 14. Using the dictionary if necessary, find the meaning for the words given below. Write each meaning after the proper number on your paper.

1. inhospitable
2. retouch
3. perspire
4. inhumane
5. perennial
6. transfusion
7. antecedent
8. contravene
9. contraband
10. antedate
11. intervene
12. reassure
13. incompatible
14. transitional
15. incoherent

23f. Increase your vocabulary by learning the companion forms of a word.

Many nouns, verbs, and adjectives in English have closely related companion forms used as other parts of speech. The noun *boy* has the companion forms *boyish* and *boylike,* which are adjectives. The verb *reflect* has the companion noun *reflection.* The adjective *happy* has for companion forms the noun *happiness* and the adverb *happily.* English is rich in relations of this sort. If you keep this in mind, you will find that you can often learn two or three new words as easily as one.

Knowing the companion forms of a word can also be an aid in spelling. If you have trouble remembering that there are two *a*'s in *capable,* the companion form *capacity* gives you the clue you need. *Dividend* should be easier to spell correctly if you remember that it is closely related to *divide.*

EXERCISE 15. Number your paper 1–10. For each verb, write the companion noun meaning the action itself or condition. Use the dictionary if necessary.

EXAMPLE 1. place
          1. *placement*

1. abandon   6. impeach
2. accuse   7. inquire
3. alter   8. persist
4. appraise   9. rebel
5. defy   10. seize

EXERCISE 16. Number your paper 1–10. For each verb, write the companion noun that names the person who does the action indicated. Use the dictionary if necessary.

EXAMPLE 1. act
          1. *actor*

1. agitate   6. serve
2. assist   7. survey
3. instruct   8. survive
4. pursue   9. torment
5. reflect   10. usurp

EXERCISE 17. Number your paper 1–5. For each noun or adjective write the companion verb. Use the dictionary if necessary.

EXAMPLE 1. short
          1. *shorten*

1. active   4. human
2. central   5. sweet
3. diverse

EXERCISE 18. Number your paper 1–10. For each noun write a companion adjective. Use the dictionary if necessary.

1. algebra
2. zeal
3. atom
4. caprice
5. circle

6. luxury
7. medicine
8. navy
9. suicide
10. triumph

USING NEW WORDS

23g. Use the exact word to express your meaning in describing people and things.

English has so rich a vocabulary that there are words to describe hundreds of kinds of people and things. It is only people with very poor vocabularies who describe everything of which they approve as "nice," and everything of which they disapprove as "terrible." Does "nice" mean pleasant, attractive, agreeable, excellent? Or does "terrible" mean ugly, unfortunate, evil, distasteful? Using the word to convey the exact shade of meaning you have in mind makes your speaking and writing more mature and interesting.

EXERCISE 19. The following sentences are uninteresting and lack force because the italicized word or words in each one do not convey any particular shade of meaning. Number your paper 1–10. After the proper number, write a word or words which can replace the italicized ones and make the sentences more meaningful. Use your imagination.

EXAMPLE 1. The inquisitive puppy *fell* down the stairs.
    1. *tumbled*

1. Visiting the Grand Canyon was a *good* experience.
2. The diamond necklace *shone* in the sunlight.

3. We all had a *fine* time at Gloria's party.
4. Skiing is a *nice* sport.
5. The column of soldiers *walked* down the road.
6. Yesterday was a *bad* day.
7. What a *terrible* movie!
8. The dancer *moved* across the stage.
9. During the storm thunder *was heard* and lightning *was seen*.
10. *Great* waves splashed against the coast.

In addition to facts and skills, you learn new words in your mathematics, science, and social studies classes. Some of these words are completely new; others are familiar words which have special meanings in a particular subject. It is important that you know the meanings of such words, for often they are essential to understanding the important concepts.

The new words you encounter in your textbooks will often be italicized or in heavy type the first time they appear. Pay special attention to words marked in this way. The writer is showing you that they are important. Often, a new word will be defined on the spot. Many textbooks also include glossaries — short dictionaries of the special words of a subject. Be sure to use this feature of your textbooks when it is available. Just because a glossary is in the back of a book, don't conclude that it is not important.

EXERCISE 20. The words below figure prominently in mathematics books designed for students of your age. Write each word on your paper, and follow it by a short definition. Then write a short sentence using each word correctly. Look up any words you do not know in your textbook or in a desk dictionary.

addend	dividend	equation
cube	divisor	fraction
decimal	equality	multiply

multiplicand	percentage	root
operation	power	set

EXERCISE 21. The following words are likely to appear in your social studies assignments. Follow the directions for Exercise 20.

History: alien, amendment, caucus, colony, elector, emancipate, embargo, impeach, legislature, ratify, secede, sedition, tariff, territory, veto.
Geography: arctic, contour, delta, estuary, hemisphere, latitude, longitude, promontory, temperate, torrid.

EXERCISE 22. The following words are likely to appear in your science assignments. Follow the directions for Exercise 20.

artery	eclipse	molecule
bacteria	environment	nucleus
calorie	hybrid	parasite
cell	invertebrate	vertebrate

23h. Use the words from specialized vocabularies in your everyday speaking and writing.

Many of the words you learn in your study of mathematics, science, and other subjects have extended meanings which are appropriate for use elsewhere. You will often encounter words like *multiply, ratio,* and *factor* outside of books on mathematics and *nucleus, artery,* and *eclipse* in books that have little to do with science. Learn to use the extended meanings of the words you learn in your school subjects appropriately in the other writing and speaking you do.

EXERCISE 23. The following words from mathematics, science, and social studies have extended meanings useful in general writing and speaking. Use these words appropriately after the numbers on your paper which correspond to the blanks below. You will not use all of the words in the list.

alien	equality	parasite
artery	fraction	temperate
cell	latitude	territory
dividend	multiply	torrid
eclipse	nucleus	veto

1. The name of Graham McNamee, once known to millions of radio listeners, has been ——d by more recent radio and television personalities.
2. Harry sometimes eats too much, but Frank is always —— at the dinner table.
3. I would like to go to the movies tonight, but I am afraid that my father will —— the idea.
4. The American Telephone and Telegraph Company has declared a yearly —— on its stock.
5. Carson Boulevard is the main —— through which the city's traffic flows.
6. A person who enjoys the benefits of this country but contributes nothing to its welfare or improvement is a ——.
7. Because Sally does her best when she is allowed to work freely, the teacher gave her much —— in writing her report.
8. Our club's membership will quickly —— after we give our first party.
9. I could look in my sister's room, but she tells me that it is forbidden ——.
10. Only a small —— of the people are familiar with the political promises of the two candidates.

REVIEW EXERCISE B. The words listed below are selected from the words you have studied in this chapter. Number your paper 1–20. Beside each number, write the letter of the word that is closest in meaning to the numbered word.

1. alien a. rapid c. in poor health
   b. foreign d. untruthful

2. deem a. demand c. happen
   b. think d. regret

3. elude a. hit c. oil thoroughly
   b. escape from d. perceive

4. veto a. agree c. invite
   b. delay in making d. refuse to ap-
   up one's mind prove

5. antisep- a. unsociable c. germicide
   tic b. ugly d. illness

6. maternal a. motherly c. anxious
   b. ever-increasing d. ancestral

7. temper- a. quick-tempered c. moderate
   ate b. tropical d. too cold

8. contra- a. illegal goods c. unlikely
   band b. disliking music d. mysterious

9. caliber a. dimensions c. shade
   b. character d. quality

10. contro- a. open to debate c. disliked
    versial b. unanimous d. complicated

11. profound a. bookish c. foolish
    b. difficult d. deep

12. parasite a. telescope c. native of Paris
    b. one that lives d. protective
    at the expense shield
    of another

13. illusion a. picture c. false impres-
    b. light sion
    d. a pattern of
    stars

14. maim a. cripple c. frighten
    b. capture d. threaten

15. perpetual a. wearing away c. seldom
    b. desirable d. lasting forever

16. lenient a. melodious c. soothing
    b. transparent d. not severe

17. novice   a. expert   c. beginner
           b. something new   d. priest
              and strange
18. humane   a. living   c. valuable
           b. conscientious   d. kind
19. authen-   a. antique   c. genuine
     tic   b. literary   d. false
20. carica-   a. scene in color   c. slight damage
     ture   b. circus per-   d. cartoon
              former

Word List

In your reading you will frequently encounter the words in the following list. Make this list the basis of your vocabulary work throughout the year, and learn about ten words a week. The following plan is one way to study the list. Your teacher may have additional suggestions.

1. *List the words* in your notebook, ten at a time, leaving a space of two lines between words.

2. *Look up each word* in the dictionary, and write after the word a short definition or a synonym. If a word has several meanings, your teacher will tell you which meaning or meanings to record and learn.

3. *Write* on the lines below the definition a sentence in which you use the word correctly.

4. *Copy in your notebook* any sentences showing good context clues to the meanings of these words.

5. *Take a test.* When your teacher dictates the words, write them correctly spelled, and after each word write its meaning.

Vocabulary List

abate	abominable	abrupt
abhor	abridge	abstain

accord
acute
adhere
adopt

advocate
aggravate
alien
ally
alternate
amends
anguish
anticipate
antiseptic
appease

approximate
assail
audible
austere
authentic
avarice
avert
banish
beguile
blemish

bravado
burnish
caliber
candid
caricature
challenge
cherish
clamber
coincide
compassion

compensate

competent
comply
compute
condescend
confirm
conform
congregate
conspire
contemplate

contraband
controversial
credible
crucial
debris
deem
defiant
deliberate
delusion
deplore

diligent
diminish
discretion
disperse
distort
distract
dubious
economical
elaborate
eloquent

elude
emancipate
enhance
entice
era
eventual
exclude

exotic
expand
exultant

faculty
fascinate
feign
fluctuate
frivolous
frugal
furtive
futile
gaudy
genial

grandeur
gratify
grimace
grotesque
guarantee
haggard
homage
hostile
hover
humane

hypocrite
hysterical
illusion
illustrious
impair
impartial
incompatible
incredible
indispensable
inert

infinite
intolerable

intricate
irritable
jostle
judicial
languish
legacy
legitimate
lenient

loiter
lucid
lure
maim
malicious
manuscript
maternal
meditate
mercenary
moderate

mythology
nocturnal
notorious
novice
nurture
obsolete
obstinate
omen
opponent
parasite

partial

paternal
perennial
perilous
perpetual
pestilence
pious
placid
plausible
pompous

ponderous
prate
precarious
prestige
profound
protrude
prudent
quell
query
rapture

rebuke
recoil
refrain
refute
relent
renounce
repel
replenish
resolve
retaliate

sanction
satellite
segregation
sequel
signify
speculate
spontaneous
subsequent
subside
subtle

sumptuous
surmise
temperate
temporary
terminate
tranquil
transgress
transient
turmoil
uncanny

uncouth
unscrupulous
utility
valiant
vanquish
velocity
versatile
veto
vivacious
zealous

Chapter 24

Spelling

Improving Your Spelling

Spelling is easy for some people and hard for others. It is a necessary skill because one's education is sometimes judged by ability to spell. With a little effort you can master some useful spelling rules and a few important exceptions.

GOOD SPELLING HABITS

1. *Keep a list of your own errors.*

Spelling, as you probably have discovered, is a very personal matter. What is a hard word for one person is easy for another. You should keep a list of the words that you misspell, either as a part of your English notebook or in a separate spelling notebook. When you misspell a word, follow these three steps:

a. See the word correctly spelled. Make a mental picture of what the word looks like.
b. Hear the word. Pronounce the word correctly by syllables several times.
c. Write the word correctly. Write the word on your spelling list, dividing it into syllables and putting in the main accent mark. Then write the word several times on a sheet of scratch paper.

2. *Use the dictionary as a spelling aid.*

When in doubt about the spelling of a word, look it

up. Guessing is much easier, but if you wish to be sure, open the dictionary. After a while you will have the dictionary habit.

3. *Spell by syllables.*

Break down long words into short syllables. It's not possible to spell all words by syllable, but if you make a habit of using that method, you'll find that your spelling will quickly improve.

4. *Avoid mispronunciations that lead to spelling errors.*

Good spelling often results from good pronunciation. If you say *gov-ern-ment,* it's more than likely that you will spell the word correctly. If you say *arc-tic,* you probably will remember to include the first *c.* Poor spelling often results from these errors in pronunciation:

a. the omission of a letter: reconize for recognize, suprise for surprise
b. the addition of a letter: ath*a*lete for athlete, enterance for entrance
c. the substitution of letters: chim*b*ley for chi**m**ney, e*x*cape for escape
d. the interchanging of the position of letters: ca*l*vary for cavalry, p*r*espiration for perspiration

5. *Revise to avoid careless spelling errors.*

Many spelling errors are a result of carelessness rather than ignorance. Reread your papers and correct errors that you may have made in haste.

SPELLING RULES

Many words fall under one or another of the following spelling rules. If you master these rules, you will help yourself to spell correctly. Remember, however, that there are many exceptions, and you must simply memorize words that do not follow the rules. List such words in your notebook, and review them often.

ie and *ei*

Words containing these pairs of letters have probably appeared on everyone's problem list at some time.

24a. Write *ie* when the sound is long *e*, except after *c*.

   EXAMPLES   chief, brief, believe, yield, receive, deceive

EXCEPTIONS   seize, leisure, neither, weird

Write *ei* when the sound is not long *e*, especially when the sound is long *a*.

   EXAMPLES   sleigh, veil, freight, weight, height

EXCEPTIONS   friend, mischief

You may find this time-tested verse a help.

> *I* before *e*
> Except after *c*,
> Or when sounded like *a*,
> As in *neighbor* and *weigh*.

If you use this rhyme, remember that *i* before *e* refers only to words in which this combination of letters stands for the sound of long *e*, as in the examples under 24a.

EXERCISE 1. Write the following words, supplying the missing letters (*e* and *i*) in the correct order. Be able to explain how the rule applies to each. Do not write in the book.

1. s .. ze
2. n .. ther
3. rec .. ve
4. h .. ght
5. fr .. nd
6. br .. f
7. dec .. ve
8. l .. sure
9. misch .. f
10. w .. ght
11. .. ght
12. rec .. pt
13. sl .. gh
14. fr .. ght
15. th .. r
16. n .. ghbor
17. c .. ling
18. shr .. k
19. r .. gn
20. p .. ce

–cede, –ceed, and –sede

24b. Only one word in English ends in *–sede—super-sede;* only three words end in *–ceed—exceed, proceed,* and *succeed;* all other words of similar sound end in *–cede.*

EXAMPLES   concede, recede, precede

PREFIXES AND SUFFIXES

24c. When a prefix is added to a word, the spelling of the word itself remains the same.

A *prefix* is a letter or a group of letters added to the beginning of a word to change its meaning.

EXAMPLES

in + audible = inaudible
im + mature = immature
dis + appear = disappear
mis + sent = missent

il + legal = illegal
un + natural = unnatural
over + run = overrun
un + tied = untied

EXERCISE 2. Write the numbers 1–20 on your paper. Then write these words in order, spelled correctly.

1. il + legible	11. im + mortal
2. un + avoidable	12. mis + spell
3. in + appropriate	13. over + ripe
4. il + logical	14. over + run
5. mis + spent	15. dis + satisfy
6. over + rated	16. dis + approve
7. un + necessary	17. im + passable
8. un + counted	18. mis + understand
9. im + partial	19. over + rule
10. in + offensive	20. mis + sent

24d. When the suffixes *–ness* and *–ly* are added to a word, the spelling of the word itself is not changed.

A suffix is a letter or group of letters added at the end of a word to change its meaning.

EXAMPLES sudden + ness = suddenness
truthful + ly = truthfully
final + ly = finally

EXCEPTIONS Most words ending in *y* do not follow this rule. Instead, the *y* is changed to *i*.
kindly + ness = kindliness
day + ly = daily

24e. Drop the final *e* before a suffix beginning with a vowel.[1]

EXAMPLES drive + ing = driving
love + able = lovable

EXCEPTIONS Words ending in *–ce* and *–ge*, however, usually keep the silent *e* when the suffix begins with *a* or *o* in order to preserve the soft sound of the final consonant.
notice + able = noticeable
change + able = changeable

[1] Vowels are the letters *a, e, i, o, u*, and sometimes *y*. All other letters of the alphabet are *consonants*.

24f. Keep the final *e* before a suffix beginning with a consonant.

EXAMPLES   care + less = careless
state + ment = statement
plate + ful = plateful
false + hood = falsehood

EXCEPTIONS   argue + ment = argument
true + ly = truly

EXERCISE 3. Write correctly the words formed as follows.

1. hopeful + ly
2. care + ing
3. sincere + ly
4. write + ing
5. desire + able
6. smile + ing
7. true + ly
8. hope + ing
9. advance + ment
10. shave + ing

24g. With words ending in *y* preceded by a consonant, change the *y* to *i* before any suffix not beginning with *i*.

EXAMPLES   pry + ed = pried
happy + ness = happiness
bounty + ful = bountiful

Words ending in *y* preceded by a vowel do not change their spelling before a suffix.

EXAMPLE   key + ed = keyed

24h. With words of one syllable ending in a single consonant preceded by a single vowel, double the consonant before adding *–ing, –ed,* or *–er*.

EXAMPLES   sit + ing = sitting
hop + ed = hopped
dip + er = dipper

With a one-syllable word ending in a single consonant which is *not* preceded by a single vowel, do not
double the consonant before adding *–ing, –ed,* or
–er.

EXAMPLES   reap + ed = reaped; heat + ing = heating
[The final consonant is preceded by two
vowels.]

EXERCISE 4. Write correctly the words formed as
follows.

1. bay + ing
2. silly + ness
3. drop + ed
4. slam + ing
5. embody + ment
6. swim + er
7. cry + ed
8. hurry + ed
9. tap + ing
10. leap + ed

THE PLURAL OF NOUNS

English is a peculiar language in its formation of
plurals. You learn a half-dozen rules—then you encounter an exception! You usually add *–s* to form a
plural; but you know that the plural of *sheep* is *sheep.*
The plural of *goose* is *geese,* but the plural of *mon-
goose* is *mongooses.* The plural of *radius* is *radii,* but
the plural of *circus* isn't *circi.*

Here are a few rules that *will* help you. Learn them
and their exceptions, and you will be well on your way
to mastering the formation of plurals.

24i. Observe the rules for spelling the plural of nouns.

**(1) The regular way to form the plural of a noun is to
add an *–s.***

EXAMPLES   girl, girls   task, tasks

(2) The plural of nouns ending in _s, x, z, ch,_ or _sh_ is formed by adding _–es_.

The _e_ is necessary to make the plural form pronounceable.

EXAMPLES   moss, mosses   birch, birches
wax, waxes   dish, dishes
waltz, waltzes

EXERCISE 5. Write the plural of the following nouns.

1. box   3. stitch   5. church 7. buzz   9. miss
2. crash 4. address 6. fox   8. witch 10. tax

(3) The plural of nouns ending in _y_ preceded by a consonant is formed by changing the _y_ to _i_ and adding _–es_.

EXAMPLES   lady, ladies   guppy, guppies

(4) The plural of nouns ending in _y_ preceded by a vowel is formed by adding _–s_.

EXAMPLES   toy, toys   tourney, tourneys

(5) The plural of most nouns ending in _f_ is formed by adding _–s_. The plural of some nouns ending in _f_ or _fe_ is formed by changing the _f_ to _v_ and adding _–s_ or _–es_.

EXAMPLES   Add _–s:_
gulf, gulfs   belief, beliefs
Change _f_ to _v_ and add _–s:_
knife, knives   life, lives
Change _f_ to _v_ and add _–es:_
half, halves   thief, thieves
loaf, loaves   wolf, wolves

(6) The plural of nouns ending in _o_ preceded by a

vowel is formed by adding –*s;* **the plural of nouns ending in** *o* **preceded by a consonant is formed by adding** –*es.*

EXAMPLES *o* preceded by a vowel — add –*s:*
  patio, patios   ratio, ratios

  o preceded by a consonant –add –*es:*
  tornado, tornadoes   hero, heroes

EXCEPTIONS Eskimo, Eskimos   silo, silos

Notice that the plural of most nouns ending in *o* and pertaining to music is formed by adding –*s:*

  piano, pianos   alto, altos
  solo, solos   trio, trios

  Some of these are exceptions to the rule; others are not.

(7) The plural of a few nouns is formed in irregular ways.

EXAMPLES child, children   mouse, mice
  woman, women   foot, feet
  ox, oxen   tooth, teeth

EXERCISE 6. Write the plural of the following nouns.

  1. turkey   11. valley
  2. loaf   12. self
  3. studio   13. contralto
  4. woman   14. chimney
  5. chief   15. potato
  6. journey   16. baby
  7. monkey   17. ditty
  8. soprano   18. tomato
  9. thief   19. child
  10. puppy   20. echo

(8) The plural of compound nouns consisting of a noun

plus a modifier is formed by making the modified noun plural.

EXAMPLES   sister-in-law, sisters-in-law
coat-of-arms, coats-of-arms
man-hour, man-hours

(9) The plural of a few compound nouns is formed in irregular ways.

EXAMPLES   eight-year-old, eight-year-olds
tie-up, tie-ups
drive-in, drive-ins

(10) Some nouns are the same in the singular and the plural.

EXAMPLES   deer, sheep, salmon, Sioux

(11) The plural of numbers, letters, signs, and words considered as words is formed by adding an apostrophe and –s.

EXAMPLES   1800   1800's
B   B's
&   &'s

EXERCISE 7. Write the plural of the following expressions.

1. side-wheeler
2. moose
3. mother-in-law
4. 1930
5. m
6. thirteen-year-old
7. trout
8. governor-elect
9. Chinese
10. commander-in-chief

REVIEW EXERCISE A. Write the plurals of the following nouns. After each plural, write the number of the rule (1–11) that applies. Use the dictionary if you are in doubt.

1. wish	18. thief
2. elf	19. squash
3. rally	20. radio
4. twelve-year-old	21. loaf
5. valley	22. pulley
6. roof	23. appendix
7. rodeo	24. mouth
8. briefcase	25. scenario
9. child	26. church
10. goose	27. camera
11. mix	28. lady
12. house	29. buffalo
13. volcano	30. ax
14. hero	31. alley
15. leaf	32. box
16. p and q	33. motto
17. woman	

WORDS OFTEN CONFUSED

The words that follow are often confused with each other. Study the explanations and do the exercises that follow. Make sure that you can spell and pronounce each word correctly and that you know the part of speech of each word as it is used in the example sentence.

accept	*to receive; to agree to* The Lanfords would not *accept* our gift.
except	*with the exclusion of; but* Everyone *except* Lauren agreed.
advice	*a recommendation for action* What is your mother's *advice?*

advise   *to recommend a course of action*
She *advises* me to take the camp job.

---

affect   *to act upon; to change*
Does bad weather *affect* your health?

effect   *result; consequence*
What *effect* does the weather have on your health?

---

already   *previously*
We have *already* studied that chapter.

all ready   *all prepared* or *in readiness*
The launching crew is *all ready* for the signal to blast off.

EXERCISE 8. Write the numbers 1–10 on your paper. After each number, write the word from the pair in parentheses that will make the sentence correct.

1. By the time Jody arrived, Peter had (already, all ready) cooked supper.
2. One of the purposes of the Cabinet is to (advice, advise) the President.
3. The soft music had a soothing (affect, effect) on the worried man.
4. The girls were (already, all ready) for the sleigh ride.
5. The supply of oil has an important (affect, effect) on driving habits.
6. The snow has melted everywhere (accept, except) in the mountains.
7. The doctor's (advice, advise) was to take a vacation.
8. She was happy to (accept, except) the invitation to the party.
9. Our reading usually (affects, effects) our composition.

10. Your (advice, advise) got me into trouble!

altar	*a table or stand at which religious rites are performed* There was a bowl of flowers on the *altar*.
alter	*to change* Another hurricane may *alter* the shoreline near our town.
altogether	*entirely* It is *altogether* too cold for swimming.
all together	*everyone in the same place* Will our class be *all together* on the trip?
brake	*a device to stop a machine* I used the emergency *brake* to stop the rolling car.
break	*to fracture; to shatter* Don't *break* that mirror!
capital	*a city, the location of a government* Do you know the *capitals* of the fifty states?
capitol	*the building in which a legislative body meets* [usually capitalized] Nearly every visitor to Washington goes to the *Capitol*.
cloths	*pieces of cloth* I need some more cleaning *cloths*.
clothes	*wearing apparel* I have outgrown all of my *clothes*.

EXERCISE 9. Write the numbers 1–10 on your paper. After each number, write the word from the pair in parentheses that will make the sentence correct.

1. My summer (cloths, clothes) are loose and light.
2. In England one can still see remains of (altars, alters) built by early tribes.
3. A bicyclist can wear out a set of (brakes, breaks) going down a steep mountain.
4. You should use soft (cloths, clothes) to clean silver.
5. The cold weather did not (altar, alter) her plans for a vacation at the beach.
6. Sacramento is the (capital, capitol) of California.
7. Put the pieces of the vase (altogether, all together) and I will try to repair it.
8. A nation may (brake, break) a treaty that no longer serves its interests.
9. On the dome of the (capital, Capitol) stands a large bronze statue of Freedom.
10. The audience was (altogether, all together) charmed by the speaker's wit.

coarse *rough, crude, large*
The *coarse* sand acts as a filter.

course *path of action; series of studies;* also used in the expression *of course*
What is the best *course* for me to take?
You may change your mind, *of course.*

complement *something that completes*
A predicate nominative is one kind of *complement.*

compliment *to praise someone; praise from someone*
Mrs. Bryant *complimented* Jean on her speech.
Thank you for the *compliment.*

council *a group of people who meet together to discuss or advise*
The mayor's *council* has seven members.

councilor   *a member of a council*
The mayor appointed seven *councilors*.

counsel   *advice* or *to give advice*
You need legal *counsel* on this matter.

counselor   *one who advises*
Mrs. Higgins is the guidance *counselor* for the seventh grade.

---

des'ert   *a dry, barren, sandy region; a wilderness*
The cactus is a common flower in the *desert*.

desert'   *to abandon, to forsake; to leave without permission*
Good sports do not *desert* their teammates.

dessert'   *the final course of a meal; usually a sweet course*
Let's have ice cream for *dessert*.

EXERCISE 10. Write the numbers 1–10 on your paper. After each number, write the correct one of the words in the parentheses.

1. The city (council, counsel) will not meet unless seven of the ten (councilors, counselors) are present.
2. The patient received (council, counsel) from the doctor on the best (coarse, course) to a speedy, safe recovery.
3. Mustard and relish are the usual (complements, compliments) of hot dogs.
4. We are eager to see the new puppy, of (coarse, course).
5. Peter is preparing the (desert, dessert) tonight.
6. Marilyn made a skirt out of (coarse, course) burlap.

7. The leader would not (desert, dessert) his men.
8. I want your (council, counsel), not your (complements, compliments).
9. After several days on the hot (desert, dessert), they began to see mirages.
10. Our camp (councilor, counselor) advised us to eat fruit for our (desert, dessert).

---

formally *with dignity; following strict rules or procedure*
We must behave *formally* at the reception.

formerly *previously; at an earlier date*
Formerly, people thought travel to the moon was impossible.

---

hear *to receive sounds through the ears*
You can *hear* a whisper through these walls.

here *this place*
How long have you lived *here?*

---

its a personal pronoun showing possession
That book has lost *its* cover.

it's contraction of *it is* or *it has*
It's the coldest winter anyone can remember.

---

lead *to go first, to be a leader* [present tense]
Can she *lead* us out of this tunnel?

led past tense of *lead*
Elizabeth Blackwell *led* the movement for hospital reform.

lead *a heavy metal*
There is no *lead* in a *lead* pencil.

---

loose *to unfasten, to free; to be free; not tight*

Loose that rope, please.
How did the dog get *loose?*
This belt is too *loose.*

lose   *to suffer loss*
Fran will *lose* the argument if she doesn't
check her facts.

---

passed   *went by; past tense of pass*
Three ice cream trucks have *passed* in the
last five minutes.

past   *that which has gone by; beyond; by*
A good historian makes the *past* come alive.
That era is *past.*

EXERCISE 11. Write the numbers 1–10 on your paper.
After each number, write the word from the group
in parentheses that will make the sentence correct.

1. The woman who (formally, formerly) (lead, led)
   the band moved to Alaska.
2. We do not expect to (loose, lose) any of our back-
   field players this year.
3. We (passed, past) three stalled cars this morning.
4. "Why did you (lead, led) us (hear, here)?" the
   boys demanded.
5. Can you (hear, here) the difference between your
   speakers and mine?
6. We have been (lead, led) into a trap.
7. How did the ship get (loose, lose) from the side
   of the dock?
8. The guests are to dress (formally, formerly) for
   the party.
9. "I think (it's, its) time for a quiz," announced
   Mrs. Ferrari.
10. Has the school bus gone (passed, past) the street
    where you live?

peace   *quiet order and security*
World *peace* is the goal of the United Nations.

piece   *a part of something*
Here is a pretty *piece* of silk.

plain   *unadorned, simple, common;* also *a flat area of land*
Blue jeans were part of his *plain* appearance.
A broad, treeless *plain* stretched before them.

plane   *a flat surface; a tool; an airplane*
Use an inclined *plane* to move that chest.
I have just learned how to use a carpenter's *plane*.
Have you ever flown in a *plane?*

principal   *the head of a school;* also *chief, main*
The *principal* spoke of the *principal* duties of students.

principle   *a rule of conduct; a fundamental truth*
Action should be guided by *principles*.

quiet   *still and peaceful; without noise*
The forest was very *quiet*.

quite   *wholly or entirely;* also *to a great extent*
Some students are already *quite* sure of their career plans.

shone   past tense of *shine*
The moon *shone* softly over the grass.

shown   *revealed;* past participle of *show*
Ms. Cross has *shown* me how to do the experiment.

EXERCISE 12. Write the numbers 1–10 on your paper.

After each number write the word from the group in parentheses that will make the sentence correct.

1. Each drop of water (shone, shown) like crystal.
2. Motor vehicles are one of the (principal, principle) sources of air pollution in our cities.
3. If you don't hurry, you'll miss your (plain, plane).
4. The (principal, principle) of trust can lead to world (peace, piece).
5. Jan has (shone, shown) me how to change a tire.
6. It is clear that Luisa is acting on (principal, principle), not from personal motive.
7. On Christmas Eve we always have eggnog and a (peace, piece) of fruitcake.
8. "What a (quiet, quite) Fourth of July," Miss Bascom remarked.
9. "For once," the (principal, principle) announced with a smile, "you don't have to be (quiet, quite)."
10. (Plain, Plane) fruits and vegetables can make a nutritious meal.

---

stationary   *in a fixed position*
Is that gear *stationary?*

stationery   *writing paper*
Have you any white *stationery?*

---

than   a conjunction used in comparisons
Alaska is bigger *than* Texas.

then   *at that time*
If she will see me after class, we can talk about it *then.*

---

their   possessive form of *they*
Can you understand *their* message?

there   *a place;* also used in the expression *there are*
Let's meet *there.*
There are three new girls in gym class.

they're   contraction of *they are*
                They're all from California.

threw   past tense of *throw*
                Ted *threw* me the mitt.

through   a preposition
                I can't see *through* the lens.

EXERCISE 13. Write the numbers 1–10 on your paper. After each number write the word from the group in parentheses that makes the sentence correct.

1. That noise is from a jet plane going (threw, through) the sound barrier.
2. The stars seem to be (stationary, stationery), but we know that (their, there, they're) moving at speeds up to forty-eight kilometers per second.
3. Is Lake Erie larger (than, then) Lake Huron?
4. The pitcher (threw, through) a curve.
5. A (stationary, stationery) store usually sells pens, twine, and other items, too.
6. She would rather live now (than, then) in the Middle Ages.
7. The girls brought (their, there, they're) displays for the science fair.
8. A moving target is harder to hit (than, then) a (stationary, stationery) one.
9. Betty can't get (threw, through) to Rochester because the circuits are busy.
10. (Their, They're, There) first rehearsal will be after school today.

to   a preposition
        We are going *to* California.

too   *also; to an excessive degree*
        Audrey is going, *too*.
        I ate *too* much pie.

two	a number We caught *two* fish.

weak	*feeble; not strong* May's illness has left her very *weak*.
week	*seven days* Let's practice again next *week*.

weather	*the condition of the air, the atmosphere* The *weather* seems to be changing.
whether	*a conjunction expressing* doubt We don't know *whether* it will work.

who's	contraction of *who is* or *who has* *Who's* going to the museum?
whose	possessive form of *who* *Whose* report was the most original?

your	possessive form of *you* What is *your* middle name?
you're	contraction of *you are* *You're* expected at the Wallaces in an hour.

EXERCISE 14. Write the numbers 1–10 on your paper. After each number, write the word from the parentheses that makes the sentence correct.

1. (Who's, Whose) the present Secretary of State of the United States?
2. We built (to, too, two) snow forts on our front lawn.
3. "(Your, You're) late," my friend complained.
4. Would you be able to stand the (weather, whether) in Alaska?
5. That sounds like a (weak, week) excuse to me.
6. (Your, You're) dog is (to, too, two) sleepy to do its tricks.

7. "(Who's, Whose) boots are these?" Mrs. Allen asked.
8. The pilot had to decide (weather, whether) to parachute to safety or try to land the crippled plane.
9. Final exams start next (weak, week).
10. We are driving (to, too, two) New Orleans for Christmas.

REVIEW EXERCISE B. Write the numbers 1–20 on your paper. Copy the words from the parentheses that will make the sentences correct.

You may have heard of the play *Macbeth,* a tragedy by William Shakespeare. The (**1.** principal, principle) character, Macbeth, was (**2.** altogether, all together) (**3.** to, too, two) ambitious for his own good. When he heard three witches prophesy that he would be the new king, he (**4.** accepted, excepted) (**5.** their, there, they're) prediction as true and decided to bring it to pass immediately. His wife did not remain (**6.** quiet, quite). She was willing for Macbeth to kill the king. Her (**7.** advice, advise) was to act at once. In fact, her (**8.** council, counsel) was largely responsible for his (**9.** coarse, course) of action.

When the king visited Macbeth's castle, Macbeth and his wife greeted him with (**10.** complements, compliments). They were (**11.** already, all ready) to proceed with their plan. That night, while the king was sleeping, Macbeth slipped (**12.** past, passed) the guards and (**13.** threw, through) the door into the king's chamber. As the king slept, Macbeth plunged a dagger into his heart. Nothing now could (**14.** altar, alter) Macbeth's plan to be king. But this deed had its (**15.** affect, effect) on Macbeth's conscience. He gained the throne but lost his (**16.** peace, piece) of mind. From that night on, while others slept, Macbeth lay awake. Macbeth had murdered the king, and he had murdered sleep, (**17.** to, too, two). His bloody deed (**18.** lead, led) him on to still other crimes which eventually caused Lady Macbeth to (**19.** loose, lose) her sanity and Macbeth to (**20.** loose, lose) his life.

REVIEW EXERCISE C. Write the numbers 1–20 on your paper. Copy the words from the parentheses that will make the sentences correct.

Last March my family could not decide (**1.** weather, whether) to visit Boston or Philadelphia. Finally we decided on Boston, the (**2.** capital, capitol) of Massachusetts. We drove (**3.** to, too, two) the city in three days. Even my parents could not conceal (**4.** their, there, they're) excitement. We did not (**5.** loose, lose) a moment. Boston (**6.** formally, formerly) was "the hub of the universe," and we discovered that (**7.** it's, its) still a fascinating city. Everyone in my family (**8.** accept, except) me had eaten lobster, and I had my first one in Boston. I was not (**9.** altogether, all together) certain how to eat the lobster, but this doubt did not (**10.** affect, effect) my appetite. My parents insisted that a banana split was a strange (**11.** desert, dessert) to follow lobster, but I would not (**12.** altar, alter) my order. After the banana split, I wanted a small (**13.** peace, piece) of pie, but my father told me to be (**14.** quiet, quite).

While in Boston we often walked up and down the streets just to (**15.** hear, here) the strange accent of the Bostonians. (**16.** Their, There, They're) especially noted for (**17.** their, there, they're) pronunciation of *a*'s and *r*'s.

We had not been in Boston long before the (**18.** weather, whether) bureau predicted a big snowstorm for the area. Since we had not taken the proper (**19.** cloths, clothes) for snow, we decided to return home. On the way back we were (**20.** already, all ready) making plans for another visit to Boston.

COMMONLY MISSPELLED WORDS

No matter how many spelling rules you learn, you will find that it is helpful to learn to spell certain common words from memory. The fifty "demons" below are words that you should be able to spell without any hesitation, even though they all contain spelling problems. Study them in groups of five until you are sure of them.

The longer list that follows contains words that you should learn this year if you do not already know them. They are grouped by tens, so that you may conveniently study them ten at a time. In studying each list, pay particular attention to the letters printed in heavy type. These letters are generally the ones which offer most students the greatest difficulty in correctly spelling each word.

FIFTY SPELLING DEMONS

ache	easy	shoes
again	every	since
always	friend	straight
answer	guess	sugar
blue	half	sure
built	hour	tear
busy	instead	though
buy	knew	through
can't	know	tired
color	laid	tonight
cough	minute	trouble
could	often	wear
country	once	where
doctor	ready	women
does	said	won't
don't	says	write
early	seems	

TWO HUNDRED SPELLING WORDS

absence
absolutely
acceptance
accommodate
accumulate
achieve
acquire
across
advertisement
against

aisles
among
announce
anxiety
apology
apparent
appreciation
arctic
arguing
argument

arithmetic
assistance
associate
attacked
attendance
attitude
attorney
basis
beginning
believe

benefit
bicycle
bough
bouquet

brief
brilliant
bureau
business
candidate
career

careless
carrying
ceased
ceiling
choice
college
committee
completely
conceive
conscience

conscious
control
correspondence
courteous
criticize
curiosity
decision
definite
describe
description

desirable
divide
divine
efficiency
eighth
eliminate
embarrass
equipment

especially
exactly

excellent
execute
existence
experience
experiment
explanation
extremely
familiar
favorite
February

field
fierce
finally
foliage
foreign
fortunately
forty
fourth
genius
genuine

government
governor
grammar
guarantee
height
heir
heroes
humorous
hungrily
icicles

imaginary

immediately
independent
inoculate
intelligence
interest
interpret
judgment
knowledge
laboratory

leisure
license
liquor
loneliness
luxury
magazine
marriage
mathematics
meant
medicine

mischief
muscle
museum
necessary
nervous
nineteen
ninety
occasion
occur
occurrence

opinion
opportunity
originally
particularly

patience
perceive
performance
permanent
personal
physical

picnic
possess
preferred
privilege
probably
professor
pursue
realize
receive
recommend

referred
religion
repetition
rhythm
safety
satisfy
scene
schedule
seize
sense

separate
shining
similar
society
speech
strength
studying

stupefy
succeed
success

surprise
suspicion
sympathy
technique
temperament
temporary
theory
thorough
tongue
tragedy

transferred
treasury
tries
university
unnecessary
unusually
useful
using
vacuum
vague

various
veil
vicinity
villain
violence
warrior
wholly
whose
writing
yield

Speaking
and
Listening

PART SEVEN

Chapter **25**

Speaking

Introductions, Giving Directions, Preparing and Delivering a Talk

As you grow older, you encounter new types of social situations. Often you are expected to take part in social conversations and to make and acknowledge introductions. In school you may give a talk in class or make a report to a club.

Learning how to speak effectively in front of a group is not difficult. You need only a few rules — and some practice.

INTRODUCTIONS

Knowing how to introduce people helps to put yourself and others at ease.

25a. Follow the customary methods of making and responding to introductions.

When you are introducing friends your own age, you may be informal and use first names.

EXAMPLES   "Alice Durgin, Jack Burke"
            "Jack, Alice Durgin"

The expressions *may I introduce* and *may I present* are formal. You probably will not have many occasions to use them. You should use whatever words come naturally to you. The important thing is for each person to learn the other's name.

(1) In introducing a younger person to an older person, if there is a distinct difference in ages, speak the older person's name first.

EXAMPLES   "Mom, this is Mary Malone. Mary, this is my mother."

"Mr. Kent, these are my brothers Tom and Matt. This is my science teacher, Mr. Kent."

(2) Introduce boys to girls and men to women.

An easy way of doing this is to speak the female name first, even if there is a distinct difference in ages.

EXAMPLES   "Mrs. Blair, may I present Mr. Jordan? Mr. Jordan, this is Mrs. Blair."

"Julie, I'd like to introduce my grandfather, Mr. Hopkins. Grandfather, Julie Gomez."

When someone is introduced to you, be sure to listen for the name. Respond with a smile and a friendly greeting. To people of your own age, you probably say "Hi" or "Hello." "How do you do?" is a customary response in formal situations. Repeating the name of the person who has been introduced will help to fix it in your mind.

EXAMPLES   "Hello, Judy."
"Hi, Mike and Bud."
"How do you do, Mrs. Fullerton?"

EXERCISE 1. Practice making introductions, using the following situations.

1. A mother introduces her seventh-grade son to the new owner of the house next door.
2. A father brings home the chief partner of his firm and introduces his daughter, who has been sitting in a chair, reading.
3. Two cousins, Roberto and Maria, are introduced to each other by their grandmother.
4. A son sits in a restaurant with his parents. A couple the parents know comes to their table. The son is introduced.
5. Michelle introduces Franklin, a new student in her science class, to two friends, Laura and Gracie.

(3) On some occasions, it is convenient and proper to introduce yourself.

Sometimes you will have occasion to introduce yourself. Simply say: "Hello. I'm Betty Perkins," or "Hi. I'm Jim Blake from Central High," or "How do you do? I'm Charles Blunt from Clifton."

(4) In introducing a newcomer to a roomful of people, do not present everybody at once (it is hard to remember all the names), but introduce small groups.

EXAMPLES "John Cagle, Al Newlin, this is Ed Benton."

"I would like you to meet Edith Saunders. Edith, this is Irene Newsom, Louise Ames, and Doris Allen."

(5) Respond to an introduction properly.

When a younger person is introduced to an older person, the older person takes the lead in handshaking. When one person extends a hand, it is the natural and gracious thing for the other to shake it. It is polite to rise from your seat when being introduced to someone.

(6) Help to start a conversation when you make an introduction.

When you introduce people, add a friendly remark. Say something that will help to put the two strangers at ease and give them something to talk about.

EXAMPLES   "Mom, this is Ellen Knorr. Ellen just entered our school today."

"Rick, this is my friend Jack Simon from Eastern High. Jack is planning to go out for track, too."

EXERCISE 2.   Make introductions according to the following situations.

1. Write on a piece of paper your name, a magazine you read, a book you've just read, and a hobby or special interest. Select from the class two of these slips of paper. Introduce the two writers to each other, using some of the information on the papers to start a conversation.
2. Newcomers with a daughter about your age move in next door. You see her for the first time and introduce yourself.
3. You are waiting to catch a bus. Standing near you are two young people of your own age, also waiting. You've seen them before but have never talked to them. Introduce yourself.
4. You take your cousin Glenda to a party. The young people are all sitting at tables, playing a game. You introduce your cousin.
5. In the following introductions, a clue is provided to start a conversation between the people introduced. How would you begin a conversation?

   a. "Nora Bates, Sally Morris. Nora, Sally just moved here from Honolulu." (What might Nora say?)

b. "Ed, I'd like you to meet Jeff Roberts. This is Ed Kindy. Ed, Jeff's dad works for a circus." (If you were Ed, what could you say?)

c. "Joan, this is Pete Sims. Joan Ryan. Joan, Pete was asking about the 4–H Club here. He used to be a member in Colorado." (What might Joan say?)

CONVERSATIONS

For all of us, there are times when we can't think of a thing to say, particularly with people we don't know well. A good rule to follow is to focus on the other person's interests, not your own. Sometimes the person who has introduced you will give you a clue to the stranger's interests. If you don't know anything about your companion, ask a question.

25b. Learn to converse easily and naturally.

(1) Do your part to get a conversation started.

EXAMPLES   "Dorothy, this is Celia Stern. Dorothy Hannen. Celia, Dorothy's new here. Her folks just moved near you. She doesn't know anybody yet."

"Hi, Dorothy. Welcome to Franklin Park! Did you move into that blue house on the corner?"

"Loren, this is Ed Bender. Ed, this is my brother."

"Hi, Ed. Do you live in this part of town, or are you visiting?"

Look at the person with whom you are talking and follow the conversation. Do not glance around the room or think about something else. Give your companion the courtesy of your full attention.

(2) Do your part to keep a conversation going.

Once a conversation has been started, be alert to keep it moving. Ask an occasional question to draw out further information, and contribute some ideas of your own on the subject being discussed.

Good manners in conversation are based on kindness and thoughtfulness. Bad manners usually arise out of carelessness. You can do much to build a habit of being tactful, considerate, and pleasant in talking to people.

Here are a few tips for conversing:

1. *Give the other person a chance to talk.* Try not to talk about yourself. Ask questions or mention subjects that the other person will want to talk about.

2. *Use a conversational tone.* Do not mumble and do not shout.

3. *Listen to the other person.* Pay close attention to whatever a person has to say.

4. *Be good-natured.* Try to be pleasant, even though you may disagree. Be patient and do not interrupt while someone is speaking.

EXERCISE 3. Hold a short conversation with a classmate by using one of the following situations as a guide. The rest of the class may evaluate the conversational manners of the speakers.

1. You are meeting a friend at his or her home to go to a movie. Your friend's mother answers the door and invites you to wait for a minute in the living room.
2. On a short bus trip, you meet a teacher whom you have not seen since last year.
3. At a baseball game, you realize that the person sitting next to you is a classmate you do not know well.

4. On a field trip or tour of a museum, you sit down in a lunchroom next to someone who is in your group but whom you do not know at all.

TELEPHONING

The telephone is so crucial in our lives that it is important to know how to use it efficiently and considerately.

25c. Learn to use the telephone correctly.

When you are talking on the telephone with someone who does not know you, your listener forms a mental image of you. You can influence this image by what you say and how you say it. Here is a list of rules for good telephone manners.

When making calls

1. Be sure you know the correct number and the correct method for placing the call. If you get a wrong number, apologize briefly for disturbing the person who answers.

2. Try not to telephone at mealtime or bedtime unless it is an emergency.

3. Identify yourself promptly when someone answers the telephone. If the person you are calling is not there, leave your name and number and, if you wish, a brief message.

4. Speak clearly. If you mumble or shout, or have the telephone too far away from you, conversation is difficult.

5. Have a pencil and a piece of paper at hand in case you wish to write down some information.

6. Do not talk too long. It is the responsibility of the person who makes the call to end it.

When receiving calls

1. Answer promptly and identify yourself.
2. Listen carefully and take notes of anything you will have to remember.
3. If the call interrupts you when you do not have time to talk, ask if you may return the call later.
4. Take a message if the call is for someone who is out. Write it down, and then repeat it to be sure you have the message straight. Check the spelling of names and addresses. Be sure to leave the message where the person called will find it.

EXERCISE 4. Prepare correct telephone dialogue with a classmate. Use one of the following suggestions for the dialogue.

(1) A student is calling to congratulate a friend for having been elected class president. (2) A baby sitter is at the home of Dr. and Mrs. A. R. King. Before leaving, the doctor gives instructions for locating him in case of an emergency call. The baby sitter receives such a call five minutes after he departs. (3) You have been asked to spend a few days with a friend in another town. Telephone him or her to discuss the details of your arrival by plane or bus.

GIVING DIRECTIONS AND EXPLANATIONS

All of us occasionally have to ask for help in finding a person or a place in a strange locality. We may be called on by others for such help, too. Or we may be asked to explain how to make fudge, repair a bicycle tire, sew on a button, or start a campfire. Giving clear, concise directions is a useful skill for everyone to have.

25d. Give directions and explanations that are orderly, complete, and accurate.

(1) Arrange information in a clear and logical order.

Before giving information to anyone, go over it in your own mind to simplify the steps and leave out unnecessary ones, and to arrange them in a sensible order that will be easy to remember.

UNCLEAR	"Just drive to the center of town, take one of the main streets east—if you go right on Boynton you'll have a detour—cross the river, go down the embankment to the motel district. You'll find the Riverside Motel in the middle somewhere."
CLEAR	"Drive straight ahead on Center to Main Street. Go right on Main, about one mile, to Riverside Road. Your motel is just beyond the yellow blinker, on the right."

(2) Give complete information.

When giving directions or explanations, make sure that you have included every necessary step. Obviously, by leaving out one necessary step, you can confuse the person you are trying to help.

(3) Review the steps.

If you are giving directions, go over them twice to give the other person a chance to remember them. You might then ask your listener to repeat them to you. In this way you can check on how well your instructions are understood. If necessary, you can correct a mistake or add any necessary detail.

EXERCISE 5. Select a well-known building or place of interest in your community and write a set of directions for reaching it from school. In class, the teacher will call upon individuals to read the directions aloud. The class will judge each set on how well

it would enable a stranger to reach the place concerned.

EXERCISE 6. Prepare directions or an explanation
for one of the following incidents.

1. The phone rings and you answer it. A friend of
   your parents' has just driven into town. He is tele-
   phoning from a drugstore on the outskirts of the
   city. Give directions to your house.
2. You are mowing your front lawn. A car stops at
   the curb, and the driver asks how to get to the
   bus station.
3. A new family has moved in next door. A member
   of the family, who is your age, asks you how to
   go to the post office, the junior high school, and
   the nearest movie theater.
4. A friend calls up to ask where a picnic could be
   held. Tell how to get to your favorite picnic site.
   (If you do not have one, invent one.)
5. You and a friend are on a fishing trip. Tell your
   friend how to clean a fish.
6. You and a friend are hiking in the country. You
   notice some poison ivy. Give directions for identifying poison ivy.
7. You and your sister have agreed to meet at a local
   department store. She is not familiar with the store.
   Tell her where inside the store to meet you and how
   to get there.

PREPARING AND DELIVERING A
SHORT TALK OR BOOK REPORT

Occasionally you may be called upon to deliver a
short talk or book report in one of your classes or at
a club meeting. Your task will be easier and more
enjoyable if you learn some basic methods of preparing and delivering a talk.

25e. Select a suitable topic.

Choose a topic that's part of your interests and your experience. Your enthusiasm for the subject will make your presentation more interesting to others.

Think how you can get your listeners interested in the subject. You may spend hours at a hobby, for example, but your audience will not have the same enthusiasm unless you express the pleasure and excitement the hobby gives you.

Once you have a topic that interests you and that you think will interest your audience, your next step is to narrow your topic so that you can cover it in a short time.

Suppose, for example, you are interested in water sports and want to talk about them. Obviously, you cannot cover all water sports in a short talk. You therefore decide to limit your topic to swimming.

List on a piece of paper some ideas that occur to you about swimming: the fun and excitement, the advantages of knowing how to swim, the various kinds of strokes, ways to improve your swimming, outstanding swimmers and their records. As you write these, you see that the subject is still too large. You narrow it further and decide to talk on the various types of swimming strokes.

When you are sure of your topic and have thought about what you will say, you are ready to organize your talk.

25f. Organize your material so that your listeners can easily follow you.

At this stage, you may jot down some notes to refer to as you are talking. Write them on 3 × 5-inch cards so that you can hold them easily in your hand. Remember, however, that you are giving a talk, not reading a speech. Don't write down everything that you will say. A few words or a sentence will remind you of each part of your talk.

A talk may be divided into three sections: (1) the introduction, (2) the body, and (3) the conclusion. These are the beginning, the middle, and the end.

The Introduction

The first thing you want to do is to attract your listeners' interest and attention. Do not waste your opening statement by saying something like, "This topic is one I have always been interested in." Such a sentence is not likely to draw your listeners' attention.

Instead, you might have an opening sentence that gives a general statement about swimming or asks a question about it. In a book report, your opening remark might refer to the main character or setting of the book.

EXAMPLES   Why is the dog paddle the first stroke most swimmers learn?

Queenie Peavy by Robert Burch is the story of a young girl growing up in Georgia in the 1930's.

Make the theme or purpose of your talk clear in your introduction. Do you want to explain a topic to your audience? Do you want to persuade your audience to do something? Do you want to convince your audience that your opinions are correct?

The Body

When you are trying to persuade or to influence your listeners, you may indicate your arrangement of arguments in your opening sentence or paragraph.

EXAMPLE   Conserving energy is every person's duty.
There are three important ways each of us
can save energy.

This introduction makes it clear that the body of your
talk will present the three ways to save energy.

When you are telling a story or giving an oral book
report, relate the events in the order in which they
happened. This arrangement of incidents is called a
time, or chronological, arrangement.

If your talk is to persuade or influence your listeners, cover all the points you want to make, one at
a time. It is usually better to proceed from your least
important point to your most important point.

EXERCISE 7.   Some of the following topics are suitable for a short talk, while some topics are too broad
in range or too narrow in interest. Choose a topic and
adapt it, if necessary, to make it more suitable. Then
think of an introduction for a short talk about it. Be
sure to think of the purpose of the talk and the points
your talk will make.

1. Solar power
2. Choosing a career
3. Sports
4. *Huckleberry Finn*
5. Recycling trash
6. Ten-speed bicycles
7. Horror movies
8. Training animals
9. Art
10. Space travel

The Conclusion

Make the conclusion a brief restatement of your talk's
purpose. If you are expressing an opinion, remind your
audience of your point of view. If you are persuading
your listeners to take some kind of action — vote for a
particular candidate, perhaps, or support some action
or cause — remind them of what you want them to do.

EXAMPLES   Each of these swimming strokes is easy to learn, as I've explained. Each is clearly more fun than the dog paddle.

Our energy needs can't wait. I urge you to take these energy-saving steps.

EXERCISE 8.   Analyze the following concluding remarks. Which are suitable? Which are weak?

1. In conclusion, I want to say thank you for your patience and good manners during my talk, and I'm sorry that I took longer than I intended.
2. I think everyone with an interest in jet planes should read this book, even though it is hard to understand in some places.
3. So you see, I've learned the hard way, and I'll be more cautious next time.
4. These are three of the reasons why major league baseball is more interesting if you choose one team to follow.
5. Bicycling is fun and it's a good way to get around. Unfortunately, not everyone has a bicycle.

Nonverbal Communication

How you say something can often be just as important as what you say. If you are delivering a speech and you look again and again at the clock, or lean casually against a desk or a wall, then these *nonverbal,* or unspoken, gestures will distract or possibly irritate your audience. A good speaker chooses nonverbal signals carefully and uses them to communicate effectively with the audience.

25g. Learn to deliver a talk effectively.

Look at your audience as you speak. Move your glance slowly from one side of the room to the other and try to focus on the faces of your listeners. Look for their reactions; they may indicate that you are speaking too fast or too softly, or that you might have to repeat something for emphasis.

If you are holding note cards, glance — but do not stare — at them as you speak. You should be looking at your audience during most of the talk, not at your notes.

As you speak, stand firmly — but not stiffly — on both feet. Keep your shoulders back and your head high.

Gestures will improve a speech if they are natural and help emphasize your words. Any movement you make while giving a speech is a gesture, and your audience will "read" your gestures as they listen to your words. If you scratch your head, the audience may think you are not sure of what to say next. If you shift your weight from one leg to another, your audience may think you are anxious to finish the talk. Many gestures such as these can be distracting. Try, as you speak, to control your gestures and use them to reinforce your words.

EXERCISE 9. Copy the following list of gestures on your paper. Next to each, write what you think the gesture means. Which gestures would be appropriate in a short talk? Be ready to explain your answers.

1. Pacing back and forth across the room
2. Putting one hand, palm down, under the chin
3. Putting one hand over each ear
4. Looking at the ceiling
5. Smiling
6. Yawning
7. Extending one hand, palm out, toward the audience
8. Cupping one ear with a hand

9. Putting thumb and forefinger on the chin
10. Leaning against something, such as a chair or a desk

EXERCISE 10. Each of the following topics is too general for a short talk. Narrow each topic to make it suitable for a short talk.

1. Pets
2. Music
3. Travel
4. Dancing
5. Farming
6. Cooking
7. Television
8. The future
9. Cars
10. Pollution
11. Mass transit
12. Growing up
13. Human rights
14. Good health

EXERCISE 11. Using the topic that you developed in Exercise 7 or one from Exercise 10, prepare and deliver a two-minute talk before the class.

Chapter 26

Listening

Listening Manners and Skills

How well we learn, how well we get along with others, even how successful we are in life, can depend in many ways on how well we listen. You can build good listening habits and improve them by practice.

26a. Show good listening manners in an audience and in conversation.

To show good listening manners:

1. Look at the speaker. Your expression and posture reveal your interest and appreciation.
2. Do not interrupt the speaker.
3. Do not doodle, read, whisper, or fidget.
4. Ask questions when they are invited, after the talk. Address the speaker politely, and show by your questions that you have listened carefully.

EXERCISE 1. During the next week, observe the listening manners of audiences you are in: at a movie, in church, at talks in school, and so on. When you get home, write down what you noticed. Be prepared to share your observations in class.

26b. Learn some useful techniques of listening.

Whether you are listening to some informal remarks or a prepared speech, you can put good listening techniques to work for you.

(1) Listen for the speaker's purpose.

A speaker may be giving information, expressing ideas or opinions, or trying to persuade you to do something. Usually the speaker will begin by stating the purpose. If you keep this purpose in mind as you listen, you will be able to follow the main points and to evaluate what you hear.

(2) Learn to follow a speaker's main points.

After the speaker's purpose is clear, your task is to follow the main points in the speech. In an informal discussion, when there are several speakers, the ideas may not be well organized. You must think as you listen, separating the main ideas from the details and illustrations.

Listening to a prepared talk is easier, because the main points are presented in a more organized form. The opening remarks may be like these: "There are three outstanding qualities that make this book memorable," or "What benefits will result from the passage of this bill?" Sometimes a speaker even numbers the points *first, second, third.* Some speakers pause as they introduce each important idea or use transitional words or phrases, such as:

so	however
next	furthermore
therefore	finally

Before concluding, a speaker may review the main points in the speech. Such a summary provides you with a double check.

(3) Take notes when necessary.

Whenever you want to be sure to retain the information you are hearing, you should jot down notes.

When you take notes, keep these questions in mind:

1. What is the speaker's purpose?
2. What do I want to get out of this talk?
3. What are the main points?
4. Is there support for the main points?

Do not try to write down everything a speaker says. Train yourself to listen for the main points and make notes of these. Use whatever words come quickly and naturally to you. Probably they will be a combination of the speaker's and your own. Do not worry about complete sentences or about punctuation — use abbreviations and whatever shortcuts you think of. Your purpose is to jot down quickly the essence of what the speaker is saying.

EXERCISE 2. Ask one student to read aloud to the class the first three or four paragraphs of any chapter in a science or social studies textbook. The other students will take notes as they think necessary. Compare the notes. Do they identify the main ideas?

26c. Listen carefully to instructions.

It is important to listen carefully when you are receiving class assignments, work instructions, or directions for doing something.

(1) Take down class assignments and instructions accurately and follow them correctly.

1. Jot down each step of the instructions.
2. Do not interrupt with questions while an assignment or a set of instructions is being given. If there

is something you do not understand, ask a question as soon as the speaker has finished.

3. Be sure that you have all the instructions and understand them. Repeat them aloud, if necessary.

EXERCISE 3. Your teacher will read the following instructions to you, pausing only briefly between instructions. Close your book and carry out the instructions as you hear them. You will need pencil and paper.

1. Write 9, no matter what the sum of 5 and 6 is.
2. If tomorrow is not the day after yesterday, write your name without capitals.
3. If you were born in the first six months of the year, multiply your age by 3; if you were born in the last six months of the year, subtract 3 from your age.
4. If you think whales are fish, write the weight of a kilogram of whalebone; if you think whales are mammals, how many centimeters in a meter?
5. Write *yes*, if the following statement is in error: You are listening to these instructions in German.

EXERCISE 4. The teacher or a student will read the following instructions to the class. No one is to take any notes during the reading. After the reader finishes, the group will write down the directions from memory. When everyone has finished, the reader will re-read the instructions, and each student will write whatever corrections and additions are necessary and will add up the number of changes.

I am going to read some instructions on how to fight fires. To burn, a fire needs air, fuel, and heat. Remove one of these three elements, and you put out the fire.

Take away the fuel: if possible, remove the burning material before the fire spreads.

Take away air: smother the fire with a wet rug or blanket, or shovel sand or dirt onto it.

Take away heat: cool the fire by pouring water on it. If, however, the fire is caused by electric wires that have shorted out because of bad insulation, do not use water until you have switched off the current. If that is impossible to do, smother the fire with sand or dirt.

(2) Get directions straight.

You can easily learn to follow directions by observing three rules:

    1. Listen alertly.

    2. Memorize the steps.

    3. Repeat the steps aloud to make sure you know them in the right order.

EXERCISE 5. With a classmate, complete the following activities in giving directions. The person receiving the directions should listen carefully, repeat them aloud, and take notes if necessary.

1. Tell a friend who doesn't know your neighborhood how to go from school to your home.
2. Outside your classroom, a woman, wearing a hat and coat, stops you. She wants to find the music teacher. Tell her how to find that person.
3. Using a map of your state, tell a friend how to drive from your town to the state capital. If you live in the state capital, explain how to drive to a city over one hundred miles away that is not on a main route.
4. Tell a friend where to get a bicycle tire patched, and how to get there.
5. Tell a friend how to find a novel written by Rose Wilder Lane in the main library of your town.

26d. **Learn to listen critically.**

There is no point in listening attentively unless you also evaluate what you hear. You should examine critically any speech that is intended to influence your thoughts or actions. Ask yourself:

1. Who says so? Does the person cite facts or speak from personal experience?

2. Is the information up to date?

3. Do the statements seem reasonable? Do they agree with what I already know about the subject?

4. Does the speaker have strong personal opinions? Do they affect the speaker's conclusions?

(1) Distinguish between fact and opinion.

When you listen to someone expressing an opinion or point of view, distinguish between words that report facts and words that express feelings or opinions. You can check facts to find out whether or not you should accept them. Do not accept another person's *opinions* without doing some thinking of your own.

Examine the following statements of fact and opinion. What might result if a careless listener took some of the opinions to be facts?

FACT   There are more students taking typing this year than last.

OPINION   All sensible students are taking typing nowadays.

FACT   Some sharks are not dangerous.

OPINION   People shouldn't be afraid of sharks in these waters.

As a listener you should be alert to statements that are *partly* factual and may be misleading. Careful speakers will use such words as *often, probably, many,* and so on, to qualify their assertions. They will be careful to name the sources of their information.

MISLEADING	Everybody thinks that the new school is too crowded.
CLEAR	Many people think that the new school is too crowded.
VAGUE	Experts say that one-way traffic will reduce tie-ups at rush hours.
CLEAR	Commissioner Harris and other members of the mayor's traffic control board predict that one-way traffic will reduce tie-ups at rush hours.

(2) Evaluate the reasoning.

When someone expresses an opinion, you have a right and a responsibility to think about the reasoning behind it. You should ask:

1. Is the speaker's thinking logical?
2. Is it supported by examples or other evidence?

Suppose you heard someone say, "Vote for Jeanne for class president. She would be good; she has the best grades in the class." Examine the reasoning. Does the job require someone with excellent grades? Do grades make any difference at all in this job? Before you accept a speaker's reasoning, make sure that it is based on sound logic.

EXERCISE 6. Imagine yourself listening to the following opinions. Which of them seem to be based on sound reasoning? Discuss your answers in class.

1. "In my experiments I found that white mice require a balanced diet. Those that were deprived of certain vitamins became nervous and irritable and showed other signs of malnutrition."
2. "No wonder he has such a good voice; his father was a singer."
3. "Our neighbor's police dog bit a child once, but I don't think all police dogs are vicious."

4. "Cars made in the United States are the best in the world."
5. "A lake is much better than the ocean for swimming."

26e. Learn to evaluate television.

Television plays an important role in our lives. Consider, for example, how much information television gives. It delivers up-to-the-minute news and the latest weather. It presents special educational programs for people of all ages. It advertises thousands of commercial products.

How much of the information on television do you remember? How much of this information do you accept without questioning, without asking yourself, for example, "Is this program based on fact or fiction?" Whenever you watch television, it makes sense to evaluate, or judge, what you see and hear. First, plan ahead and consult the television schedule. Decide beforehand which shows you will watch. Second, sum up your impressions of each show. Decide whether the show was worthwhile and whether you will watch it again. Third, distinguish between fact and opinion on television. Claims made in commercials, for example, should never be accepted without question. When viewing commercials, apply what you have learned about critical listening from pages 498–499.

EXERCISE 7. Choose any advertisement on television and, using your memory or notes of what the ad said, answer these questions: (1) Does the advertisement offer facts or opinions about the product? Give examples. (2) Does the advertisement offer evidence for its claims about the product? Give an example.

(3) Based on what the advertisement says, do you think the product is worthwhile? Why or why not?

EXERCISE 8. Consult the television schedule for the next week and underline one show you think the entire class should watch. Make a list of your reasons and be prepared to announce your choice of television show and list of reasons to the class.

Index and
Tab Key Index

Index

Tab Key Index

Key to
English Workshop Drill

To supplement the lessons in *English Grammar and Composition, First Course,* additional practice in grammar and usage, punctuation, capitalization, composition, vocabulary, and spelling may be found in *English Workshop, First Course.* The following chart correlates the rule in the textbook with the appropriate lesson in *English Workshop.*

Text Rule	Workshop Lesson	Text Rule	Workshop Lesson	Text Rule	Workshop Lesson
1a	1	7c	77-82	14e	107, 108
1b	2			14f	109
1c	4	8a-b	87, 88	14g	109
1d	2	8c-d	89, 90		
1e	3			16h	85
1f	5	9b	26		
1g	5	9c	26	17a	111
1h	6			17b	112, 119
1i	6	10a	56	17c-f	111, 116, 123
		10c	57		
2a	10	10d	58	18a	113
2b	11	10e	58	18b	113
2c	12	10f	59	18c	114
				18d	114
3a	13	11a-c	1	18f	115, 119
3b	14	11f	39	18g	123
3c	16	11g	39		
3d	5	11h	40	20a-c	124
		11i	41	20d	125
4a	31	11j	42	20e	126
4b	31				
4c	32	12e	98	22b	37, 45, 62,
4d	33	12f	98		74
		12g	99	22c	37
5a	24	12h-j	98	22d	37
5c	25	12k	99		
		12l	99	23a	37
6a	64	12o-q	95	23b	8, 20, 29
6b	65	12r	96	23c	37, 45
6c	66			23d	38, 46, 63
6d-f	67	13a	47	23e	38, 46
6g-i	71	13b	51	23g	85, 93
6k	69				
6n	70	14a	103, 104	24a	21
		14b	105	24c	38, 46
7a	76	14c	105	24 d-h	55, 63
7b	76	14d	106	24i	9

Correction Symbols

ms	error in manuscript form or neatness
cap	error in use of capital letters
p	error in punctuation
sp	error in spelling
frag	sentence fragment
ss	error in sentence structure
k	awkward sentence
nc	not clear
rs	run-on sentence
gr	error in grammar
w	error in word choice
¶	You should have begun a new paragraph here.
t	error in tense
∧	You have omitted something.